# REDEFINING ISLAMIC POLITICAL THOUGHT

## A Critique in Methodological Perspective

# REDEFINING ISLAMIC POLITICAL THOUGHT

## A Critique in Methodological Perspective

**Dr. Obaidullah Fahad**
*Reader, Department of Islamic Studies*
*Aligarh Muslim University*
*Aligarh (India)*

SERIALS PUBLICATIONS
NEW DELHI

**First Published - 2006**

ISBN: 81-8387-019-8



*Published by*

**SERIALS PUBLICATIONS**
4830/24, Prahlad Street, Ansari Road
Darya Ganj, New Delhi-110002 (India)
Phone : 23245225
Fax : 91-11-23272135
E-mail: serials@satyam.net.in

**To**

*Mr. Kabir Ahmad Khan*

*Who*

*Completed this incomplete*

# Acknowledgements

My thanks are due to the organizers of the various seminars who provided me chances from time to time to concentrate upon some important methodological issues relating to Islamic political thought and to present them in the intellectual gatherings. I would also like to express my thanks to the editors of the various journals and proceedings and volumes in which some of these articles were originally published.

I must also thank to my research students: Mr. Imtiazul Hoda, for preparing the bibliography, glossary and index of the volume and Mr. Shahzada Ashraf for his assistance in reading the proof and for many constructive suggestions provided by him; to my friends Dr. Rashid Shāz, Chairman Milli Parliament of India for his technical advice regarding the title and sub-titles of the book; Dr. Faizan Ahmad for his keen judgement and wise counsel; to my son Masna Faris for help of various kinds and to Mr. Naimuddin Khan for the care and skill with which he tended this book from the first draft to the final published version; and in the Last to Almighty Allah whom I pray wholeheartedly:

رَبّ زِدْنی علماً

My Lord ! advance me in Knowledge (The Qur'an, 20: 114)

# CONTENTS



**PART ONE**

**PART TWO**

*****

# INTRODUCTION

I agree with the opinion expressed by Dr. Abu Sulayman in his book entitled "Crisis in the Muslim Mind" that the crisis in the Muslim society is basically intellectual and academic; it lies in the methodology and approach adopted by Muslim Ulama, reformers, intellectuals and researchers in their studies on Islam and Islamic history. The Muslim mind, therefore, has remained a captive of those concepts and basic approaches that doom it remain bound by past mistakes and digressions and bereft of the ability to penetrate, distinguish and amend its own course, or to plumb the depths of the issues confronting it. Thus it is unable to boldly chart a course for the future, for it sits bound and blindfolded in a dusty corner of the distant past.[1] If the methodology of thought does not undergo change and if its approaches are not rectified, the Muslim mind will remain unable to take a critical or penetrating look at anything. Instead, it will continue to gravitate from one failed solution to the next. There can be little doubt that continuing along this path can only lead to further disintegration and collapse, the author has concluded.[2]

## Totalitarianism in Islam

The best example of the intellectual crisis among the Muslim leaders is that of Jamaluddin Afghani (1838/39-1897) the famous writer and Pan-Islamist political activist. Controversial during his life-time, he has become since his death one of the most influential figures in the Muslim world. His political thought was impelled by hostility to British rule in foreign, especially Muslim lands. His anti-British speeches and writings were extended to a more general anti-imperialism that has increased in the Muslim world since his time. His theory of Pan-Islamism as a barrier to further European conquest of Muslim territory became especially strong after the British conquest of Egypt in 1882, the French protectorate of Tunisia in 1881, and the European taking of Muslim territories in the Russo-Turkish war and the Congress of Berlin in 1877-1878.[3] The man of such a calibre like Afghani misinterpreted the relationship between the social and political systems at the time of Rashidun caliphs and concluded that the leadership needed by Ummah was 'a just dictatorship' (*mustabidd aadil*).

This confusing statement of Afghani is self-contradictory. The dictatorship and justice are the two opposite poles. This is in violation with the clear cut *Qur'ānic* teachings, in which all such tendencies of tyranny and dictatorial authority are criticized:

> Nay, but man does
> Transgress all bounds.
> In that he looks
> Upon himself as self-sufficient. [(4)]
>
> It is part of the Mercy
> Of God that you do deal
> Gently with them.
> Were you severe
> Or harsh-hearted,
> They would have broken away
> From about you: so pass over
> (Their faults), and ask
> For (God's) forgiveness
> For them; and consult
> Them in affairs (of moment).
> Then, when you have
> Taken a decision,
> Put your trust in God. [(5)]
>
> Those who hearken
> To their Lord, and establish
> Regular prayer; who (conduct)
> Their affairs by mutual consultation. [(6)]

The same mistake was repeated by Inayatullah Khan Mashriqi (1888-1936) the founder of *Khaksar* Movement in India who provided a naval interpretation of Islam in his famous book *Tazkirah*. Following fascism in Germany as the model, he called for Islamic revolution and emphasized mainly on the strict system of order and discipline, military organization and hardwork. He treated the leader of Islamic society an authoritative dictator to be followed by the community willingly or unwillingly like that of the Prophets. To him "The *amir* (Leader) of the Muslims is a powerful *amir*. He is above all the checks and balances. He is responsible to Allah and His Apostle only. Only Allah and His Apostle can deal with him. He should consult the Ummah but none can share his power and authority. He is the ruler above all the partnerships and associations. He is bound to Allah, Shariah and Sunnah and this boundation is due to his own discretion not because of the opinion of the Muslim community."[7]

The totalitarian approach advocated by Mashriqi believes in dominance and victory. It explains the religion as the tool of power and authority, the main objective of Islam and *Iman* to overcome others and subordinate them. "The first and the last clause of the constitution of God reads that *Iman* (faith) is equated with victory and triumph and *Kufr* (rejection of God) means defeat and decline."[8]

This totalitarian view was taken by Hameeduddin Farahi (1862-1930) the famous commentator of the *Qur'ān* and ideologue of the *Qur'ānic* order and coherence (*nizam al-Qur'ān*) when he discussed *Khilafah* as the noblest and highest system of government and *mulukiyah* (Kingship or monarchy) as the workable and affordable one. He supported the latter – though as the lowest system of government – in order to check the disorder and lawlessness in the society. He further theorized that when a nation loses its basic character, there emerges a king – be it a tyrant and totalitarian – as the benevolence from God. The intellectuals do afford him and obey the authoritative government since there remains no way out.[9]

Farahi, in order to provide some legal and historical evidences in his favour, states that a monarch usually emerges in a non-suitable and un-eligible society and inspite of his religious nature and practicing Islamic behaviour, he soon turns into a dictator and authoritative (*aamir wa mustabidd*).[10] He has quoted the Prophet Sulayman and Dhul Qarnayn as the notable examples and declared them dictators and totalitarians, and has referred the holy *Qur'ān* in this context.[11]

It was very amazing to me when I was discussing the Islamic system of government and was criticizing Farahi in this regard in the national seminar at Madrasatul Islah Azamgarh (dated 8-10 October 1991) on the *Life and Thought of Allamah Hameeduddin Farahi*, the scholars like Prof. Hakim Altaf Ahmad Azmi (Jamia Hamdard, New Delhi) and Dr. Mohd. Enayatullah Subhani (the then teacher at Jamiatul Falah Azamgarh) raised objections against me and supported Farahi's views unhesitatingly.

More interesting in this case were the footnotes on my article added by the learned editor of the minutes of the seminar published later on in association with one of his friends (namely Dr. Ghulam Qadir Loan, the author of *Mutalah Tasawwuf* in Urdu a research study based on original sources on anti-Islam mysticism/Sufi Thoughts prevalent in Islamic history, as the author told me later on privately). In these footnotes Shaykhul Islam Ibn Taimiyah and Shah Wali Allah of Delhi were quoted in favour of totalitarianism in Islam but not a single verse of the *Qur'ān* was discussed. The Learned editor (or editors) felt it necessary to conclude that "this theory, as advocated by Farahi, is in total accordance with the *Qur'ān*, the Sunnah, and the consensus of opinion in Islamic history and more feasible and practicable in the light of the historical facts."[12]

The striking feature of these notes is the confession of the editor (in the preface of the book) of his shortcomings in the field of political science and his humble acknowledgement that he is not acquainted even with the alphabets of political thought. Even then he managed to support the authoritarian approach in Islamic political thought and to provide some even irrational justifications in his favour.

More bewildering studies in this respect are those presented by Alam Khundmiri (1922-1983) an impressive intellectual figure of Hyderabad who alongwith his friends founded *Comrades Association* in 1939 in order to disseminate the Marxist ideology. The Association also functioned as a front for the Communist Party of India during its formative phase and was a key factor in inaugurating and intensifying the Marxist movement in Andhra Pradesh. Khundmiri in his articles published in the periodicals, emphasized upon an ideology-free Islam because ideology-based Islam always treats the golden past as the dominating passion. "It still remains a dominant passion of the activist elements in the world of Islam, whether it is the Jama'at e Islami or the Ikhwan al-Muslimun which have assumed a completely fascist colour. The fascist ideology of the minority groups contributes to the fostering of a climate of regression, which may ultimately make ineffective the share of the minority community in the actual task of change and progress. It might even become suicidal, as a neurotic personality may sometimes find solace in complete withdrawal or suicide",[13] as Khundmiri proposes his Marxist scheme.

Very fascinating in this context is the confession of the author that "the social philosophy and political theory of early Islam do not reveal any tendencies which can be identified as fascistic, in the strict sense of the term. It is primarily because early Islam itself contained radical solutions to the contemporary issues of the day. In this sense it was not an infantile regression but a march forward,"[14] as he has historically analysed.

"The political theory in Islam", as he further explicity elaborates, "even in the days when the Khilafat was replaced by monarchy, retained its dislike for an exclusive authoritarian outlook, as is evidenced in the theory of the state by Abu Yusuf, the famous jurist of Al-Harun's time."[15]

Apart from glorious history, as Khundmiri suggests, "Islamic ideology will adapt itself to an emerging democratic idea, which means that it will have lost its ideological character. It will not give political legitimacy to the emerging democratic regimes, but it might give to the democratic idea a spiritual content and that will be the greatest contribution of Islam to the modern world." The medieval Islam in his view, could not provide a soil for the growth of a humanistic tradition in Islam, though it was a hidden possibility in the *Qur'ānic* Vision, such a humanistic tradition can only grow in a democratic soil. But medieval Islam is a great resistant to the growth of democracy. After analysing the issue in the context of entire Islamic history from a Marxist point of view, he very clearly exposes his hidden intentions when he suggests the Muslims to reject 'Islam as an ideology' and believe in 'the Islamic vision'. A younger generation of Muslims may succeed if they relate this vision to democratic-humanistic traditions of the contemporary world,[16] he concludes.

The entire scheme of the analysis in this progressive Marxist paradigm is based upon the assumptions – mostly misleading and also confusing – that the Islamic history or medieval Islam' as Khumdmiri calls it, flourished under the umbrella of fascism/totalitarianism; that whole legacy of Islamic learning developed in a dictatorial atmosphere and even the modern Muslims and their associations and institutions allow no democratic procedure and therefore, they should turn into democratic – humanistic people, have they any desire to progress and development.

## Islamic Objectives

Due to these random unsystematic studies from within the Muslim community, the Western scholars of Islam and communal Hindus alike, whenever they speak of Islam they speak of fatalism, authoritarianism, terrorism and fundamentalism, the religion having no scope of pluralism, democracy and political participation. They speak of the excesses of the slave trade and the degradation of women. They proclaim that Islam ensures no fundamental right, no freedom and equality, no human values. It admits no respect and dignity to human values. It allows no concession to others. These people knowingly or unknowingly proclaim that Islam is no more than the practices of the contemporary Muslims, their myths and fabrications, ignorance and superstitions. The Islamic ideals, objectives and fundamental principles are generally neglected, while it is very important to realize that the shortcomings in the behaviour and attitude of Muslims are in no way attributive to the values and objectives of Islam. The later are clearly reflected in the texts of the *Qur'ān* and Hadith. These values and objectives are universally recognized and firmly established facts. No one can deny them.

**Concept of Unity**:

No son did God beget,
Nor is there any god
Along with Him: (if there were

Many gods), behold, each god
Would have taken away
What He had created,
And some would have
Lorded it over others![17]

O mankind! We created you
From a single (pair)
Of a male and a female,
And made you into
Nations and tribes, that
You may know each other
(Not that you may despise
(Each other), Verily
The most honoured of you
In the sight of God
Is (he who is) the most
Righteous of you.[18]

**Proposeful Life, and Sense of Responsibility**:

God commands justice, the doing
Of good, and liberality to kith
And Kin, and He forbids
All shameful deeds, and injustice
And rebellion: He instructs you
That you may receive admonition.
Fulfil the Covenant of God
When you have entered into it,
And break not your oaths
After you have confirmed them;
In deed you have made
God your surety.[19]

O mankind! revere
Your Guardian – Lord,
Who created you
From a single person,
Created, of like nature,
His mate, and from them twain
Scattered (Like seeds)
Countless men and women;
Adorate God, through whom
You demanded your mutual (rights)
And reverence the wombs
(That bore you): for God
Ever watches over you.[20]

**Human Dignity**:

We have honoured the sons
Of Adam; provided them
With transports on Land and sea;
Given them for sustenance things
Good and pure; and conferred
On them special favours,
Above a great part
Of Our Creation.[21]

And He has given you shape –
And made your shapes
Beautiful, - and has provided
For you sustenance,
Of things pure and good, -
Such is God your Lord.
So Glory to God,
The Lord of the Worlds.[22]

That which is on earth
We have made but as
A glittering show for the earth,
In order that We may test
Them – as to which of them
Are best in conduct.[23]

**Freedom and Tolerance**:

Let there be no compulsion
In religion: Truth stands out
Clear from Error: whoever
Rejects Evil and believes
In God has grasped
The most trustworthy
Hand-hold, that never breaks.[24]

Say: O ye
That rejects faith!
I worship not that
Which you Worship.
Nor will you worship
That which I worship.
And I will not worship
That which you have been
Want to worship.
Nor will you worship
That which I worship.
To you be your way,

And to me mine.[25]

**No Persecution:**

Let those fight
In the cause of God
Who sell the Life of this world
For the Hereafter.
To him who fights
In the cause of God, -
Whether he is slain
Or gets victory –
Soon shall We give him
A reward of great (value).
And why should you not
Fight in the cause of God
And of those who, being weak
And ill-treated (and oppressed)?-
Men, women and children,
Whose cry is: "Our Lord!
Rescue us from this town,
Whose people are oppressors;
And raise for us from You
One who will protect;
And raise for us from you
One who will help!"
Those who believe fight in the cause of God,
And those who reject Faith
Fight in the cause of Evil:
So fight you against the
Friends of Satan: feeble indeed
Is the cunning of Satan.[26]

God forbids you not,
With regard to those who
Fight you not for (your) Faith
Nor drive you out
Of your homes,
From dealing kindly and justly
With them: For God loves
Those who are just.
God only forbids you,
With regard to those who
Fight you for (your) Faith
And drive you out
Of your homes, and support
Others in driving you out,
From turning to them

(For friendship and protection).
It is such as turn to them
(In these circumstances)
That do wrong.[27]

**Justice, Equity and Cooperation**:

Forget not your portion in this
World: but do you good,
As God has been good
To you, and seek not
(Occasions for) mischief in the Land:
For God loves not those
Who do mischief.[28]

O Ye who believe!
Stand out firmly
For justice, as witnesses
To God, even as against
Yourselves, or your parents,
Or your Kin, and whether
It be (against) rich or poor:
For God can best protect both.
Follow not the lusts
(Of your hearts), lest you
Swerve, and if you
Distort (justice) or decline
To do justice, verily
God is well-acquainted
With all that you do.[29]

O ye who believe !
Stand out firmly
For God, as witnesses
To fair dealing, and Let not
The hatred of others
To you make you swerve
To wrong and depart from
Justice. Be just: that is
Next to piety: and fear God,
For God is well-acquainted
With all that you do.[30]

Help you one another
In righteousness and piety,
But help you not one another
In sin and rancour:
Fear God: for God

Is strict in punishment.[31]

**Resistance against Mischief and Disorder:**

O my people ! worship God:
You have no other god but He.
And give not
Short measure or weight:
I see you in prosperity,
But I fear for you
The Penalty of a Day
That will compass (you) all round.
And O my people ! give
Just measure and weight,
Nor withhold from the people
The things that are their due:
Commit not evil in the Land
With intent to do mischief.[32]

Those who break
The covenant of God, after
Having plighted their word hereto,
And cut as under those things
Which God has commanded
To be joined, and work mischief
In the Land; - on them
Is the curse; for them
Is the terrible Home.[33]

**Truthfulness, Honesty and Good Conduct:**

For Muslim men and women, -
For believing men and women,
For true men and women,
For men and women who are
Patient and constant, for men
And women who humble themselves,
For men and women who give
In charity, for men and women
Who fast (and deny themselves),
For men and women who
Guard their chastity, and
For men and women who
Engage much in God's praise,-
For them has God prepared
Forgiveness and great reward.[34]

Those who spend (freely),
Whether in prosperity,
Or in adversity;

Who restrain anger,
And pardon (all) men;-
For God Loves those
Who do good.[35]

Did you see one
Who denies the Judgement
(To come)?
Then such is the (man)
Who repulses the orphan
(With harshness),
And encourages not
The feeding of the indigent.[36]

And what will explain
To you the path that is steep? –
(It is:) freeing the bondman;
Or the giving of food
In a day of privation
To the orphan
With claims of relationship,
Or to the indigent
(Down) in the dust.
Then will he be
Of those who believe,
And enjoin patience (constancy,
And self-restraint), and enjoin
Deeds of Kindness and Compassion.[37]

**Acquisition of Knowledge:**

Proclaim ! (or read !)
In the name
Of your Lord and Cherisher,
Who created –
Created man out of
A (mere) clot
Of congealed blood;
Proclaim ! And your Lord
Is most Bountiful, -
He Who taught
(The use of) the Pen,-
Taught man that
Which he Knew not.[38]

Say: are those equal, those who know
And those who do not know?
It is those who are educated

With understanding
That receive admonition.[39]

Those truly fear God
Among His Servants
Who have Knowledge.[40]

**Construction and Rehabilitation:**

Travel through the earth
And see how God did
Originate creation; so will
God produce a later creation:
For God has power
Over all things.[41]

It is out of His Mercy
That He has made for you
Night and Day, - that you
May rest therein, and that
You may seek of His grace;-
And in order that you
May be grateful.[42]

God has promised, to those
Among you who believe
And work righteous deeds, that He
Will, of surety, grant them
In the Land, inheritance
(Of power), as He granted it
To those before them; that
He will establish in authority
Their religion – the one
Which He has chosen for them;
And that He will change
(Their state), after the fear
In which they (lived) to one
Of security and peace.[43]

And say: "Work (righteousness):
Soon will God observe your work,
And His Apostle and the Believers.[44]

If anyone does evil
Or wrongs his own soul
But afterwards seeks
God's forgiveness, he will find
God Oft-forgiving,
Most Merciful.[45]

And ask forgiveness
Of your Lord, and turn
Unto Him (in repentance):
For my Lord is indeed
Full of mercy and Loving-kindness.[46]

These ideals and objectives, quoted from the *Qur'ān*, are incorporated and explained well in the traditions of the Prophet (SAW) as well.[47] The two basic sources of Islam cover all the aspects and dimensions of a successful life. The Islamic coverage of the values and objectives is more reliable, authentic and more comprehensive than the other religions, theories and philosophies.

## Classical Methodology

The shortcomings in the methodology of Islamic thought applied by the modern Muslim intellectuals, owe their origin in the traditional approach of the history popularly known as *Usul al-Fiqh* (jurisprudential source methodology), the best application of which was made during the period of the Caliphs when revelation was treated as main source of guidance and direction and when reason and *ijtihad* were used both as tools for understanding and explaining revelation, as well as for dealing with the living events and issues of the society and developing responses and policies.

On the basis of the classification of the principles of Islamic Law (*fiqh*) into two: primary and secondary and defining first as those studies related to the *Qur'ān*, the *Sunnah*, *ijma* (the consensus of Ulama) and *Qiyas* (analogy), and the last as those sources to be used in the primary as the basis for *ijtihad* most particularly *Istihsan* (the more reasonable analogy), *masalih mursalah* (the wider interests of the community), *sadd al-dhariah* (the obstruction of ostensibly legitimate means to illegitimate ends), *urf* (custom and legal usage), the sayings of the companions, and the practices of the people of Madinah, all the Islamic sciences were divided since the very beginning into Shariah and non-Shariah sciences.

Islamic Law accompanying both the types of sources from the founders till the present day has been representing both the traditionalism and rationalism toward the realities of life. With the separation of the committed intellectual leadership from all real forms of authority and institutions of wider influence – due to various reasons mostly political – Islamic thought, however, turned away from using its *usul al-Fiqh* for the development of sciences and disciplines dealing with the organization and well-being of society, preferring instead to focus on the spiritual and ritualistic needs of the individual Muslim, as Dr. Abu Sulayman has assessed.[48]

This is the reason why the social sciences could not be developed as the independent disciplines in the Islamic history. Well, the door of ijtihad was not closed as the scholars of today do claim wrongly; but it was mostly confined to the area of individual life. There are a number of outstanding contributions in the social and collective institutional fields. Ibn Khaldun[49] (1332-1406) is an important name in the classical period whose pioneering work *Muqaddimah* and the original theories of sociology (*Ilm al-Umran*) and contribution in the philosophy of history are worldwide recognized. Dr. Ali Shariati[50] (1933-1970) of Iran, and Engineer Malek Bennabi[51] (1903/1905-1973) of Algeria are very prominent in the civilizational studies of the contemporary Muslim world. These are the individual contributions and do not constitute any intellectual movement.

## Imported Approach

Imported modernizing approach – just opposite to the classical one – is another method that is popularized in the Muslim world. Historically it was first adopted over two centuries ago, when the Turkish Ottoman empire was confronted by the military might of Europe. Under Salim III, the empire began a policy of imitating Europe, thinking that this was the way to renew their declining power. The foreign technical knowledge and experience were imported and the traditional military corps were actually massacred in their barracks when they resisted the plans to 'modernize' the army. This could not be proved successful in restoring the power and dignity of empire but the westernization process continued and the trend of transforming Western science, technology and culture to Turkey increased. This resulted in many liberal political and social reforms in the latter half of the nineteenth century known as Midhat Pasha's constitution. This attempt of reformation too was no more successful and consequently Sultan Abdul Hamid II marched ahead and took the charge of the entire state to revive the Islamic model of government but in vain.

The reform movement in Turkey now introduced a new dimension: the Turkish nationalism that encompassed all speakers of Turkish language in Western and Central Asia. This pan-Turkish nationalism was theorized and supported with the rational arguments borrowed from the Western literature by the ideologue Zia Gokalp (1875-1924). The Union and Progress Party later on challenged the Ottoman Empire, overthrew Sultan Abdul Hamid II and took the reign of power under the leadership of Mustafa Kamal Ataturk (1881-1938) who carried foreign imitation to its farthest extremes, abolished the role of Islam and Islamic culture in the society and endorsed the European concept of secularism.

Inspite of all the efforts made by the Turkish leaders they were not successful in restoring the former power, dignity and status. On the contrary, the deterioration was so complete that in 1960 Adnan Mindaris was hanged in the first of a series of military coups that would eventually lead to dictatorship and repression. The famous Islamist leader Najmuddin Erbakan and his political parties (formed by him after one another in order to bring a democratic Islamic change in the society) had been banned again and again. The Turkey is still today, as was in the past, the "sick man of Europe". In fact Turkey is worse than sick. It is the perennial Western Camp-follower that has no hope of ever improving its lot in life.[52]

## Secularism and Secularization

The imported model of secularism and secularization and the idea of the separation of religion from politics was first theorized in the Muslim world by Shaykh Ali Abdul Raziq in his book entitled *al-Islam wa Usul al-Hukm* published in 1925 a year and a few days after the abolition of the Caliphate in Turkey (March 1924), when he was a judge in Shariah courts in Egypt.

The summary of Shaikh Ali Abdul Raziq's views is that the government of the Islamic State can be of any kind – it can be an autocracy or bureaucracy; a monarchy or republic; a dictatorship or constitutional or consultative government; it can be democratic, socialist or Bolshevik; that Prophet (SAW) was nothing "but a *Rasul* (Messenger) for a religious call, purely for the sake of religion, unblemished by any tendency to rule or call for (the formation of) a state;" and that "Islam is a religious unity, and the Prophet called for that unity and had actually achieved it before his death and that for the sake of that unity he struggled with his tongue and his sword and Allah's help and victory came to him." He also says that it should be realized that "*al-Risalah* (the Message of Islam) in itself required the Prophet (SAW) to acquire some form of leadership and power over his people. But this is very far from the leadership of the Kings and their power over their subjects. Hence, one must not confuse the leadership of *al-Risalah* with that of the King", and that "the rule of the Prophet (SAW) over the *muminin* was the rule of *al-Risalah* which is untainted by (any urge to) rule".[53]

In support of these views, Shaikh Abdul Raziq cited verses of the *Qur'ān* and some traditions of the Prophet (SAW). Further more, he added – what he thought to be proof of his claim – that it is conceivable that the whole world could be organized under one single religion and that the entire humanity could be regulated within one religious unity, but to put the whole world under the rule of one government and gather it in a single political unit would seem to be almost outside the scope of human nature and is not related to the will of Allah."[54]

These views were severely criticized by the Muslims not only from Egypt where the book was published, but also from Arab and other Muslim countries. Consequently in 1925, Al-Azhar's Ulama in a major statement condemned the secularizing views of Ali Abdul Raziq, stating that "...this theory is absolutely false. *Qur'ān* and Sunnah contain numerous precepts of a temporal character... According to the unanimous consensus of the Muslims Islam is the totality of the precepts transmitted by the Prophet in regard to doctrine, cult and legal relations among the people. These precepts form one whole and can not be disassociated from one another.[55]

Inspite of all these academic refutations, most of the Muslim countries are following secularism as the best model and have confined the role of religion to the private sector or to the celebrations.

Modernization and secularization - the two western models paved nothing to the decline of Muslim society. They rather intensified the frustration, degradation, dissatisfaction and deterioration in the Muslim society. It is very important to note that "each nation has its own motivations, psychology and history, has its own composition in terms of its values, beliefs and concepts. Unless these are understood correctly, it is next to impossible to deal with a nation in a way that will inspire it to realize all its hidden potential for progress".[56]

## Islamic Socialism

The book in hand is in no way a systematically arranged and orderly chapterized composition. It is rather a reflection, a contemplation and an analysis that has occupied me since a long time.

As a research scholar in the Department of political science A.M.U., Aligarh, I found most of the researchers and academicians in the field of Islamic political thought confused and frustrated while discussing the Islamic state and government. I saw the Islamists like Mustafa Sibai (1915-1964) the leader of *al-Ikhwan al-Muslimun* in Syria, in his famous book entitled *Ishtirakiyah al-Islam* (Socialism of Islam) published from Damascus in 1960, very much influenced with the alien ideologies. He blessed the basic philosophy underlying the Egyptian socialism, the essence of socialism is neither nationalization nor expropriation of capital. What socialism really aims for is the elimination of capitalistic exploitation of the masses, and the building of a social system in which the society will be based on social equality as well as economic justice in the distribution of wealth. Islamic socialism is derived not only from the specific institution of Zakah, but also stems from the common goals of social justice found in Islam and socialism.[57]

Sibai saw Islamic socialism as conforming with human nature, based on five natural rights: life, freedom, knowledge, dignity and ownership. God is the ultimate owner of all, and man is deputized to make use of property through honest labour. The state plays a regulatory function through nationalization (*tamim*) of essential public services, implementation of Islamic laws on mutual social responsibility (*al-takaful al-ijtimai*), and sanctions (*muayyidat*). This theory of Islamic socialism created an uproar because of its opposition to capitalism, its association of Islam with socialism, and its ostensible support of Nasser's ideology at a time when al-Ikhwan of Egypt was suppressed.[58]

It was very appreciating to me that Muhammad al-Bahi al-Kholi, the famous Islamic scholar and activist in Egypt was convinced that the *Qur'ān* reveals that God wills that man be active in development of the wealth of the nation and participate and share in the community economical activities. Earth is God's gift to its inhabitants, and it is man's duty and his purpose in life, first to worship God, and second to "cultivate the earth and establish various and magnificent civilizations, with a full exploitation of the riches of the earth for man's prosperity and happiness... constructive work, in the light of modern science, is not confined to agriculture or architecture only; it also means the full exploitation of the mineral wealth and the expansion of industry."[59]

This interpretation brought a fresh emphasis on the role of Islam in ensuring the social justice and certainly it is fully in keeping with basic Islamic notions, but it became violative and contradictory to the spirit and objectives of Islam when these notions were collaborated with socialism and a new term of "Islamic socialism" was coined in order to make a compromise between the two systems.

This combination of Islam and socialism, as Dr. Khurshid Ahmad has well explained, sounds strange to many and is seditious in its effect. If the mentality at work behind this is studied analytically, the following issues confront the readers: (i) Socialism and Islam are not in conflict with each other. They can be brought together. (ii) One form of coming together may be that they are complementary, in which case it will have to be admitted that Islam is imperfect and must be complemented with socialism. (iii) Another sense of bringing them together may be qualificatory or elucidatory to present the characteristic of Islam that it is a supporter of socialism. But in this too, apart from the question raised in, another pertinent question also arises whether Islam is divisible in a manner that any of its integral parts may be taken a part as distinguished from others, and even then it may retain its balanced and harmonious identity as a perfect system. Also, that in such a case, the combination should be "Socialistic Islam" and not in the reverse order "Islamic Socialism".

This term is extremely confusing and misleading. We do not mean to that all those using it are necessarily dishonest. But they are certainly guilty of mixing up issues. This slogan has been raised mostly by the following groups: (i) The communism who know very well that they can never push the bitter pill of communists down the throat of the people in an Islamic country without sugar-coating it. They are fully cognizant of the differences between the two systems, but in pursuit of Lenin's policy, they consider this trade in subterfuge necessary for their success. (ii) Those who are satisfied with the limited concept of religion and take it for granted that religion concerns only individual life and its limited sphere. And in collective affairs any existing system can be adopted. But this concept may be acceptable to the votaries of other religions but not to the followers of Islam. (iii) Those sincere people who have neither studied Islam in detail nor socialism, they are over-awed by the popular slogans and assertions of communists based on equality and justice, under the impression that since Islam is the upholder of justice, these two can come together. Their sincerity, however, can not avail them as a substitute for knowledge and realism. (iv) Those who are interested neither in socialism nor in Islam. But since through socialism, political and economic powers get concentrated in their hands, they seek support in it to maintain and strengthen their political despotism.

Every one of these four positions is wrong and based on falsehood and can never yield correct results.[60]

## May Woman Join The Masjid?

Another issue agitating to Muslim mind is the controversy that arose between the Muslim intellectuals and Ulama of various schools of thought in India few years back over the problem whether a woman may join or not the congregational prayers in the Masjid in her locality. Some women from Kerala and Tamil Nadu states decided to build their own separate Masjids and to appoint lady Imam therein. The Ulama of Deoband school reacted sharply against the issue and declared a total ban upon joining the Masjid for the women. Mufti Jamil Ahmad Naziri of Jamiah Arabiyah Mubarakpur, Azamgarh had already opposed the issue tooth and nail and had given his legal opinion against it on the ground that just after the death of the Prophet (SAW), both the companions and she-companions used to prohibit the women from joining the Masjid because the situations were entirely changed and the provocatives and disorders were intensified.[61] Very interesting, however, is that he has quoted only one statement in his favour – that of Hazrat Aishah who is reported to have said, 'in case the Prophet was alive and would see the conduct and behaviour of the people he would have certainly checked the women from joining the masjid as the women of Bani Israil were checked in the past'.[62]

Mufti Naziri himself admits that the Prophetic traditions do permit the women to join the masjid though the performance of prayers in their own residences is counted desirable and supererogatory for women. By following the juristic opinion of Imam Abu Hanifah, he is adamant to oppose the issue, though the next part of the tradition of Hazrat Aishah, that Mufti Naziri himself has quoted in his favour, explains that the joining masjid was declared unlawful and illegal exclusively for the ladies of Bani Israil (and not for any other else).[63] Hazrat Aishah has expressed her disliking in this issue in fact and has not declared any legal verdict/fatwa, because it was the common practice of the ladies at that time.

Refuting the claims of Mufti Naziri in this context, and advocating the usefulness of the Prophetic practice even in the modern times, Maulana Muhammad Rais Nadvi, a senior teacher then in Jamia Salafiah, Varanasi has referred the case of

one of the wives of Umar al-Farooq who did not see suitable for ladies to join the masjid. She was asked by anyone why does she regularly join the masjid inspite the disliking of her husband. She responded spontaneously why did he not check me if he was against it? They said, your husband did not do so because of the Prophetic tradition that declared:

لا تمنعوا إمآء الله من المساجد

(Do not prohibit the she-slaves of Allah from the Masjids !)[64]

Maulana Muhammad Rais Nadvi, then concluded that this tradition reflects upon the full cognizance of the companions in general with the permission of Shariah to ladies to join the Masjid accompanying the opposite gender, and in pursuance of this, Umar did not prohibit his wife.[65] Maulana Rais also refutes the statement of Aishah-quoted above-and counts it wrong and contradictory to clear-cut Islamic text. It is quite possible that Aishah might have heard it from any Israeli ignorant narrator who was unaware of his religious issues, since the statement is in clear opposition to scriptures of Bani Israel, as Maulana Rais has very boldly criticized.[66]

Another advocate of the usefulness of the prophetic practice, Maulana Mukhtar Ahmad Nadvi, former amir of Jameat Ahl Hadith of India and the patron of Majallah Al-Balagh Mumbai, nullifies the suspicious and undue reservations that few Ulama had in their minds in this issue. He declared that hanafid Ulama's approach is a clear violation of Shariah, an undue interference in the religion and a deviation from and opposition to Sunnah.[67]

If the Muslim women are prohibited due to captivation and fascination in the society from joining the Masjid, then on the basis of the same ground and keeping in view the same arguments why are they not checked from visiting the holy Kabah and performing the pilgrimage at Makkah while the latter is full of dangers; the chances of scandal and defamation are more therein, and their mixing with the opposite sex may be intensified? The Masjid al-Haram at Makkah and the al-Masjid al-Nabawi at Madinah also qualify a Masjid in which Muslim

ladies of these followers of classical jurists perform the prayers in group and group ! Why this ban is not applied on the two sacred Mosques (Haramayn Sharifayn)? Why is it so contradiction in the matters of religion? It is very amazing that same argument is treated legal and justified in one matter and illegal and unjustified in the other. It is being played a game with the Shariah. He appealed the entire Muslims to practice directly the Book of Allah and the Sunnah of the Prophet and be independent of all these unnecessary limitations.[68]

The modern-educated Muslim intellectuals like Sayyid Shahabuddin former M.P. and now President of All-India Muslim Majlis Mshawarat, think it discretionary to the women. Now the working women have two options; either they perform prayers in their working places in time or in the masjid in locality along with the men in congregation or they postpone the performance till they reach to their residences when the work is over and then do the due. Apparently there is no reason why the ladies like gents can not join the masjid. Sayyid Shahabuddin has warned the orthodox Ulama that instead of issuing the fatwa they must resolve the issue and decide clearly what is legal and what is not. He is of the view that growing tendency of feminism in the Muslim society may be intensified. The deviations and distortions emerged before that in the Muslim society died their death. Today we are living in the age of information technology and every event of change may affect the society globally. In case the orthodox Muslims continued to push the ladies from the masjids and their economic, social and educational equal rights were still violated, the western feminist movement would enchant the Muslim women entirely and there would be no way out then, he very earnestly concluded.[69]

## Textualizing Islamic Thought

A balanced approach in the controversial juristic issues lies in the method of following only the *Qur'ān* and the Sunnah and of benefiting from all the juristic views independently, as elaborated in detail by various delegates of the international seminar on 'the collective ijtihad and its contemporary requirements' held at Islamabad (Pakistan) on 19-22 March 2005. The Muslim scholars out of the realm of madrasahs are now confident that the challenges can not be successfully met out unless the distance between various schools of thought is removed. Professor Shabbir Ahmad Jamei, Department of Islamic Studies Bahawal Pur University, emphasized on the point in detail. He said:

> "To create the spirit of tolerance among all the groups of ahl-al-Sunnah wa al-Jamaah is incumbent. The people must avoid talk in terms of Hanafid, Ahl al-Hadith, Shafi'i and Hanbali; Islamic fiqh, be it founded by Abu Hanifah, Malik bin Anas, Muhammad bin Idris Shafii or Ahmad bin Hanbal is our own fiqh. All these Imams are our common Imams. We should not be biased against or in favour of any one of them. The appropriate method is to follow that ijtihad of any one among them which is more closer to the *Qur'ān* and the Sunnah and more suitable to the circumstances and the public interests. We are obligated to it only. In the issues of discretion Islam did not guide us to follow Abu Hanifa, Shafii or other jurists appointedly; it has rather ordered us to follow only that ijtihad which is more convenient to the *Qur'ān* and the Sunnah."[70]

Hafiz Salahuddin Yousuf, another eminent delegate of the same seminar, while referring Shah Wali Allah from his notable works entitled *Musaffa* and *Iqd al-Jid*, emphasized upon following a *fiqh* more suitable to the requirements of the time and more convenient to the people, be it Hanafid, Shafiite, Malikite or Hanbalite. The main point is the superiority of the *Qur'ān* and the Sunnah and the convenience of the masses. We must discourage the traditional imitation, the juristic bias and the communal grouping that are counted barriers in the implementation of Islamic system of life, as Hafiz Yousuf assessed.[71]

Dr. Mahmud Ahmad Ghazi, Rector of International Islamic University Islamabad, offering an extension lecture in the said seminar introduced a new term '*Cosmopolitan Fiqh*' which is the immense need of today's Muslim world. Now the whole Muslim Ummah is in march toward this new kind of *fiqh*. It is a growing tendency to think all the juristic schools and the entire legacy of Muslim jurists as the common intellectual and academic legacy and to benefit from them as that of the common heritage. This *fiqh* may not be titled a Hanafid, Hanbalite or Shafiite; instead it may titled as 'Islamic *fiqh*'. In the next 50 years this 'cosmopolitan *fiqh*' will dominate the entire Muslim world and various classical schools of jurisprudence would be recorded as a historical phenomenon only, he forecasted.[72]

I agree with the opinion expressed by Hafiz Hasan Madani, the editor of *Muhaddith* Lahore that those scholars and Ulama who are not confronted with the changing situations of time and space, and who are confined within the traditional issues of Muslim society, do not feel the urgency of the need and far reaching consequences of the intellectual crisis in the Muslim mind. Soon they will face the challenges they will realize the gravity of the issue and will be convinced to rethink, reassess and re-examine the issues in the right perspective.[73]

Since these chapters of the book are written over a period of time, certain quotations as well as arguments are something repeated. Most of the topics in the book appeared in periodicals of one sort or another, ranging from learned quarterlies to monthly magazines, and their topics correspondingly range from problems of political thought in Islam covering the classical period to medieval and modern history of thought. Some were papers presented in the national or international seminars/workshops and originally published in the proceedings. Some of these are published for the first time in the present volume; these have not previously been printed in any form. With a few minor changes, I have kept all these papers in the original form. In a few places, I have made cuts, usually to avoid overlaps and repetitions, occasionally to remove matter no longer of any general interest because of being confined into local situations. Some times few additions are made to make the study updated and coherent. All the papers in this volume however, deal with the Islamic political thought in one form or another.

The book is divided into two parts. The first part begins with a critical discussion of the methodology applied in classical political thought of Islam. The whole legacy of political thought prepared by the thinkers and politicians in Islamic history reflect more or less the status quo to be maintained, since most of the books were composed either on the advice of the rulers or as the suggestions proposed to them in order to reform and strengthen the government. Apart from the lack of independent thinking there is no system and order applied in the approach. This chapter follows a critique of our classical and medieval political thinkers who appear to have tried to relate interpretation of political theories and concepts to their own contemporary conditions. The third chapter deals with the Islamization of Political Science in methodological perspective. It declares a value-neutral social science as advocated by behaviourlists, as against the spirit of goal-oriented Islam. It emphasizes upon a balance between the material and spiritual aspects. It necessitates to keep in mind the Islamic values while forming methodology in social sciences.

The second part of the study deals first with the issue of national movement or liberation struggle launched by the Mujahidin in India and discusses its main objectives, organization and process in detail. The remaining chapters speak in Islamic perspective the main challenges of modern time to Islamic political thought and the approach and methodology applied by the Muslim thinkers and activists of the contemporary world. Nationalism in the Arab world (*Urubah*) was reconciled with the Islamic tenets by the Islamists and reformists while the nationalist Muslims treated their religion subservient to modern nationalistic trends. This controversy has been confronted with the entire Arab world even in the present time. Western democracy and Islamic *Shura* are studied in this work comparatively and the democratic spirit and procedure of Islam is highlighted in detail without forming any apologia. The plural spirit of the *Qur'ān* and the Sunnah is theororized in proper perspective in order to cope with the challenges in a global society without any withdrawal from the values and objectives of Islam.

This part of the study may create various questions about the traditional approach. We may, however, form a true Islamic methodology to study Islam and Islamic political thought in the contemporary perspective with the approach of Islamic *Asalah* that denotes the innovative application of original Islamic principles to changing circumstances, as coined by Dr. Abul Hamid Abu Sulayman.[74] We the Muslims must remember that:

> "Islam potentially inherits the qualification that it may provide solid foundations to economic justice, social equality and democracy under the umbrella of the belief of Unity of God (*Tawhid*). It broadens the field to plural society through its commitment with the ideals of freedom and religious tolerance for the non-Muslims. In other words, the expectations and aspirations created by the globalization in the mind of the people especially of Asians and Africans, may be fulfilled only by Islam. This noble dream may be converted into reality only when Muslims change their present attitude and behaviour and turn into the true representative of Islam. Muslims must seek a new identity based upon (*tawhid*) the unity of God, the good conduct, the social equality, the economic justice and the true democracy."[75]

May Allah Most High grant that this study proves to be as useful as we hope it to be; and He is the granter of success!

All praise be to Allah, Lord of the Universe!

Date: 31.08.2005

**Obaidullah Fahad**
Qasr-e-Fahd,
University Fort Enclave,
Barauli Road,
Aligarh-202002 INDIA

## NOTES AND REFERENCES

1. Abu Sulayman, Abdul Hamid A., *Crisis in the Muslim Mind*, Eng. Trans. Yusuf Talal Delorenzo, Herndon, IInd Edition, 1994, p. 28. See for detail the Urdu Trans. Dr. Obaidullah Fahad, Fikr Islami Ka Buhran, Lahore, 2001, pp. 55-56.
2. Ibid., pp. 28-29.
3. See for detail, *The Oxford Encylopaedia of the Modern Islamic World*, Oxford, 1995, Vol. I, pp. 23-27.
4. The *Qur'ān* 96: 6-7.
5. The *Qur'ān* 3: 159.
6. The *Qur'ān* 42: 38.
7. Mashriqi, Inayatullah Khan, *Maulavi Ka Ghalat Mazhab*, No. 4, p. 20: The text reads:

   الغرض مسلمانوں کا امیر امیر ناطق ہے۔ امت کی ہر گرفت سے آزاد ہے۔
   اس کا مقابلہ صرف خدا اور رسول سے ہے۔ صرف خدا اور رسول ﷺ ہی اس سے
   نبٹ سکتے ہیں۔ اس کو چاہئے کہ مشورہ کرے لیکن خود خدا کی مانند لا یُشرِکُ فی حُکمِہٖ
   احدًا کا مصداق ہے۔ لاشریک حاکم ہے۔ صرف اللہ، شریعت، رسول، سنت کا پابند
   ہے اور وہ پابندی بھی امت کی رائے سے نہیں خود اس کی اپنی تمیز سے ہے۔

8. Mashriqi, Inayatullah Khan, *Tazkirah*, Lahore, Tazkirah Publications, 1980, p. 71. The Original Text reads:

   خدا کے قانون کی پہلی اور آخری دفعہ یہی ہے کہ ایمان بہر نوع فتح ونصرت کے
   مترادف اور کفر بہر حال شکست اور زوال کے ہم معنی ہے۔

9. Farahi, Abdul Hameed, *Fi Malakut Allah*, Azamgarh, 1391 A.H., p. 26.
10. Ibid., pp. 26-27.
11. Ibid.
12. Farahi, Ubaidullah, *Allamah Hameedudin Farahi: Hayat wa Afkar*, Azamgarh, 1992, p. 497 (footnote) also pp. 498-499 (footnote).
13. Khundmiri, Alam, Secularism, Islam and Modernity, ed. M.T. Ansari, New Delhi, 2001, p. 265.
14. Ibid., p. 261.
15. Ibid.
16. Ibid, p. 272.
17. The *Qur'ān* 23: 91.
18. The *Qur'ān* 49: 13.
19. The *Qur'ān* 16: 90-91.
20. The *Qur'ān* 4: 1.
21. The *Qur'ān* 17: 70.
22. The *Qur'ān* 40: 64.
23. The *Qur'ān* 18: 7.

24. The *Qur'ān* 2: 256.
25. The *Qur'ān* 109: 1-6.
26. The *Qur'ān* 4: 74-76.
27. The *Qur'ān* 60: 8-9.
28. The *Qur'ān* 28: 77.
29. The *Qur'ān* 4: 135.
30. The *Qur'ān* 5: 8.
31. The *Qur'ān* 5: 2.
32. The *Qur'ān* 11: 84-85.
33. The *Qur'ān* 13: 25.
34. The *Qur'ān* 33: 35.
35. The *Qur'ān* 3: 134.
36. The *Qur'ān* 107: 1-3.
37. The *Qur'ān* 90: 12-17.
38. The *Qur'ān* 96: 1-5.
39. The *Qur'ān* 39: 9.
40. The *Qur'ān* 35: 28.
41. The *Qur'ān* 29: 20.
42. The *Qur'ān* 28: 73.
43. The *Qur'ān* 24: 55.
44. The *Qur'ān* 9: 105.
45. The *Qur'ān* 4: 110.
46. The *Qur'ān* 11: 90.
47. For example about the good intention, conscience and human responsibilities, see the following traditions:
    The deeds solely depend upon the intentions. For every one is what he has intended for. (Bukhari & Muslim).
    Indeed Allah does not see your bodies and features; He instead sees your hearts and deeds (Muslim, Ahmad, Ibn Majah).
    There is no superiority for an Arab over a non-Arab except because of the piety from you. (Ahmad)
    Tell the truth be it bitter. (Baihaqi)
    The man who lags behind due to his deeds, can not advance by his affinity. (Ahmad, Ibn Majah).
    The respect of a man is his piety, the intelligence his manliness, and the good conduct his affinity. (Baihaqi & Al-Hakim).
    The godliness means the good conduct; the evil is that agitated by your heart and is painful to you when ever is circulated to others (Bukhari, Muslim & Tirmidhi)
    The rulership is a trust and would convert into insult and regret on the Day of judgement except when ruled with truthfulness and sincerity (Al-Hakim)
    Everyone of you is shepherd and is responsible of his sheeps. (Bukhari & Muslim).
    The noblest jihad is telling the truth before a tyrant ruler. (Ahmad).

My people will never agree with a misgiving unitedly. Whenever you see any conflict or internal war you must behold the huge majority of the people. (Ibn Majah).

Whenever anyone of you see an evil he must replace it with his hand, if unable to do it he must do it with his tongue, if unable he must do it through his heart and this is the lowest rank of the Faith. (Ahmad & Muslim).

The traditions about soft-heartedness, kindness, social services selflessly, being advantageous to humanity are very clear and explicit. The Prophet is reported to have said:

"It is better for a ruler to pardon one than to punish him unconsciously". (Al-Hakim & Baihaqi).

Fear from God be you anywhere, replace the evil with the good and behave with the people gently. (Ahmad, Tirmidhi, Al-Hakim).

Allah loves the leniency in everything. (Bukhari & Muslim)

One who is deprived of kindness, is deprived of every good. (Muslim, Ibn Majah & Ahmad).

Do facilitate, do not render difficult. Tell the news and messages in a rejoining way; do not frighten the people. (Bukhari).

Be compassionate for those who are on the earth would be Compassionate to you One who is on the sky. (Hakim & Tibrani).

One who does not show compassion would not be compassionable on the day of judgement (Bukhari).

The whole human being is the family of God. Most desirable to God is one who is most useful to humanity. (Tibrani).

By Allah, he is not a Muslim whose neighbour is not safe from his disasters (Bukhari).

He is not among us who does not respect our elders, does not show compassion to our youngers and does not pay due to our scholars. (Ahmad & Hakim).

The prophetic traditions emphasizing upon ensuring the justice, generosity and fraternity are countless. Some of these are as follows:

"Avoid the injustice because the injustice will turn into the sole darkness on the Day of Judgement. Avoid the greed because the greed destroyed those passed away before you; it persuaded them to kill the others and made their forbiddens lawful". (Muslim).

The Prophet used to seek the protection by God from the curse of the oppressed man. (Nasai).

The Prophet is reported to have prayed in these words:

"And I seek the protection by You from committing any injustice or being victim of injustice". (Nasai).

Avoid the curse of the oppressed man be he an unbeliever, because nothing can check it to rush towards God". (Ahmad).

Those who ensure justice in this world, would be installed on a pulpit of light near God on the Day of Judgement (Muslim).

The most desirable of the people to Allah on the Day of Judgement and the nearest in sitting to Him would be a Just ruler; and the most hated to Allah and the most distant from Him would be an unjust ruler. (Tirmidhi).
It suffices for a man to be sinful that he spoils those for whose maintenance he is responsible. (Bukhari & Muslim).
The higher hand is better than the lower hand. (Sihah Sittah).
One who takes his rope and collects the wood from the jungle is better than one who begs others humbly and it rests upon them to give him or not. (Bukhari & Nasai).
The best and purest livelihood is one that is earned honestly through one's own hand. (Tirmidhi & Abu Dawud).
The Muslim is not bitten twice from one hole. (Bukhari & Muslim).
A man dishonest is not among us. (Tirmidhi)
The best among you is one who is best for his family. (Tirmidhi & Ibn Majah).
If the Doom is about to occur and any one of you has a plant of date in his hand he must plant it. (Ahmad).
All these traditions are taken from Abu Sulayman, Abdul Hamid A., Azamat al-Aql al-Muslim, Urdu trans. Fahad, Obaidullah, *Firk, Islami Ka Buhran*, Lahore, 2001, pp. 71-74.

48. Abu Sulayman, Abdul Hamid A., *op. cit.*, pp. 43-44.
49. See for the Life and Contribution of Ibn Khaldun, Bukhsh, S. Khuda, *Ibn Khaldun and His History of Islamic Civilization*, Islamic Culture Hyderabad, 1927; Enan, Mohammad Abdullah, *Ibn Khaldun: His Life and Works*, Lahore, 1941; Rosenthal, Erwin, Ibn Khaldun: A North-African Muslim Thinker of the Fourteenth Century, John Rylands Library, *Manchester Bulletin*, 1940, Vol. 24; Sattar, E.M., *Ibn Khaldun: The Author of the Muqaddimah*, Dacca, 1980.
50. See for the Life and thought of Dr. Ali Shariati in detail, Ahsanul Haq, *Reinterpreting Islam in Iran: Life and Thoughts of Ali Shariati*, Aligarh, 1995.
51. For a brief study of Malek Bennabi See, Asma Rashid Malek Bennabi, *International Seminar on Malek Bennabi* (Programme Leaflet), University of Malaya, Kualalumpur, 1991, pp. 17-18; Fawzia Bariun, Malik Bennabi and the Intellectual Problems of the *Muslim Ummah, American Journal of Islamic Social Sciences*, Herndon, Vol. 9, No. 3, 1992, pp. 325-337.
52. See for the whole analysis of Turkey in detail, Abu Sulayman, Abul Hamid A., *op. cit.*, pp. 7-11; Gibb, H.A.R., and Eowen, Harold. *Islamic Society and the West*, Oxford, 1957, Vol. I, Part II, pp. 159-61; Berkes, Niyazi, *Development of Secularism in Turkey*, McGill, 1964.
53. Ali Abdur Raziq, Sheikh, *Al-Islam wa Usul al-Hukm*, Beirut, al-Hayat Library, 1966, pp. 82-83, 136, 141 and 142 quoted from El-Awa, Muhammad S., *On the Political System of the Islamic State*, Indiana, 1980, pp. 66-67.

54. Ali Abdur Raziq, *op. cit.*, p. 153.
55. Von Grunebaum, Gustave E., *Modern Islam, The search for Cultural Identity*, New York: Random House, 1964, p. 307.
56. Abu Sulayman, Abdul Hamid A., *op. cit.*, p. 10.
57. Al-Sibai, Mustafa, *Ishtirakiyah al-Islam*, Damascus, Muassasah al-Matbuaat al-Arabiyah, 1960. 423 pp.
58. Dekmejian, R. Harair, in *The Oxford Encyclopaedia of the Modern Islamic World*, ed. John L. Esposito, Vol. 4, pp. 71-72.
59. Al-Kholi al-Bahi "On Property and Ownership between God and Man", in *Minbar al-Islam* (English edition, Cairo, January 1962) pp. 25-26.
60. Ahmad, Khurshid Dr., *Socialism or Islam*, English trans. Sharif Ahmad Khan, n.d. distributed by Muslim Welfare Society Jammu & Kashmir, pp. 251-253, footnote No. 252.
61. Naziri, Mufti Jamil Ahmad, *Rasul Akram ka Tariqaah Namaz*, Jamiah Arabiyah, Mubarakpur, Azamgarh, Safar 1408 A.H./October 1987, p. 95.
62. Bukhari, *Al-Jame al-Sahih*, Vol. I, p. 120; *Muslim al-Jame al-Sahih*, Vol. I, p. 183 quoted in Naziri, *op. cit.*, p. 95.
63. Fath al-Bari, Vol. II, p. 350.
64. Ibn Abi Shaibah, *Kitab al-Musannaf*, Vol. 2, p. 383.
65. Nadvi, Rais Muhammad, *Rasul Akram Ka Sahih Tariqah Namaz*, Varanasi, Jamiah Salafiah, 1417AH/1996 AD., p. 233.
66. Ibid., pp. 230-232.
67. Nadvi, Mukhtar Ahmad, Majallah *Al-Balagh* Monthly, Mumbai, Vol. 15, No. 9, Safar, 1426AH/April 2005, p. 53.
68. Ibid., p. 53. See for a detailed study, Nadvi, Mukhtar Ahmad, *Kiya Musalman Khawatin Ka Masjid Mein Aana Fitnah Hai*? (Is joining Masjid a captivating for Muslim Women?) Mumbai, Al-Dar al-Salafiah.
69. Shahabuddin, Sayyid, *Muslim Muasharah Huquq Niswan Ki Maghribi Tahrik Ki Zad Per* (Muslim Society: The Target of Western Feminist Movement), *Roznamah Rashtriya Sahara* (Urdu), 23 May 2005, p. 03.
70. Jamii, Shabbir Ahmad, Ijtimai Ijtihad Ke Asaalib (Styles of Collective Ijtihad), in *Maqaalaat Seminar bar Ijtimai Ijtihad*, pp. 75-76, quoted by Madani, Hafiz Hasan, Monthly Muhaddith, Lahore, Vol. 37, No. 4, Rabiul Awwal 1426 AH/April 2005, pp. 10-11.
71. Ibid., p. 12.
72. Ibid., p. 10-11.
73. Ibid., p. 14.
74. Abu Sulayman, Abdul Hamid A., *op. cit.*, p. 4. This term of *Islamic Asalah* should not be confused with "fundamentalism" used by the West to defame Islam and Muslims and to portray them as reactionary, non-tolerant and terrorist.
75. Siddiqui, Nijatullah Dr., *Maqasid Shariat*: Yek Asri Mutalah, *Tarjuman Darul Uloom*, New Delhi, Vol. 1, No. 4, December, 2004, p. 18.

*****

# 1

# CLASSICAL POLITICAL THOUGHT

When we use the expression 'Islamization of knowledge' the scope of discussion often becomes limited and we tend to refer to the intellectual and cultural re-orientation of the West alone. In proclaiming this, we have been highlighting the Western sciences developed in accordance with the peculiar intellectual, academic and ideological requirements. Or course, these sciences, social or human, physical or chemical, comprise a set of notions and informations arranged and systematised according to the ideas and beliefs, outlooks, dispositions, social conditions and intellectual environment of the West and we have to bring them in harmony with Islamic moral principles and thereby achieve intellectual autonomy.

We can not, however, ignore the fact that the whole legacy of Islamic thought too was prepared in the intellectual atmosphere and with the implicit assumptions that are no longer valid at present.[1] In discussing Qur'anic exegesis, Ismail R. Faruqi touched upon the problem when he said:

> It is needless to point out that our ancestors completed remarkable studies constituting a tremendous wealth of insight, though none of them followed this method (axiological systematization). We can not do without their work nor can we afford to overlook the insight of their research or the wisdom of their vision... (though) none of them achieved the axiological systematization we need today.[2]

Fazlur Rahman agrees with this, although he sees it in a different context:

> A most fundamental and striking feature of our *Fiqh* is that its various parts and legal points and enunciations do not actually tie up with one another to make it (a really) well-knit system.[3]

The lack of comprehensive systematization is clearly apparent in the field of law and Islamic social sciences. The entire legacy of Muslim political thought requires a thorough examination. There are two key problems which are very important and which frequently agitate the minds of researchers:

a) Lack of truly Islamic independent thinking; and

b) Lack of a comprehensive approach.

## Lack of Independent Thinking

While considering the problem of Islamization of the discipline, it should remain in our mind that the dichotomy between the political and intellectual leadership through the ages resulted in an intellectual and cultural legacy that did not adhere strictly to the spirit and objectives of Islam. The whole literature of political thought has been prepared, more or less, under the supervision or in accordance with the will of the Muslim rulers.

During the period of the Prophet (SAW) and the reign of the righteous Caliphs, the rulers struck a harmonious balance between religion and politics. The Caliph's faith and practices were in consonance with the Islamic values and objectives and there was no dichotomy or conflict between the temporal and the spiritual. But in later days, when kingship was introduced in the society, the gulf between religion and politics widened and this brought about an intellectual pomposity which lacked seriousness especially in the field of political thought. If we make a close study of its heritage we may reach to the conclusion that in that age political science was understood in a very limited sense referring to the qualities which should be possessed by the Sultan, the faults from which he should be free in order to be a capable ruler and so on. As for monarchy, it was treated from the point of view of the conditions which should be legally found in the Imam or Sultan and it referred to those qualities which render him unfit to rule. It also took into account the monarchical functions, such as posts of ministers, emirates, and the various departments (diwans). From Ibn Qutayba al-Dinawari (d. 889 A.D.) to Shah Waliullah Dehlavi (d. 1762 A.D.) most of the political thinkers deal with the subject in the form more of counsels than a critical exposition. Al-Farabi

(d. 950 A.D.) al-Mawardi (d. 1058 A.D.), al-Turtushi (d. 1126 A.D.), al-Ghazali (d. 1112 A.D.), al-Tiqtaqa, Ibn Khaldun (d. 1337 A.D.) and others have discussed these but confined them to monarchical politics.[4]

It is commonly understood that 'The Ordinances of Government' (Al-Ahkam al-Sultaniyah) by Al-Mawardi is the standard account of the Islamic political thought. But it is not so. This book was commissioned by one of the Abbasid caliphs and from points in its treatment, it is argued that 'it must have contemporary relevance.'[5] In fact, this work defends the position of the caliph against the Buwaihids who were ruling in Baghdad, and against the Fatimids ruling in Cairo, who then claimed to be the rightful rulers of the whole Muslim world. The scholars view that al-Mawardi later began to move along the path of compromise and that under subsequent writers this path brought Sunni political theory to a collapse.[6]

The writers[7] on Islamic political thought see the discipline as reaching its highest point in the writings of al-Farabi (d. 950 A.D.), Ibn Sina (d. 1037 A.D.), and Ibn Rushd (d. 1198 A.D.). These scholars were, of course, outstanding in metaphysics and other branches of philosophy, and their political writings, as part of their general philosophy, reached a high level of technical competence. But if, as is suggested, it was the study of Platonic philosophy which gave their own philosophy its character and its form,[8] sometimes modified by the ideas of Aristotle and later commentators, then we shall not expect these writers to be the best guides to the distinctive aspects of Islamic political thought.[9]

## A Case Study of Ibn Taimiyah

Ibn Taimiyah (d. 728 A.H./1328 A.D.) whose writings on Islamic political thought are considered to be seminal and who had severely criticised the innovations and deviations in religious conceptions and consequently, faced the clossal opposition from the different classes of 'Ulama – the Sunni, the Rawafid, the mystics and the Ahl al-Bid'ah, and was subjected to constant political persecution by the state too, does not have much modern relevance nor does he represent the Qur'anic uncompromising political teachings in his approach and expression.

He is the first thinker in the Muslim history who has asserted that Islam has given no principle of state and that the establishment of State is not one of the functions of Prophecy. In his opinion, the Prophet was a prophet first and a prophet last and the state he established was an incidental affair, an outcome of the historical situation, not essential to his mission. In fact, most of his ideas about the state are found in his famous book Minhaj al-Sunnah written in refutation of the Shi'ite thought of Ibn al-Muttahhar al-Hilli. It is not a systematic work on politics but a book of polemics. Therefore, the political ideas are interwoven with hair-splitting discussions on scholastic theology, *Qur'ānic* and hadith texts, jurisprudence, philosophy and mysticism. Ibn Taimiyah has commented on Ibn al-Muttahhar's Minhaj al-karamah which was written to persuade Uljaytu Khan, the Mangol emperor, to embrace Shiism, and observed that these people made only a hypocritical show of Islam but were in fact a species of the Batiniyah heretics:

> ... who do not enjoin submission to the faith of Islam, and do not prohibit submission to other religions, but regard the different religions as different schools of thought and varieties of politics which may be suitably adopted, and who regard prophecy as a kind of just polity, evolved for the common good in this world.[10]

Thus, it seems that Ibn Taimiyah's real intention was just to oppose the Shias, for whom the *Imamah* is the first article of faith and the whole of religion depends on the proclamation of this dogma. Ibn Taimiyah wanted to condemn this theory in the strongest of terms. He pointed out that faith, and not state, is the foremost consideration in religion and that the aim of the Prophet was not to create a mere political order.[11]

In fact, in the first chapter of the first part of *Minhaj al-Sunnah*, Ibn Taimiyah has not only made a great endeavour to refute the Shi'ite theory of *Imamah*, but has also incidentally made remarks on the general political theory in Islam, which, if not interpreted properly, may lead to serious misunderstandings.[12]

One great weakness in Ibn Taimiyah's thought was that he gave the idea of *Shura* and *Shawkah* – the two opposite poles at the same time. He, on the one hand, advocates the theory of consultation and suggests to the caliph to take advice on each and every governmental problem from *Ahl al-hall wa al- 'aqd* (people at the helm of affairs) and, on the other, justifies the *status quo* however tyrannical and unjust it might be. He holds the view that the *Khilafah* is not conditioned by any thing except the support of the *Ahl al-Shawkah*, and as regards the common people they are only the means by which the purposes of the *Ummah* are realised.[13] For him, *Ahl al-Shawkah* are all those persons who, irrespective of their profession and station in life, command the respect and obedience of the community. Ibn Taimiyah, though, has interpreted the concept of *Imamah* not in terms of mere force, authority and power, instead he has emphasised the common profits, social peace and constitutional guarantees of the law.[14] Yet he, by giving the idea of *Shawkah*, has minimised the role and contribution of the Muslim community within the institution of *Imamah*. In his opinion, the common people cooperate in achieving the fundamental aims of the state, but so far as the *Imamah* is concerned it is only the *Ahl al-Shawkah* who count.

The idea of *Shawkah* was, perhaps, first introduced by Abu Hamid al-Ghazali. In his time the Saljuq Turks were the real masters of Baghdad who ruled with the title of Sultan. To maintain the integrity of the Muslim world, he endeavoured to strengthen the compromise theory of caliphate. He said that the *Khalifah* might be instituted either by a text from the Prophet, or by a will of the reigning caliph for his successor or by the delegation of authority to a powerful person whose obedience and delegation might be able to command the agreement of others and hasten them towards *Mubayaah*.[15] Al-Ghazali writes, "Then indeed according to us the *Imamah* instituted by the *Shawkah*, is established by the *Mubayaah*.[16] In another passage he declares, "The *Shawkah* cannot be achieved except with the support of the majority of the reliable persons of the age."[17] Indeed, he had in mind the Saljuqs of Baghdad who were the actual guardians of the caliphate. He, therefore, developed the theory of *Shawkah* only to strengthen the theory of delegation of authority (*Tafwid*). The same theory was subsequently to be transformed by Ibn Khaldun into his famous theory of the Asabiyah[18] (solidarity) who has given basically no new idea except his elaboration of the *Asabiyah*-structure.[19]

Although Ibn Taimiyah has rejected the traditional theory of the caliphate and although he has developed an independent theory of the state, yet his concept of power-state is totally against the natural law, reason or the *Shariah*. No doubt, his support to Mumluks who had halted the onslaught of the Mongols and pushed the Crusaders to take defensive position, was of vital importance but his justification to power-state theory and condemnation of all kinds of rebellion can not be testified.

Hence, the advocates of Islamization of political science should realise these inadequacies and must review the whole legacy in the light of the Qur'an and the *Sunnah* and in consonance with the need of time and place. Secondly, the Qur'an does not give any indication as to the definition of an ideal state and does not prescribe any political principles as part of the fundamentals of religion for organizing the state.[20]

## Varying Definitions of Khilafah

The Muslim thinkers have discussed this problem in different ways. For example, the Shiahs say that the *Imamah* is the *lutf* (grace of Allah towards His people)[21]. And all that brings the believers near to obedience and keeps them away from sins is technically termed *lutf*. From this it is clear that the necessary effective appointment of the *Imam* is a grace of God towards the realization of the obligatory responsibilities.[22] So the Shi'i stand is: since God is the absolute ruler of the universe and has placed certain responsibilities on mankind for the good for His creation, it is, therefore, incumbent upon Him to appoint some one as *Imam* to enforce His law and execute His decrees, because He does not look into all these affairs personally.[23]

The Orthodox Sunni view, as given by al-Iji, is that "the *Imamah* is not one of the fundamentals of faith and religious practice, as the Shi'ites believe, but it is one of the details (*furu'*) connected with the acts of the believers, because they think that the appointment of *Imam* is enjoined on the Ummah by *al-Sam* (tradition)[24]."

The Mu'tazili view of the problem is entirely opposed to the Sunni view, which holds in general, that the necessity of the *Imamah* is proved by reason and not revealed by God.[25] This opinion is mainly of the Basrah school led by Wasil, al-Asamm, al-Fuwati, al-Jubbai and others. The Baghdad school is heavily inclined towards Shi'ism. The difference between the two views is vital, because a function that is not demanded by the Shari'ah, but is only based on reason, carried a wide latitude for interpretation and adjustment.

The Khariji position in this controversy is very interesting. They attach no importance to the question whether the *Imamah* is ordained by reason or revelation. They are interested only in the application of *Shar'*. If this law can be applied by the community without the help of a superior authority there is no need for an Imam.[26] The Khawarij as a whole allow that there may be no Imam in the world at all.[27]

Al-Baghdadi (d. 429 A.H.) defines Khalifah as one "who implements the rules of *Shari'ah* amongst the Muslims, establishes *hudud*, dispatches expeditions, arranges marriages of widows and distributes the booty among the public.[28] Al-Mawardi giving a more comprehensive definition says that Khilafah is the succession (*Niyabah*) to the Prophet (SAW) in the protection of religion and looking after the worldly affairs of the people.[29] According to al-Juwayni (d. 478 A.H.):

> The *Imamah* is a perfect authority and general leadership over the people, commons as well as notables, in all important religious and temporal affairs, the defense of the territory of *Dar al-Islam*, looking after the interests of the community, establishing Islamic *Dawah* by providing evidence and proof and even by using force, denouncing the deviation, abstaining from inequity and oppression, providing help and support to the oppressed against transgressors and recovering the dues from those who refuse to be paid to those who were deprived of their rights.[30]

Abu al-Hasan Ash'ari is of the opinion that the *Imamah* and *Shari'ah* are twins, and the implementation of *Shari'ah* depends on the establishment of the *Imamah*.[31] Ibn Taimiyah holds the view that the Imam is a protector of the Ummah,[32] a statement which is derived from a well known *hadith*.[33] According to al-Taftazani (d. 791 A.H.) "The *Imamah* is a general leader (*riyasah aammah*) in religious and temporal affairs, as vicegerent of the Prophet (SAW)[34]." Ibn Khaldun, in this respect, stresses the religious aspect, because the religious commitment and fervour strengthens the power and solidarity of the believers. The politics based on religious values, as viewed by him, contributes to the good in this world as well as in the Hereafter.[35]

Shah Waliullah Dehlavi has explained the Khilafah as follows:

> It is general authority as vicegerent of the Prophet (SAW) for the establishment of *Din* by reviving the religious sciences, establishing the pillars of Islam, carrying out the *Jihad* and what is necessary for *Jihad*, such as organizing the army and paying the stipends to soldiers and allocating the *fay*, establishing justice, implementing the *hudud*, eliminating oppression, enjoining the good and forbidding the evil.[36]

It is clear from the definitions cited above, that Fuqaha hold divergent views regarding the status and position of *Khalifah*. Al-Juwayni's definition is different from that of al-Mawardi. The first had included the words *riyasah aammah* and *ziaamah aammah* which have differentiated between the *Khilafah* and *imarah*. The *Khilafah*, according to al-Juwayni, too, testified this definition. These two scholars confer the *Khalifah* with much authority and hence this definition was not popularized in Muslim society because it was the Prophet (SAW) only who being the Messenger of Allah, held such an extensive authority.[37]

Some *fuqaha* suggest the ability of *ijtihad* as a necessary qualification for the *Khalifah*. In this capacity he has the right to exercise *ijtihad*.[38] But there are some scholars who assert that the basic function of *Khalifah* is to preserve religion and hence he has no right to make any change or amendment or even to introduce any new interpretation to fundamentals of *Din*.[39]

The *fuqaha* have a contradictory opinion on the qualifications necessary for *Khalifah*. Mostly the *fuqaha* stress upon knowledge, soundness of character, capacity of social and political organization, military expertise and descent of the Quraysh.[40] The condition of being a descendent from the Quraysh is mentioned as the last one by al-Baghdadi, al-Mawardi and al-Ghazali. Al-Iji discusses it as being disputed, the Khawarij and some of the Mu'tazilah do not accept this condition. He criticises this condition in the historical context.[41] Ibn al-Farra puts this condition as the first one. He mentions a tradition from Ahmad b. Hanbal saying that *the Khalifah* whould not be a non-Qurayshite. He is strict about this condition and lenient about others[42] while some scholars view that the condition of being a descendent of the Quraysh was not a permanent one and the *hadith*, oft-repeated in this regard, only expresses the political dominance held by the Quraysh and does not lay down any legal rule of permanent nature.[43]

In view of this controversy it is not easy to derive any specific definition of Islamic State. It is, therefore, necessary to give a precise definition of it.

## Lack of Comprehensive Approach

One of the important problems in the legacy of Islamic political thought is perhaps, the superficiality, inaccessibility and general lack of specialized studies in the field. The misconceptions about original text books and basic sources of Islam have created chaos in our political perceptions. If we realize the nature of problems affecting Islamic thought as a result of its methodological deficiencies, we can easily understand the inadequacy of Islamic political thought.

For example one of the most misunderstood concepts in the field of political science is the system of *Shura*. Most of the scholars hold the opinion that the ruler is not obliged to act in accordance with the opinion rendered by the majority of the members of *Shura*. It is sufficient that he consults the advisors and then acts according to the best judgement whether or not it is in conformity with the views of *Shura* members.[44] These scholars rely on the interpretations of some *Mufassirin* of the *Qur'ān* which provides that:

> So, pardon them and ask forgiveness for them and consult with them on the matter and when you decide, put your trust in Allah.
>
> (al-*Qur'ān*, 3:159)

They construe this verse --- *faiza Azamta fatawakkal al Allah* – as giving the Prophet (SAW) a choice to accept or reject the view of the *Shura* members. They cite some situation in which they did not find *Shura's* final opinion as binding either on the Prophet (SAW) or on his Companion, Abu Bakr and 'Umar. The most important of these was in the case of the peace treaty of al-Hudaibiyah in which the Prophet (SAW) signed and ruled out the objections of some of his companions: then in Abu Bakr's in dispatching Usamah's army despite the disagreement of the rest of the Companions on the matter: and again in his action in waging war against the apostates in which his companions did not agree with him. Another stand was that of 'Umar in the distribution of the land in Iraq.[45]

But if we take the verse in its proper context we will reach to the conclusion that this required adherence only to the conclusions resulting from the consultation because *al-azm* (decisions of resolutions) can be reached only after consultation has taken place. Thus al-Qurtubi, in his interpretation of the view in question related from Qatada has said that "*al-azm* is a matter carefully checked and considered. To follow one's view without consideration is not '*azm*'."[46]

There is no contradiction between what is said above and the meaning of "Put your trust in Allah", as one who is not putting his trust in their advice will not be guided by Allah for "trust in Allah" means asking Allah for support and guidance which can come only from Him whose hands hold the reins of everything. The role of consultation, however, is limited to presentation of views which come closest to being correct and are most worthy of being followed.

We can also support this view by citing al-Tabari in his *Tafsir* in which he said that *al-Azm* and *al-Tawakkul* (trust) in Allah applied only to a matter on which the Prophet was given a revelation, commanding him to do a certain thing. In such a case, the Prophet was not allowed to consider the views of the people of his *Shura*, but was required to execute the command given to him whether or not it agreed with their view. Commenting on this, al-Tabari interprets the verse in the following manner:

> When you have firmly resolved with our confirmation and directive to you in any of your groups on worldly or religious matters, you must go forward in executing our Order to you, whether it agrees with the view of your companions and with what they have advised you.[47]

It is clear here that one must resolve firmly in all matters revealed in *Wahy* without consideration of *Shura* or its conclusions. This verse does not apply to matters in which no *Wahy* is given and, therefore, the rulers in regard to such matters are to remain basically bound by *Shura*.

Those who claim that *Shura* is not a binding have based their arguments on the previously mentioned situations. However, they seem to have been unsuccessful in interpreting and explaining these situations and as such shall be seen from the following details, even in reporting them.

(a) The subject of the peace treaty of al-Hudaybiya was never, at any stage, subject to *Shura*. From the beginning to the end, the actions of the Prophet (SAW) were inspired by *Wahy*. What had happened, however, was that 'Umar b. al-Khattab inquired from the Prophet (SAW) why the Muslims would accept the peace . In reply, the Prophet (SAW) said: "I am Allah's slave and His *Rasul* – I will not oppose His order, and He will not abandon me."[48] Even before this discussion with 'Umar, the Prophet (SAW) had stated that the matter was subject to revelation. For when the she-camel of the Prophet (SAW) had stopped, he said to his companions: 'The one who restrained the elephant from Makkah is keeping her back. Today I shall agree to any conditions the Quraysh may make in which they ask me to show kindness to kindered'.[49] Hence, there is no relation whatever between the events leading to the peace of al-Hudaibiyah and the subject of *Shura*, nor is there any evidence to prove that it was a binding.

(b) As for Abu Bakr's stand concerning the dispatch of Usamah's army, it should be pointed out that Abu Bakr was carrying out the decision of the Prophet (SAW) who organised Usamah's army and supervised it himself. The dispatch was delayed because of the illness of the Prophet (SAW). Thus Abu Bakr's action in this matter was to carry out the Prophet's (SAW) command according which the army departed from Madinah before his death, but when its commander (Usamah) saw the Prophet's illness worsening, he decided to encamp near by to await the outcome of this illness.[50]

(c) It is well known that Abu Bakr, among the companions of the Prophet (SAW), was the first to hold the opinion that it was necessary to fight the Arabs, who, after the death of the Prophet (SAW) had apostatized and declined to pay *Zakah*. Soon, however, several companions who had at first opposed him came round to his views. Both Bukhari and Muslim have related that 'Umar b. al-Khattab said: "By Allah, as soon as I saw that Allah the Almighty had opened the heart of Abu Bakr to fight, I knew it was the right thing." There is no doubt that the *Imam* or the ruler has the right to express his view on a matter which is subject to *Shura* and to present supporting evidence to convince the people of its rightness. This is exactly what Abu Bakr did, reasoning with the help of the *Hadith* in which the Prophet (SAW) said that "I have been ordered to fight people until they say, 'La Ilaha Illa Allah (There is no deity except Allah). Therefore, he who says 'La ilaha illa Allah' shall render himself and his property safe from me, except for what is due from him, and his accounting will be with Allah." Then Abu Bakr argued further, pointing out that "a *Zakah* is a due on property." Thereupon those who had opposed him in the beginning, led by 'Umar b. al-Khattab, came to agree with his convincing arguments and reasoning.[51]

If this is true, and no doubt it is, then it is not that Abu Bakr disagreed with the conclusions of the members of *Shura*, rather they agreed to what he had initiated and afterward to his fighting the apostates. Thus Abu Bakr was, in fact, carrying out the conclusion of *Shura* and not 'contradicting the almost unanimous view advocated by the Muslims'[52] as some researchers put it.

(d) The position of 'Umar b. al-Khattab with respect to the distribution of the lands in Iraq after its conquest is also a proof that he was acting on the conclusions reached by *Shura*, and not a proof of disregard thereof. It is reported on the basis of reliable authorities that 'Umar had consulted the Prophet's (SAW) companions on the matter and the majority of them advised him to distribute it in the same manner in which Khayber, when conquered by the Prophet (SAW), was distributed. But 'Ali b. Abi Talib and Ma'adh b. Jabal advised 'Umar against this course and to keep it as a source of income for succeeding generations of Muslims. 'Umar himself concurred with the opinion of these two, and in further discussions with the Muslims won them over to this view, gained their agreement and, therefore, did not distribute the land in Iraq. Umar's stand in this case is similar to that of Abu Bakr's in the case of the war against the apostates. Each had a view with which the majority of the companions did not agree initially, but each persuaded them with arguments, convincing them of the soundness of his view. Thus, each acted after a final decision was arrived at by mutual consultation and did not act on his own view.

Hence, the researcher of Islamic political thought should realize that the mutual consultation qualified the rule rather than exception in the life of the Holy Prophet (SAW) and during the period of *al-Khulafa al-Rashidun*. Those who think otherwise betray short-sightedness. Their failure lies in their inability to make a comprehensive study of the literature on the subject.

*****

## NOTES AND REFERENCES


1. Allal al-Fasi, *Maqasid al-Shariyah al-Islamiyah wa Makarimuha* (Morocco, 1963), pp. 82-194.
2. Al-Faruqi, Ismail Raji, "Towards a New Methodology for Qur'anic Exegesis," *Islamic Studies*, March, 1962, p. 47.
3. Fazlur Rahman, *Islamic Methodology*, p. 184.
4. Enan, M.A., *Ibn Khaldun: His life and work*, (Lahore, 1946), pp. 90-99.
5. Gibb, H.A.R., *Studies on the Civilization of Islam*, (England, 1962), p. 153.
6. *Ibid*, p. 142.
7. See for detail, Rosenthal, E.I.J., *Political Thought in Medieval Islam*, (England, 1962); Sherwani, H.K., *Studies in Muslim Political Thought and Administration*, (Lahore, 1942).
8. Rosenthal, *op. cit.*, p. 114.
9. Watt, W.M., *Islamic Political Thought—The Basic Concepts*, (Edinburgh, 1968) p. 104.
10. Ibn Taimiyah, *Minhaj al-Sunnah*, Vol. I, pp. 2-3.
11. *Ibid*, pp. 17-19.
12. Khan, Qamaruddin, *The Political Thought of Ibn Taimiyah, op. cit.*, p. 57.
13. Ibn Taimiyah, *Minhaj al-Sunnah*, Vol. IV, pp. 232.
14. Laoust, Henry, *op.cit.*, pp. 288-289.
15. Al-Ghazali, *Kitab al-Iqtisad fi al-Iitiqad*, p. 106.
16. Al-Ghazali, *Fadaih al-Batiniyah*, (Leiden, 1956), p. 66.
17. *Ibid*, p. 67.
18. Ibn Khaldun, *Al-Muqaddimah*, pp. 125-135.
19. Khan Qamaruddin, *The Political Thought of Ibn Taimiyah, op.cit.*, p. 137.
20. Ibn Taimiyah, *Minhaj al-Sunnah*, Vol. I, pp. 17, 23, al-Ghazali, *Fada'ih al-Batiniyah*, (Leiden, 1956), p. 64.
21. Al Iji, *al-Mawaqif*, Vol. VIII, p. 348.
22. Al-Tusi, Nizam al-Mulk, *Risalah Imamah* (Tehran, 1335 A.H.), p. 16.
23. *Ibid*, p. 19.
24. Ibn Taimiyah, *Minhaj*, Vol. I, p. 26, al Juwaini, *al-Irshad*, p. 410, al-Iji, *al-Mawaqif*, Vol. 8, p. 344.
25. Al-Shahrastani, *al-Milal wa'al-Nihal*, Vol. I, p. 153 (on the margin of Ibn Hazm's *al-Fisal*).
26. Elie, Abid Salem, *Political Theory and Institutions of Khawarij*, p. 51; Ibn Khaldun, *al-Ibar*, Vol. V, p. 160.
27. Al-Shahrastani, ed. by Fathullah, Vol. 2, p. 216.
28. Al-Baghdadi, Abdul Qadir, *Usool al-Din*, (Istanbul, 1928), p. 271.
29. Al-Mawardi, Abul Hasan Ali, *Al-Ahkam al-Sultaniyah*, (Cairo 1966), p. 5.

30. Al-Juwayni, Imam al-Haramayn, *Giyath al-Umam,* Mustafa Hilmi, (Alexandria, 1979), p. 15.
31. Al-Juwayni, *Usool al-Din, op. cit.*, p. 272.
32. Laoust, Henry, *Nazriyyat Ibn Taimiyah fi al-Siyasah*, Arabic tr. By M. Abdul Azim Ali (Cairo, 1979), p. 226.
33. Bukhari, *Sahih*, Cairo; (nd.) Vol. I, Part II, p. 6, Abu Daud, *Sunan*, ed. Izzat Ubaid, Hims, 1969, Hadith No. 2928, Ibn Taimiyah, *al-Siyasah al-Sharyiah*, (Kuwait, 1986), p. 23.
34. Al-Taftazani, *Sharh al-Maqasid,* (Lahore, 1981), Vol. 2, p. 272.
35. Ibn Khaldun, *al-Muqaddimah*, (Beirut, 1956), p. 38.
36. Shah Waliullah, *Izalah al-Khifa*, Urdu Tr. Abd Al-Shakur, Karachi, (ed.), Vol. I, p. 28.
37. Faruqi, M.Y., Early *fuqaha* on the Significance and Role of the *Khilafah, Hamdard Islamics,* Karachi, Vol. XIV, No. 1, p. 7.
38. See Lambton, K.A.S., Khilafah in Political Theory, in *Encyclopaedia of Islam*.
39. Al-Rayyis, Ziauddin, *Al-Nazriyat al-Siyasiyah fi al-Islam*, (Cairo, 1990), p. 121.
40. The condition of being a descendent from the Quraysh is based upon an oft quoted *hadith*, 'the leaders come from the Quraysh.' See, Ahmad b. Hanbal, *Musnad, op. cit.*, Vol. III, p. 129, Vol. 4, p. 421.
41. Al-Baghdadi, *Usool al-Din*, *op.cit.*, p. 277, al-Mawardi, *Al-Ahkam al-Sultaniyah, op.cit.,* p. 6; Al-Ghazali, al-Iqtisad (Beirut, 1969) p. 215, al-Iji, *al-Mawaqif*, *op.cit.*, p. 398.
42. Ibn al-Farra, *al-Ahkam al-Sultaniyah*, ed. Mohd. Hamid al-Fiqi (Cairo, 1966), p. 20.
43. Faruqi, M.Y., Early Fuqaha on the significance and role of the *Khilafah, op.cit.*, pp. 12-13. The author, in his support, has quoted the two *hadiths* as follows:

    > Umar once said to the Quraysh, "O people of Quraysh By Allah, even if you enter a hole, the Arabs, following your traces, will also enter the same. Therefore be mindful of Allah in their affairs."

    The second one related to Thaqifah Banu Saidah where the companions had met to select their leader. At that meeting Abu Bakr and Umar argued, "certainly the Arabs will not submit to anyone except this tribe of Quraysh." The author concludes that the *hadith* does not seek to lay down any principle or rule that the rulers or leaders should always be from the Quraysh.
44. Prof. Abdul Hamid Mutawalli has related this from *Tafsir al-Tabari* and *Tafsir al-Qurtubi*. See, his book *Mabadi Nizam al-Hukm fi al-Islam*, (Alexandria, 1964), p. 245-246.
45. Babelly, M., *al-Shura fi al-Islam*, (Beirut, 1968), pp. 81-105.
46. *Tafsir al-Qurtubi*, Vol. 4, p. 525.
47. *Tafsir al-Tabari*, Vol. 7, p. 346.

48. Sirat Ibn Hisham, with Al-Rawdh al-Unuf by al-Suhayli, Vol. 2, p. 230.
49. *Ibid* p. 226.
50. Sirat Ibn Hisham, Vol. 2, pp. 365, 369.
51. See this hadith and its Tafsir in *Sahih Muslim* with the commentary of Nawawi, Vol. I, pp. 200-210, and also in *Sahih al-Bukhari*, Vol. 2, Cairo, p. 131.
52. Abd al-Hamid Mutawalli, *op.cit.*, p. 246, F more details in this regard see, *Kitab al-Amwal*, by Abu Ubaid al-Qasim b. Salam, Vol. 1, Cairo, p. 83.

An Appended List of Political Theorists in Islamic History

The following is a list of the selected works on the history of Muslim political thought. This list is in no way complete but consists of some basic works easily available. The list includes both the classical and modern period.

1. Ibn Qayyim al-Jauziyah (d. 751) discussed the political steps and actions that should be taken by the kings for the sake of establishment of justice and administration of the country effectively. He wrote the book entitled *Al-Turuq al-Hukmiyah fi al-Siyasah al-Sharyiah*. Discussing his intention of raising the problems in his writings he has elaborated the point in the very introduction: "the administration of justice is an important, significant and profit bearing work that if ignored by the ruler or governor he will destroy many rights and if managed by him without taking Islamic *shariah* into consideration he will be oppressor and tyrant." His political ideas are given less importance than they deserved.
2. Abdullah bin al-Muqaffa who was excuted as a heretic in 757, has produced the elegant Arabic version of Persian work namely *Kalilah wa Dimnah*. In this book much traditional wisdom, some of political nature, is put into the mouths of animals. He also wrote *The lives of the Persian Kings* and *The Book of the Crown*.
3. Abu Yusuf (d. 798) wrote the book *Kitab al-Kharaj* (Book on Land tax) for Harun al-Rashid. The introductory remarks occupy some twenty pages and deal with the duties of princes and their relations to their subjects. This is available in French and Urdu translations by E. Fagnan and M.N. Siddiqui respectively.
4. Ibn Qutaybah (d. 889) one of the great Sunni polygraphs of the ninth century being both a theologian and a writer of *Adab*. He was appointed as *Qadi* of Dinawer in 851 probably because of his introduction to the *Adab al-Kātib*. In this book he gave the philosophy for the use of secretaries with an introduction which may be regarded as a politico-cultural profession of faith. In his book *Tawil Mukhtalaf al-Hadith* some of his religious and political ideas are clearly set out.
5. Abul Hasan Ash'ari (d. 935) the founder of Ash'arite theological school, has included various political discussions in his different writings. At the end of *Kitab al-Luma* he has elaborated the Sunnite theory of *Imamah* because it was customary to have a section on *Imamah* in most treatises on theology.

6. Al-Maturidi (d. 944), who is closely associated with the Hanafi legal rite, and his followers who are considered to have important influence on some later developments, contributed much to *Imamah* theory. Their early forms of the Hanafi creed are represented by A.J. Wenisick in *The Muslim Creed.* The later views on the theory of *Imamah* are translated in the creed of Najmuddin al-Wasafi (d. 1142).
7. Abu Nasr Al-Farabi (d. 950), the eminent philosopher, the statesman, wrote several treatises on politics. *Al-Madinah al-Fazilah, al-Fusul al-Madaniyah* and *Al-Siyasah al-Madaniyah* are the most important ones. The idea of 'Ideal State' propounded by al-Farabi has been compared with that of Greek philosophers. *Al-Madinah al-Fazilah of al-Farabi* gives a unique idea in the sense it introduced a best mixture of morality and politics and its ideal state is governed by the ethical and spiritual laws.
8. Qadi Al-Numan (d. 974) the spokesman of the Fatimi form of Ismaili Shi'ism elaborated the political ideas regarding *Imamah* in his book *Daaim al-Islam* (The Pillars of Islam).
9. Shaykh al-Saduq al-Qummi (d. 991) wrote an early Imami Shi'ite creed that was translated into English by A.A.A. Fyzi entitled *A Shi'ite Creed.*
10. Al-Baqillani (d. 1013) developed the Ash'arite view on *Imamah*. He included a considerable section on the subject in his general book on theology entitled the *Tamhid* or Introduction.
11. Ibn Sina (d. 1037) who played a part in politics in various minor courts east of Baghdad, even rising to be a vizier for a time, did not write any political treatise. His main concern was with human happiness and perfection, the highest stage of which consists in the contemplation of God or Truth and in mystical union with Him. It is in this context that man as a political being was considered. He, in his books *Aqsam al-Uloom*, *Kitab al-Siyasah* and others has presented the idea of a perfect ruler which is a combination of ideal state of Islam and that of Plato's philosopher-king.
12. Al-Baghdadi (d. 1037) an Ash'arite political thinker has devoted a chapter of his theological work *Usool al-Din* (The Principles of Religion) to book *Al-Farq bayn al-Firaq*) translated into English by A.S. Halkin as *Moslem Schisms and Sects.*
13. Al-Mawardi (d. 1058) an Ash'arite thinker who wrote *Al-Ahkam al-Sultaniyah* (The Ordinances of Government) to assert the authority of Abbasids against the Buwaihids who were in effective control of their state government and administration at all levels. The appointment of Khalifah, his main attributes and basic functions were the principal concern of this book. The author, as *Qadi* under the caliph al-Qaim, who entrusted him also with diplomatic missions, was actively engaged in the application and administration of *fiqh*. This helped him in his authoritative exposition of the principles of constitutional law as well. This book is the result of slending reasoning derived from the

traditional Islamic bases of law with historical and political deductions from the formative period of Islam, supported by the views of early Muslims and a realistic appraisal of the contemporary political science.

14. Ibn al-Farra (d. 1065) the Hanbali writer, produced his political thought in his book *Al-Ahkam al-Sultaniyah* but could not gain much popularity due to Al-Mawardi's book on the same topic.
15. Amir Kaykaus (d. 1082) wrote *Qabusnama* the most interesting and accessible book in Persian language. The minor prince produced the work for his son and was translated into English by Reuben Levy under the title of *A Mirror for Prince*. The author advises his son what he should do if he were to become a middle class man, how he should serve the king if he were to be raised to an exalted position, what policy he should pursue if he were to be appointed Minister of state, how he should deal with the army if he were to become the Commander-in-Chief, and how he should conduct public affairs if he were to be crowned king of the land. These are merely the headings of but a few chapters of *Qabusnamah*.
16. Al-Juwayni (d. 1085) the prominent Ash'arite (Known as *Imam al-Haramayn*) contributed a book on the subject namely *Ghiyath al-Imam* dedicating to the vizier Nizam al-Mulk Tusi. He, moreover, had a chapter about *Imamah* in his theological work Al-Irshad.
17. Nizamul Mulk Tusi (d. 1091) Chief Minister of Saljuqi realm, the powerful statesman, who laid the foundation of Madrasa Nizamiyah at Baghdad wrote two treatises on politics, *i.e.* the *Siyasat Nama* or *Siyar al-Muluk* mainly for guidance of sultan Malik Shah and the *Majma al-Wasaya* or *Dastur al-Wuzara* which was compiled for his son Fakhr al-Mulk. In both these works every principle of political conduct is substaintiated and illustrated by a large number of anecdotes mainly taken from history and tradition. His *Siyasat Nama* has been compared with Machiavelli's *The Prince* by many scholars yet there is a great difference between the two. His suggestions to the king are thought more practical and expedient but may be traced more in the non-Muslim sources than Arab or Islamic one.
18. Al-Ghazali (d. 1111) besides discussing the *Imamah* in his theological works wrote *Fadaih al-Batiniyah* at the request of Abbasid caliph Al-Mustazhir to defend him against Fatimi claims. It is surprising that his *Kitab al-Iqtisād fi al-litiqad* exposes the nature and purpose of the *Imamah* as orthodox and classical as that of al-Mawardi but his *Kitab al-Mustazhiri* is generously tempered with political realism and preparedness to make concessions to expediency. Later in his *Ihya al-Uloom* he bows to the actual power of the Saljuqs in his attempt to preserve the institution of the *Khilafah* as the symbol of the unity of the Muslim community.
19. Al-Turtushi (d. 1126) also known as Ibn Abi Randaka, the eminent lawyer and the authority on *hadith*, wrote twelve books but only three are known to us. The book *Siraj al-Muluk* is a treatise on politics and

government which contains a large collection of more or less interesting anecdotes in 64 chapters, completed at Fustat on 19 Sep. 1122 A.D. and dedicated to the author's patron, the *vizier* al-Mamun Abu Mohammed b. al-Batachi al-Umavi.

20. Ibn Bajja (d. 1138) was for many years *vizier* of a brother-in-law of the Almoravid ruler of Muslim Spain. His three treatises *Tadbir al-Mutawahhid, Risalah al-Wada* and *Kitab Ittisal al-aql bi al-Insan* discuss his ideas in detail. He is a thinker in his own right in addition to being an important influence on Ibn Tufail and a link between al-Farabi and Ibn Rushd. Ibn Bajja has used the word '*Tadbir*' for the government and said that its proper application is to city-state and households. In his political theory Rosenthal finds individualist deviation. In his extreme rationalism and in his denial of social responsibility and civic duty he stands alone among the *Falasifah*.

21. Ibn Rushd (d. 1198) the Grand *Qadi* of Qurtubah, trained in *fiqh* and representing Maliki school, was equally well-versed in theology, philosophy and medicine. In his treatise *Fasl al-Maqal* he attempted to reconcile revelation and philosophy. He vindicated philosophy as the only legitimate discipline which leads to a true understanding of the inner meaning of the *shariah*. He denied both jurists and theologians, who were restricted to the use of dialectical and rhetorical arguments, the rights or the ability to rise to demonstrative proof of the truth of revelation. To understand and evaluate his political thought one should study his commentaries on Republic of Plato, his spirited defiance of philosophy *Tahafut al-Tahafut, Fasl al-Maqal Damima* and *Kashf an Manahij al-adillah fi Aqaid al-Millah*. He is conscious of the supremacy of the *shariah* as the ideal revealed law and of its political function as the ideal constitution of the ideal state. His commentary on the Republic is a philosophers comment on and a critique of contemporary Muslim political institutions especially those in the Maghrib. According to him, it is impossible for a man to live without the state. He is convinced that man can reach his highest perfection only in the ideal state. But he insists that no man can live, let alone reach happiness and perfection, outside any kind of political association.

22. Nasiruddin Tusi (d. 1274) who wrote *Akhlaq Nasiri*, was a Shi'ite writer who witnessed the transference of power from the Ismailis to Monogols. He has incorporated into his work the Greek and Farabian conception of the virtuous city. The work is greatly influenced by earlier Muslim writers on ethics, economics and politics. This has assimilated Platonic and Aristotelian ideas and opinions as well in his Islamic environment especially the concept of law.

23. Ibn al-Muttahhar al-Hilli (d. 1325) wrote *Minhaj al-karamah fi Marifah al-Imamah* (The Path of Nobility on the knowledge on Imamate) to represent the later form of Imami shia doctrine of Imamate. The author compiled the work to persuade Iljaytu Khan, the Mongol

emperor, to embrace Shi'ism and to convince him about Shi'ite theory of *Imamah*. Al-Hilli held the view that *Imamah* is a basic and fundamental part and belief of Islam. According to him, the principal aim of the Prophet was to establish a just political state. For him, *Imamah* is an essential element in the religion and the whole of religion depends on the profession of this dogma. The book has been translated into English.

24. Ibn Taimiyah (d. 1328) the Hanbali Jurist, the voluminous writer who severely criticised the deviations and innovations in the religion and faced the strong opposition from different classes of *'Ulama* and was presecuted by the state, wrote three main treatises on politics *i.e.*, *Minjah al-Sunnah, Al-Hisbah fi al-Islam* and *Al-Siyasah al-Sharyiah*. The first book was written in refutation of Al-Hilli's concepts of *Imamah* and was not a systematic work on politics. In this book his political ideas are intricately interwoven with hair-splitting discussions on scholastic theology, Qur'an and *Hadith,* jurisprudence, philosophy and mysticism. The second work deals with the application of the principle of ordering the good and forbidding the evil, specially with reference to state administration and contains some significant statements about the nature and functions of the state. *Al-Siyasah al-Sharyiah* was compiled primarily about the Islamic rules of administration rather than politics, yet it contains very important ideas on political theory as well.

25. Ibn Jamaah (d. 1393) a Shafi'i writer, like Ibn Taimiyah may be said to be adopting Sunni Theory of caliphate to the situation created by the destruction of the Abbasid caliphate of Baghdad in 1258. He was a noted jurist, theologian and teacher and held the office of Qadi in Jerusalem (1288-91) then that of a Grand *qadi* of Cairo and (1294) of Damascus. His treatise on constitutional theory and administrative law namely *Tahrir al-Ahkam fi Tadbir Ahl al-Islam* deserves notice as a compendium of political statutes. It is based on Qur'an and *Sunnah*, the examples of the companions of the Prophet and the utterances of *'Ulama* of Muslim countries. Of its seventeen chapters the first five concern political affairs in particular, they deal with the necessity of *Imamah*, the conditions and duties of *Imam* and the regulations governing his office and those of his principal ministers. This work was edited and translated in German by Hans Kofle.

26. Ibn Khaldun (d. 1406) both a historian and statesman who has been held as one of the first to attempt a scientific study of the state and society. The North African author propounded a theory of the power-state which transcended the opinions generally held in the Middle Ages. Not only is the state an end in itself with a life of its own, governed by the law of causality, a natural and necessary institution, it is also the political and social unit which alone makes human civilization possible. It is this human civilization which is the object of his inquiry and the subject of his "new science of history". In the

*Muqaddimah* he composed a summary not of theology but of civilization, founded on that of Islamic civilization with all of whose aspects he was thoroughly familiar. His political theory is a part of his description of Umran (civilization) and politics as the art of government as apparent from his terminology, for Umran is synonymous with Madaniyah and Hadarah, settled urban life (as distinct from Badawah, rural life). His empiricism is deeply rooted in the traditional beliefs and convictions of Islam and steeped in the traditional sciences. Ibn Khaldun distinguishes three kinds of state according to their government and purpose: *Siyasah Diniyah*, government based on the divinely revealed law, the ideal Islamic theocracy: *Siyasah Aqliyah*, government based on a law established by human reason: and *Siyasah Madaniyah*, government of the ideal state of the philosophers, *Madina Fadila*, Plato's Republic. According to Ibn Khaldun, any collective and social life requires the effective support of like-minded men, held together by a common bond; in the first place, the ties of blood and family tradition which create a sense of solidarity and mutual responsibility, or a common outlook which shows itself in united action and serves as an important driving force in the formation of the state. He calls it *Asabiyah* and gives as its aim *mulk*, dominion, rule. To him, it is as necessary as association itself, for the later alone is not sufficient to protect man's life and property. (Rosenthal pp. 84-109).

27. Ibn Tiqtaqa (born in 1262) was from eighteen generation from Ali, the son-in-law of the Prophet. The son after the father was assassinated in 1281 succeeded him in the task of looking after the interests of the Shi'ites. He wrote *Al-Fakhri fi al-Adab al-Sultaniyah*, a work of history and not simply one of a large number of moralizing and entertaining examples of a literary genre. Its main theme is political and its stress is on government based on morals and power. Its utilitarian tendency is reinforced by an introduction dealing generally with royal politics. Its usefulness consists in its description of the qualities of kings and of the foundations of government and the tools of authority. The author has given advice as a moralist on the qualities, required in a ruler, his conduct, his relations with his subjects and their duties towards him. Though he considers *Khilafah* the ideal state, he is chiefly concerned with the *Mulk*, such as that over which his patron holds sway. He is not interested in the origin, character and purpose of the state, instead his observations betray a certain political realism, a realistic attitude which takes for granted the monarchy under consideration. That is why, the author has been called, a utilitarian moralist.
28. Al-Dawani (d. 1502) the Imami Shi'i writer, *Qadi* at Faras, teacher in *Madrasah al-Aitam* in Shiraz wrote philosophical commentaries and treatises, one of which is *Akhlaq Jalali* an adaptation of Nasiruddin Tusi's treatise on practical philosophy. He, separated from Tusi, has written as an eclectic harmonizer in a fluent, easy style and succeeded

in making philosophy respectable and presentable as part of a pleasant, interesting mixture of traditional beliefs and convictions with appropriate quotations from Qur'an and *Hadith* and suitable sayings from Plato and Aristotle. The book has been translated into English by W.F. Thompson as *Practical philosophy of Muhammadan people.* He is called the master of application and integration, since he has integrated Tusi's political thought with traditionalists and at the same time he has accommodated Platonic and Aristotelian ideas to Islam.

29. Shah Waliullah Dihlavi (d. 1762) a revolutionary Indian thinker, theologian, pioneer Persian translator of the Qur'an and a traditionalist the founder of Islamic revivalism in modern times, attempted the reintegration of the socio-economic and the religio-ethical structure of Islam. The reform movement outlined by him, which found full expression in the Jihad campaign of Syed Ahmad Barelvi and Shah Ismail revolved round his concept of *Maslaha, i.e.*, the establishment of a kind of welfare state based on the relationship of man's development with the creative forces of the universe. His political ideas are scattered throughout his works like *Hujjatullah al-Balighah, Asrar al-Din, Tafhimat Ilahiyah, Izalah al-Khifa an Khilafah al-Khulafa* and *Anfas al-Arifin*. He gave the idea of *fakk Kull nizam* (down with all system!). His mission failed because both he and his successors failed to assess the impact of contemporary forces and the increasing conflict of the East and West consequent on the growth of European influence in India, especially those parts of the country where Muslims dominated.

30. Ahmad Khan, Syed (d. 1898). Indian Islamic modernist writer, political thinker and activist. Immediately after 1857, the first freedom uprising against the British colony, he undertook three projects (i) to initiate an ecumenical movement in order to create understanding between Muslims and Christians, and for that he composed a commentary on the Old and New Testaments namely *Tabyin al-Kalam* (1862); (ii) to establish scientific organizations that would help Muslims understand the secret of the West's success; in that regard he founded Scientific Society in Ghazipur, All India Mohammedans Educational Conference and Mohammedans Anglo-Oriental College in Aligarh and (iii) to analyse objectively the causes for the 1857 revolt, and in this context he wrote the famous treatise *Asbāb Baghawat –e-Hind*. He on the contrary of Indian National Congress promoted a form of Muslim nationalism that accentuated a new Muslim politics in the country keeping Muslims far from Hindu politics and concentrating in the field of modern education. What made Sir Syed controversial among a group of Ulama was his emphasis on religious modernism that rejected the traditional practices and orientations of the orthodox, and his advocacy of modern education, which lured young Muslims from orthodox religious seminaries into Western-style schools and colleges.

While he was in London he for the sake of an indepth study of British educational institutions, visited the universities of Cambridge and Oxford, as well as private preparatory schools including Eton and Harrow. These educational models enabled him to develop the blueprint for the Mohammedan Anglo-Oriental College, which he established in 1875; in 1920 the college became Aligarh Muslim University.

31. Khayruddin of Tunisia (d. 1308/1890), a prominent Muslim thinker and activist who served even as the defence minister under Ottoman Empire, was called later on to the capital Constantinople by Sultan Abdul Hamid II as his advisor. His most important contribution to Islamic thought is his work *Aqwam al-Masalik fi Marifah Ahwāl Ahl al-Mamalik*. The work emphasizes upon learning from the West and makes a complain to the Muslim political thinkers in general why did they not opt this method. The main objective of this work, as elaborated by the author, lies in his invitation to adopt better resources and methodologies for the sake of reformation and construction of the Ummah. He warned the Muslims not to be conscious about benefiting positively from the useful things of the aliens, insisted upon the following of the tradition that reads: wisdom is the lost property of the Muslims. To follow the West, learn from its institutions and to be fully aware of the secrets of its success in developing the various branches of sciences and humanities is incumbent upon the Muslims, as he asserted. The scholar discusses in detail the values of freedom, and liberty as the natural instincts. He examines the factors responsible for the collapse of Islamic Empire and the negative role of Ottomans in this regard. The internal conflicts and disturbances in the Ottoman Empire owe to the injustice and tyranny of the rulers, according to Khayruddin who declared the *tanzimat* (modernization of the Ottoman institutions) as essential to progress. He highlights the golden image of Western culture and its far reaching consequences.
32. Afghani, Jamaluddin (d. 1897) writer and Pan-Islamist activist. Controversial during his life time, he became since his death one of the most influential figures in the Muslim world, even though his written output was rather small. From traditional Islamic philosophy, he drew a belief in reason and natural law, and a deity who did not contradict these. He taught what Muslim philosophers advocated: preaching orthodox religion to the masses and a kind of rationalist, natural-law deism to the elite. His political thought was impelled by hostility to British rule in foreign, especially Muslim lands. Although he expressed himself in friendlier terms toward the French and Russians, his anti-British speeches and writings could be, and were, extended to a more general anti-imperialism that has increased in the Muslim world since his time. He is treated as the harbinger of Pan-Islamism, though it was started with the nineteenth-century Ottoman Sultans and was then voiced in more progressive, anti-imperialist forms by the Young

Ottomans, especially Namik Kamal. As Afghani's works on this subject were written in Arabic, he had more influence internationally than did the Young Ottomans. Nationalism and Pan-Islamism were seen as different but not necessarily contradictory strategies for communal unity and anti-imperialism. He in his scheme of independence of Muslim countries stressed pragmatic aspects of internal reform and self-improvement, including technical and scientific education.

33. Kawakibi, Abdur Rahman (d. 1902), Islamic revivalist and advocate of an Arab Caliphate. He is best known for his two works *Umm al-Qura* and *Tabā'i al-Istibdād*. He attributed the Muslim decline to religious, political and moral factors. Influenced by the reforms of Jamaluddin Afghani and Muhammad Abduh, he advocated a return to the original purity of Islam, which had been distorted by alien concepts and currents such as mysticism, fatalism, sectarian divisions and imitation. These distortions had led to ignorance among the Muslims and their submission to stagnant theologians and despotic rulers who suppressed freedoms, promoted false religion, and corrupted the moral, social, educational and financial systems of the Muslim nation.

    Al-Kawakibi proposed the formation of a society, with branches throughout the Muslim world, to educate Muslims and promote in them aspiration for progress. Holding non-Arabs, namely the Turks, accountable for the degeneration of Islam, he called for an Arab Caliphate, which would exercise religious and cultural leadership, not temporal authority, and become the basis for revival of Islam and an Islamic federation. He stipulated that the caliphs be from the tribe of Quraysh, have limited powers, and be subject to election every three years and accountable to an elected council. He viewed the true Islamic state as one based on political freedoms and government accountability. His work *Tabā'i al-Istibdād* is an outright attack on tyranny. The author discussed the nature of despotism and its devastating effects on society as a whole. A despotic state conducts the affairs of its citizens without fear of accountability or punishment, suppresses their rights, and prevents their education and enlightenment.

    Contributing greatly to the evolution of Arab nationalist thought, Kawakibi drew a clear distinction between the Arab and non-Arab Muslims, exalted the former on the basis of their language, descent and moral attributes, and explicitly called for an Arab state.

34. Abduh, Muhammad (d. 1905), Egyptian scholar and reformer regarded as the architect of Islamic modernism. The crucial influence in his development was the impact of Afghani, the serious advocate of unitary Islam and Pan-Islamism. To achieve emancipation from the mentality of *taqlid* and yet retain Islamic authenticity was a formidable task of him. He shouldered it with patience and resistance, corroborating his scholarly credentials by earning increasing personal stature. The idea that the Shariah could be subject to wise discretion

and that even theology could be flexible within limits served to enliven theological education, to increase student initiative, and to give scope to existing ideas of *istihsān* and *istislah*. He was fully committed with the notion that revelation and reason, each rightly perceived, were inherently horminous. Was not reason one with that *fitrah* by which, the Qur'an affirms, God had made human nature fit religion, the two being combined in the very word Islam? In *Risalah al-Tawhid* he expounded his conviction that "every sound speculation led to a belief in God as He is described in the Qur'an". He also sustained the traditional case for *ijaz* of the Qur'an as conclusive evidence of its divine origin. He called for reconciliation between the Muslims and Christians on the ground of both the revealed texts e.g. the Qur'an and Gospel in his book *al-Islam wa al-Nasra niyah*.

35. Iqbal, Muhammad (d. 1938), Indo-Pakistani political and religious writer, philosopher and poet. His prose works are actually very few; the most notable among these is *The Reconstruction of Religious Thought in Islam* (Lahore, 1930). It is a collection of seven lectures delivered in December 1928 in Madras. He took three years to compose these lectures and considered them reflective of his mature philosophical and rational approach to Islam. He expected the younger generations to follow him in a responsible *ijtihād*, the interpretation of the Qur'an and Sunnah and the formation of an entirely new opinion by applying analytical deduction. His Presidential Address to the Annual Meeting of the All-India Muslim League, 1930 is a very extensive review of the interaction between the British, the All-India National Congress, and the All-India Muslim League from the perspective of a Muslim thinker who was anxious about the political and cultural future of Muslims in the Indian sub-continent. He expounded here the two-nation theory in India. Subsequently this address came to be known as the conceptual basis for the state of Pakistan, although the name 'Pakistan' was not used by him.

    Iqbal composed his poetry in both Persian and Urdu. His six Persian works include *Asrar e Khudi wa Rumuz e be khudi* (1915), *Payam e Mashriq* (1923), *Zabur e Ajam* (1927), *Jawed Namah* (1932), *Pas chih Bayad Kard ye Aqwaam e Sharq* (1926), and *Armaghan e Hijaz* (1938). His Urdu works are *Bang e Dara* (1924), *Bāl e Jibril* (1935), and *Zarb e Kalim* (1936).

    Iqbal remained a steady supporter of the founder of Pakistan, Muhammad Ali Jinnah. During 1936-37, he wrote eight letters to Jinnah, emphasizing the partition of India into two states: however during the 1920s when Jinnah was still grouping for coexistence with the All-India National Congress, he opposed Jinnah's policies.

36. Bennab, Malek (d. 1973). The most eminent and profound scholar and thinker of post-World War II Algeria, and certainly in his period, one of the foremost intellectuals of the Arab world. His first great work

*The Quranic Phenomenon* (French) published in Algiers in 1946 is a serious attempt to tie the particular case of Islam to the religious phenomenon in general, to place its Messenger as the ultimate link in the chain of the prophetic movement, and to place the Quranic doctrines as the outcome of the stream of the monotheistic thought. Consequently this method involves drawing conclusion from the Holy Qur'an and determining from the phenomenological point of view whether there is an authentic basis or not for Islam as a revealed religion. The most important work of Bennabi for our purpose, however is *Islam in History and Society* (French, written in 1949 but published in 1954 just on the eve of the Algerian Revolution, translated into English and published from Islamabad in 1988 and Kuala Lumpur in 1991). This is full expression of his socio-political philosophy that represents an incisive and quite original analysis of the crisis facing the Muslim as well as the Western world. The thinker's masterly exposition of the twin phenomena of colonisibilite and colonisation makes him one of the 'first Arab and Afro-Asian socio-political philosophers of our times", and his remarkable grasp and critical appraisal of the modern trends in the Muslim world ensures him an honourable place in the forefront of Muslim thinkers of the past century.

Bennabi, in this book provides a methodological analysis of the various stages of history and the march and evolution of civilization. Developing further the cycle theory of change and development inherent in Ibn Khaldun he represents his own theory of the cyclical phenomenon. He divides the history of Muslim society into three stages: i) the Quranic one that ended with the battle of Siffin; ii) flourishing Muslim period till the fall of al-Muwahhids; and iii) the period of stagnation and decadence. He finally shows us the glimmer of a new stage of history as reflected in the re-awakening of the Muslim world but it can not work out its destiny in isolation. The post al-Muwahhid man must still attain the material level of the present civilization, so deeply marked by the technical spirit; but his role remains, above all, spiritual, as a moderator of the excesses of modern thought and national egoism, Bennabi makes a starting forecast: the shift of the centre of Islamic Gravity from Mediterranean to Asia, where he sees conditions most propitious for a new synthesis of man, soil and time, the formation of a popular will and evocation of that dialogue between heart and mind that he discerns in Iqbal.

37. Maududi, Sayyid Abul Ā'la (d. 1979) Islamic ideologue politician, the most prominent revivalist thinker of the modern Muslim world. His interpretative reading of Islam has contributed greatly to the articulation of Islamic thought and has influenced Muslim thinkers and activists from Morocco to Indonesia. Jamaat Islami, the organization (founded by him in 1941) that has embodied his ideology over the course of the past six decades, has played a significant role in the

history and politics of Pakistan, India, Balgladesh, Sri Lanka and the South Asian communities of the Persian Gulf states, Great Britain and North America. After the collapse of the Khilafat Movement in India in 1924, he became suspicious of Indian National Congress's manipulation of nationalist sentiments to serve Hindu interests. He opposed the Indian nationalism and counted it as against the religion of Islam and its teachings of Ummah in his book *Muttahidah Qaumiyat Awr Islam*. In his work *Al-Jihad fi al-Islam*, he explained systematically Islamic response to war, peace, violence and other issues relating to international relations without offering any apology. When India was partitioned, he divided Jamaat Islami into independent Indian and Pakistani units and himself moved to Lahore to assume leadership of Jammat of Pakistan. He did much here to mobilize public opinion for the cause of Islam, pushing the Ulama to demand an Islamic constitution. Between 1948 and 1950 he was imprisoned for refusing to lend religious legitimacy to the government's military campaign in Kashmir. In 1954 he was again imprisoned, and this time sentenced to death, for his role in instigating the disturbances against the Ahmadiyah in Punjab in 1953-54. His sentence was later commuted and he was released from prison in 1955. He was incarcerated on two other occasions, in 1964 and again in 1967, for challenging the regime of Ayub Khan.

Throughout his years of political activity, Maududi continued to produce an impressive number of articles, pamphlets and books. His Qur'anic translation and commentary *Tafhim al-Qur'an* (6 volumes), begun in 1942 and completed in 1972, is one of the most widely read Qur'anic commentaries in Urdu. His writings constitute an interpretive reading of Islam that sought to mobilize faith for the purpose of political action. His ideological perspective has been influential in the unfolding of revivalism across the Muslim world. The counters of Islam's discourse with socialism and capitalism were first defined by him, as was much of the terminology associated with Islamic revivalism, including 'Islamic revolution', 'Islamic state' and 'Islam *i.e.* ideology'.

Maududi's vision was dialectic in that he saw the battle between Islam and *Jahiliyah* (paganism) – both the West and the Hindu culture of India – as the central force in the historical progression of Muslim societies. This struggle would culminate in an Islamic state, which would in turn initiate broad reforms in society, thereby erecting an Islamic order. In his conception, Islamic revolution was to unfold within the existing state structures rather than after their destruction. He disapproved the use of violence in promoting the cause of Islam and defined the ideal Islamic state as a 'theo-democracy' or a 'democratic caliphate'.

38. Khomeini, Roohullah al-Musavi (d. 1989), Iranian Shia Alim and leader of the Islamic revolution. In the 1930s he as a very confident

teacher began to expound on ethics in response to Reza Shah Pahlavi's modernization and secularization of Iran. In 1944 his first political statement appeared in visitors' book in a mosque at Yazd. By the end of the 1940s his interest in the political field, which he considered just as much part of Islam as philosophy and theology, increased. In 1962 when Ayatullah Mohammad Hosany Borujerdi died, the burden of fusing religion and politics fell on Khomeini, whose aim was more to Islamize politics rather than to politicize Islam.

The Shah's secularization policies of the early 1960s gave him his first excuse to oppose the ruler. He accused the government of aping the West and eroding Islam, and he showed great ability in mobilizing his net-work of opposition. In his book *Kashf al-Asrar* he openly attacked the Pahlavi dynasty and called for an end to imperialist influences in the country. In another work *Wilayat Faqih* he discussed the basic principles of Islamic state and analysed the following themes: i) unity of the Muslim world; ii) Islamic government in the light of the Qur'an; iii) Islamic government in the light of the traditions; iv) aims and objectives of Islamic government; v) Islamic jurisprudence; vi) Islamic fiscal system; vii) Qur'anic teachings in the social, moral and material aspects of life; viii) duties and responsibilities of the ruler and ix) Imam – the supreme authority to enforce the decrees of the Qur'an.

Because of his severe opposition to Shah regime he was arrested again and again. In 1964 he was sent into exile to Turkey but he later settled at Najaf in Iraq from 1965 to 1978. Later on he was compelled to move to Kuwait that did not accept him and then he left for Paris two years later. He returned to Tehran in February 1979 as the Imam a title used in the Arab Shi'ite world for a religious leader. He had come to serve the clergy and Iranian society which had been transformed by Islamic revolution. His main objectives for the future were twofold: to control the forces unleashed by the revolution and to consolidate his regime. He did not accept any position in the new Islamic Republic but as a father figure worked for the Islamic revolution. He could not bring about the just and virtuous society he had promised but stated in his will that "he was proud to be trying to implement the rules of the Holy Qur'an and the traditions of the Prophet (SAW)". After his death in 1989, Khamene'i was then selected as the next leader of Islamic Republic of Iran.

39. Qutb, Sayyid (d. 1966), Literary critic, novelist, poet, Islamic thinker and Egypt's most famous Islamic activist of the twentieth century, exceeding in reputation even the founder of *al-Ikhwan al-Muslimun*, Hassan al-Banna (1906-1949). His passionate writings contain powerful images of the maladies of contemporary Islamic societies and an idealization of the faith through the words of the Qur'an and Sunnah. In 1948 he was despatched to the United States by the Ministry of Education in which he was employed, to study Western methods of education. He spent about three years abroad, leaving

America in 1950 and visiting England, Switzerland and Italy on his way back to Egypt in 1951. This trip to America marked a transition from literary and educational pursuits to intense religious commitment. He in 1953 joined the Ikhwan and was appointed editor of its weekly organ. Due to his uncompromising attitude toward the Jahili system, he was arrested and tortured in jail again and again. In 1965 he was arrested on charges of terrorism and sedition. Incontrovertible evidences against Qutb were apparently not presented, as his revolutionary tract, *Ma'alim fi al-Tariq* (1964) did not explicitly called for armed overthrow of the state. Rather, it urged resistance by turning away from existing society and creating a model Ummah which eventually would establish true Islam. Despite great international pressure, the government executed Qutb and two colleagues on 29 August 1966.

Qutb regarded the leaderships of Muslim societies which he disapproved, and the societies that went along with them, to be living in a state of *Jahiliyah* which can be considered anything that is inimical to Islam. He thought of Islam as a comprehensive way of life. Islam thus provides model solutions to all aspects of human existence. In his most sustained book *Khasais al-Tasawwur al-Islami wa Muqawwamatuhu* (1962), he elaborates the characteristics of Islamic ideology in detail. One of his socio-political program is the organicism and connotations of corporatism which he calls *al-tajammu al-haraki* (dynamic concrescence). This entity is in fact the embodiment of the Ummah, which is reinforced into a living organism with attributes of thought and behaviour. He has further focussed on the *hakimiyah* verses of the Qur'an and thereby sanctioned collective action to dismiss a ruler who failed to apply Allah's revelations. He has well elaborated the concept of social justice in Islam in his book *al-Adalah al-Ijtimaiyah fi al-Islam*.

40. Ali Shariati (d. 1977) one of the most important social thinkers of twentieth-century Iran. Shariati's ideas are distinguished more by their practical impact than their intellectual content. In this regard he can be compared in stature with Jamaluddin Afghani (1838-1898). He was less a disciplined scholar than a social and political activist. By the time of his final arrest, he had given over two hundred lectures at the Husayniyah Irshad, many of which had been prepared for publication and sold thousands of copies in several printings. His early works include *Maktab-e-Wasatah* (The Middle School of Thought) that upheld Islam as the virtuous path between capitalism and communism, and *Tarikh-e-Takāmul-e-Falasifah* (The History of perfection of Philosophy) written in 1955. He was also deeply impressed with the biography *Abu Dharr al-Ghifari* by Jawdah al-Sahhār, whose protagonist, Abu Dharr (d. 957), symbolized Muslim resistance to injustice.

Shariati as an independent thinker took very public stand to promote a collectivist revolutionary course of action to bring about social justice and freedom for the downtrodden. The hallmark of his thought is his conviction that religion must be transformed from a purely private set of ethical injunctions into a revolutionary program to change the world. In this course of liberating the mind and attitude of the people, he rejected the Western image of religion. In his perspective, religion lends itself to ideological commitment for the emancipation of the individual believer from oppression. Despite the prevalence of Shi'i symbols, his cause was humanity in general, especially the masses of the third world. He believed that Western imperialism wished to transform the masses into slaves. Islam was, in his view, the answer to both Marxism and capitalism. Some of the key concepts in his discourses are *shahadah* (martyrdom); *intizār* (anticipation of the return of the Hidden Imam); *zulm* (oppression of the Imam's justice) *Jihād I'itirāz* (protest); *ijtihād* (independent judgement in adducing a rule of law); *tarikh* (the movement of history); *rawshanfikrān* (enlightened thinkers); *mas'uliyat* (responsibility); and *adālat* (social justice). From Marxism, he borrowed the notion of dialectical conflict and appropriated the term *jabr-e-tarikh* (historical determinism). From Western liberal thought, he adopted the Enlightenment's stress on reason as the corrective for the maladies of the society.

41. Nabhani, Taqiuddin, al- (d. 1977), the founder of *Hizb al-Tahrir al-Islami* in 1953 in Jerusalem, al-Azhar graduate and religious school teacher and judge from Ijzim in north Palestine. His thoughts may be studied in his works especially in the books, *Nizam al-Hukm fi al-Islam*, (1953), *Nizam al-Islam* (1953), *al-Shakhsiah al-Islamiyah* (1953) and *Al-Takattul al-Hizbi* (1953). He considers the implementation of the Shariah as the lynchpin in the restoration of an Islamic way of life and the state as a *sine qua non* for achieving this aim. He upholds the classical model of the caliphate as the only authentic form of Islamic government, which he sought to restore with its traditional accompanying institutions. To this end he drafted a constitution detailing the political, economic and social systems of the proposed state. This document vests executive and legislative powers in an elected caliph, in whom most functions of state are centralized. Citizens are encouraged to exercise their right to call the state to account through a political opposition based on the Islamic ideology and expressed through a system of party plurality. Although involvement in politics is construed as a collective religious duty (*fard al-Kifayah*), *shura* is not held to be a pillar of Islamic government. He emphasizes upon a distinction between *shura* and democracy and holds that democracy is not compatible with Islam. He also denounces nationalism as a creation of unbelief.

42. Banna, Hasan Al- (d. 1949), founder of *al-Ikhwan al-Muslimun* (The Muslim Brotherhood) and author of *Majmu'ah al-Rasail* and *Mudhakkirāt al-Dawah wa al-Dā'iyah*. He basically emphasized on the four themes; nation, state, social justice and society in true Islamic perspective. The slogans that ikhwān took up from him were: "The Qur'an is our constitution", "No other constitution but the Qur'an", and "The Qur'an is our Law and Muhammad is our model". An analysis of existing trends in the Muslim world shows Banna as accommodating and much more Westernized than he would have acknowledged. He rejected the movement for secularization begun in the nineteenth century, and also the secular Arab nationalism mapped out by Sati al-Husri (d. 1968) in the 1920s and systematized by Michel Aflaq (d. 1989) in Damascus in the 1940s. Aflaq launched the secret Arab Ba'th party in 1941 and founded it publicly in 1947, explaining that "Islam is the soul; Arabism is the body". For Banna, however, "The Arabs are the backbone of Islam, and its guardians, *Ikhwan* speaks about Arabism in the same terms as the Prophet (SAW). In effect, just as Islam is a faith and a religion, it is also a country and a citizenship that erases differences of background between men: The faithful are brothers'. Thus Islam knows no geographical frontiers, nor racial or civic differentiations. Banna considered all Muslims to exist in a sole Ummah. He did not hesitate to condemn expressly modern nationalisms especially European fascism or Nazism.

Banna did not encourage any terrorist violence. However, he asserted that war was an obligation at the time that Egyptians faced British colonial power. He interpreted jihad tradition by making it a present-day individual obligation (*fard 'ayn*) for all, rather than a collective obligation (*fard kifāyah*) in which some could represent the whole. As to Islamic criminal Law, in particular the *hudud*, he advocated its application only on the condition that an Islamic society with social justice was established, with appropriate legal interpretations required by present and future situations.

43. Abdur Rahman, Omar (b .1938), more properly spelled 'Umer Abd al-Rahman' Egyptian Muslim scholar and Jihadist leader. He was accidentally blinded at ten months age. In 1967 he obtained his graduation degree from al Azhar University and was appointed by the state as a mosque preacher in a village of Fayyum. Soon he was recognized as a firing speaker against anti Islamic theories and actions. At a public ceremony after Nasser's death on 28 September 1970, he condemned Nasser as an infidel and prohibited prayers for him. Consequently he was detained for eight months. Again soon after his return from Saudi Arabia, he was arrested for his involvement in the Jihad Organisation accused of assassinating president Sadat and was released only in 1984.

During this protracted trial (1981-84) three factors led to Abdur Rahman's emergence as the leading figure in his Islamic movement.

The first was his book *Mithāq al-Āmil al-Islami* (Charter of Islamic Action) , an explanation of his view of correct Islamic life; it marked his departure from the more moderate wing of the Muslim Brotherhood (Ikhwan) and affiliation with the radical forces informed by the concept of jihad and the necessity to overthrow the secular state in order to restore the principles of the Qur'an. Second, he married again, this time to Fātin Shu'ayb, a kinswoman of several important activists, affirming his solidarity with the *Jama'ah al-Islamiyah* in upper Egypt and lending weight to his religious status as mufti al-Jihad. Third, most of the Jihadi leaders were executed or imprisoned for life, leaving a power vacuum that Abdur-Rahman readily filled.

44. Turabi, Hasan (b. 1932) Sudanese Islamist and political leader who has never published a comprehensive account of his thought, but his various writings and pronouncements present a relatively liberal interpretation of Islam, including a belief in democracy and pluralism. He has not repudiated this line of thought; however the regime for which he regularly speaks, both in Sudan and abroad, had been widely seen as the most restrictive since independence in 1956. Parliamentary democracy was abolished by the military, which has forcibly repressed not only political parties but also many independent groups in civil society in promoting its Islamic revolution. The Ikhwan has become dominant not only in government but also in the civil service, the professions and the economy. Feared by neighbouring Arab states as a promoter of radical Islamic activism, the new regime cooperated in turn with Libya, Iraq and Iran; and the latter connection in particular supported government victories in the civil war in the south in 1992.

    Turabi has won a reputation for pragmatism and flexibility in the pursuit of resurgent Islam, which he seeks to see expand not only in Sudan but also in neighbouring African and Arab countries. His success in building the Ikhwan in Sudan before 1989 enabled the military regime to pursue his Islamizing policies. See for some of his thoughts, "The Islamic State" in The Voices of Resurgent Islam, ed. John L. Esposito, pp. 241-251; *Al-Harakah al-Islamiyah wa al-Tahdith* (in association with Rashid al-Gannoushi).

45. Fadl Allah, Muhammad Husayn (b. 1935) Lebanese Shi'i religious scholar, activist and a leader of Hizbullah. He in his works like *Al-Islam wa Mantiq al-Quwwah* (1981), *Khatawat ala tariq al-Islam* (1982), *Mafāhim Islamiyah* 12 Vols. (1982), *Al-Muqawwamah al-Islamiyah* (1985), *Ala Tariq Harakah al-quwah fi al-Dawlah al-Islamiyah* (*Al-Tawhid*, March, 1986), and others has adhered to the *usuli* (fundamentalist) tradition of modern Shi'ism that was established at the end of the eighteenth century as an alternative to the great tradition called *akhbari* (textual). He has seen *taqiyah* (dissimulation) as a rule governing concrete daily conduct without the supervision of a *marj'a taqlid*. According to him, the possibility of a violent revolution

at an appropriate juncture is not excluded, because of the breach between intangible ideal of Shariah and traditional customs and new conditions. In addition he has sought to emulate the revolutionary examples of Ali and Husayn more than the quietist examples of the subsequent Imams. He has even claimed to draw inspiration from the rebellion movements that were crushed by the Shi'i powers backed by the Ulama in the name of *taqiyah*. He made such claims as early as the first year of the civil war in Lebanon, in 1976. At the same time, he reproached the Islamic extremists with indulging in impulsive and disorganized actions – "without *taqiyah*" he said. The time of taqiyah is the time of education, preparation and organization in a party which is disciplined and adheres to firm a doctrine.

Fadl Allah addressed the status of non-Muslims in an Islamic state. For him, secular individual freedom does not exist. Going against the great Muslim tradition existing in practice as well as theory since the eleventh century, he rejects the fundamental distinction between political and religious power. He opposed his teacher who did not wish to become involved in political activity, in particular his own mentor in Najaf, al-Khoi. Fadl Allah has maintained that Christians must renounce political sectarianism. Yet, although he asserts that Muslims should do so as well, in fact the Christians' situation is seen from the perspective of strict Muslim sectarianism. The desired Muslim state is not founded on the legal equality of all people, regardless of their religious and family ties, even though these ties might be taken into account, as in the present-day Lebanese constitution. The same situation applied to the rights of women and the family. He encourages young women and even mothers to work professionally.

46. Ghannushi, Rāshid Al- (b. 1941), Islamic thinker, activist, and political leader in Tunisia. His thought reflects a masterly understanding of Western and Islamic philosophies and a genuine concern for reconciling the basic tenets of Islam with modernity and progress. He evaluates the West within the philosophical dimension of East-West dialogue. He perceives the West as an ideological counter-weight to Islamic doctrines: the West is considered neither superior nor inferior to Islam. He sees coexistence and cooperation as the basis for the relationship between the two. What sets the two worlds apart, however, is the difference in their perception of fundamental concepts, or 'effective ideas" that move their cultures: the value and place of humanity in the universe. He acknowledges that the system of democracy was a direct consequence of a particular Western experience. He perceives democracy as a method of government and as a philosophy. In his view, the Muslims' problem is not with democratic institutions themselves, but with the secular and nationalistic values behind democracy. Islamic democracy is distinguished from other systems by its moral content as derived from the Shariah.

Ghannushi makes an important intellectual contribution by linking Westernization with dictationship. He believes two common characteristics dominate the political systems of the Arab and larger Muslim world Westernization and dictatorship by ruling elites. Because of its alienation from the masses, the Westernized elite resorts to violent and repressive means to impose its foreign-inspired models and perpetuate its rule. His important works include, *Maqaalāt* (1984), *Fil Mabadi al-Asasiyah lil Dimiqratiyah wa Usul al-Hukm al-Islami* (1990), *Tariqunā ila al-Hadarah, Ma Huwa al-Gharb al-Harakah al-Islamiyah wa al-Tahdith.*

47. Siddiqi, Kalim Dr. (d. 1996), Islamic thinker and activist of Pakistan who migrated to Great Britain in the early 1950s and established the Muslim Institute in London in 1973 and the Muslim Parliament in 1992. He in all his writings and editorial notes emphasized on the formulation of an articulate and rationally satisfactory Islamic epistemological paradigm as a necessary condition in the search for alternative social, economic and political system for Muslims. The central contention of the scholar is that Revealed paradigm or Prophetic paradigm of Islam provides the constant core around which the much larger totality of human knowledge that may be called science paradigm revolves or should revolve. He was of the view that capitalism and communism are equally and totally alien to Islam and must be rejected in their entirety and no new hybrid philosophy carrying the label of Islam would be acceptable. He discussed that the design for future social and political structures and institutions in Muslim societies should arise from the conceptual frame work of Islam in its purest form. He defined the Islamic movement as the struggle of the Muslims to establish, maintain, develop, defend, extend or establish the Islamic state as an instrument to enjoin good and forbid evil, for the welfare and happiness of all mankind in this world and in the hereafter. The Islamic state is an essential and integral part of Islam. This is an act of faith and duty not an act of common consent of its citizens, as he viewed. The leadership must be confined within *muttaqi* preferably ālim elements of society. Islamic state is not a totalitarian, liberal or democratic Leviathan put together to pursue the narrowly defined national class, ethnic or colonial/imperialist interests of its leadership, government or people. It is a moral structure with equal responsibilities towards all mankind. This state is put together by those who are committed to order their individual and collective lives according to a moral paradigm defined by Allah. In the history, when Muslims deviated from their course, the situation got compounded by the impact of man-made ideologies which impaired Islam's power of regeneration. He feels that after error and deviation, Muslim thought must attempt at the correction and convergence before they could establish the Islamic state. His important works includes; *Towards A New Destiny* (1974), *Beyond the Muslim Nation-*

*States* (1977), *The State of Muslim World Today* (1980), *The Islamic Revolution: Achievements, Obstacles and Goals* (1981), *Issues in Islamic Movement* (ed.) (Vol. 1-7, 1982-87), *Stages of Islamic Revolution* (1996).

48. Bin Laden, Osama (b. 1957), The Leader of al-Qā'idah and the hero of the devastating September 11 attacks in the World Trade Centre and the Pentagon in the United States in 2001 as portrayed by Western/American media. Born in Riyadh, Saudi Arabia he is the son of Muhammad bin Laden who came to the Kingdom from South Yemen around 1930 as an illiterate labourer. He started a small construction business and went on to become one of Saudi Arabia's wealthiest construction magnates. His company received a multibillion dollar contract to restore and expand the Grand Mosques of Makkah and Madinah, raising his company's prestige throughout the Muslim world and setting the stage for the company's expansion beyond the Kingdom. Osama was educated in Madinah and Jeddah earning his degree in public administration in 1981 at Jeddah's King Abdul Aziz University, where he studied management and economics. Among his teachers were Dr. Abdullah Azzam, Muhammad Qutb and others known for their Islamic activism.

In 1986 Osama participated actively in Afghan Jihad against Soviet Russia and created Al-Qā'ida to organize and track the channelling of fighters and funds for the Afghan resistance. In this jihad he proved himself to be a selfless and dedicated mujahid. Still young he was more comfortable as an activist than as an ideologue, focused primarily on the jihad in Afghanistan rather than on Muslim international politics and activism.

After Soviet troops withdrew from Afghanistan in 1989, Bin Laden found a refuge and invested his resources in the fledgling Islamic state of Sudan led by Colonel Omar al-Bashir. Bin Laden voiced his approval for the World Trade Centre Bombing in 1993 and the killing of U.S. troops in Mogadishu Somalia. His final break with Saudi Arabia came in 1996 when the Kingdom revoked his citizenship and freezed his assets in the country because of his support for Islamic jihadists.

In 1996 Afghanistan witnessed the rise of an improbable militia that would go on to unite the whole country and declare the Islamic Republic of Afghanistan. The Talibān Leader Mulla Umar had been quick to offer sanctuary and express his admiration for Bin Laden's sacrifices and dedication to jihad. Bin Laden supported the new government wholeheartedly. Safely entrenched in this country he assumed more visible and vocal leadership role in international resistance, calling openly for jihad against America and its allies. In 1996, he issued a declaration of jihad whose goals were to drive US forces out of the Arabian Peninsula, overthrow the Saudi government and liberate Islamic cities of Makkah and Madinah, as well as support revolutionary groups around the world. In November, he again repeated his threat to wage holy war against the US and its allies if Washington did not remove its troops from the Gulf.

In 2000 Bin Laden announced the formation of the World Islamic Front for the jihad against Jews and Crusaders, an umbrella group of radical movements across the Muslim world, and issued a fatwa stating that it is the duty of all Muslims to kill US citizens and their allies. The title of the organization summed up the man and his view of the West. Because of Western abuses, the entire world has been divided, he claimed, into two regions-one of faith where there is no hypocrisy and another of infidelity, from which we hope God will protect us.

Bin Laden mobilized in his favour the Muslim sense of historic oppression, occupation and injustice at the hands of the West. After September 11, 2001 he charged, 'what the United States tastes today is a very small thing compared to what we have tasted for tens of years. Our nation has been tasting humiliation and contempt for more than 80 years." He portrays a world in which Islam and Muslims are under siege, "America and its allies are massacring us in Palestine, Chechnya, Kashmir, and Iraq. The Muslims have the right to attack America in reprisal.... The September 11 attacks were not targeted at women and children. The real targets were America's icons of military and economic power." He connected Western presence in the Gulf with the international concern: America's complicity in Israeli expansionism, its support for "Jewish and Zionist plans for expansion of what is called Greater Israel". Palestine is a primary issue for Bin Laden. His passionate statements on the plight of the Palestinians, who have been living under Israeli military occupation in violation of UN Security Council resolutions for over forty years, graphically describe, capture, and appeal to the outrage of many in the Arab and Muslim world towards Israeli policy and the complicity of international community.

Bin Laden charges that the Jewish lobby has taken America and the West hostage. He calls upon the American people to rise up against their government. He called the Muslims to defend themselves. He appeals to the Islamic teachings that jihad in the defense of Islam and to correct an unjust political order is legitimate and required. He declares the Muslim world under the siege of enemies of Islam: "They rob us of our wealth and of our resources and of our oil. Our religion is under attack. They kill and murder our brothers. They compromise our honor and our dignity and dare we utter a single word of protest against the injustice, we are called terrorists". Bin Laden, like a jurist, speaks in term of a distinction between commendable and reprehensible terrorism: "There is no doubt that every state and every citizen and culture has to resort to terrorism under certain circumstances for the purpose of abolishing tyranny and corruption... The terrorism we practice is of the commendable kind for it is directed at the tyrants, the traitors who commit acts of treason against their own countries and their own faith and their own prophet and their own nation. Terrorizing those and punishing them are necessary measures to straighten things and make them right," as he advocated.

Inspite of Bin Laden's Islamic/Qur'anic references in his favour, the Ulama of al-Azhar, Egypt and of the entire Muslim world denounced his statements as irrelevant, aberrant and as out of the context of the Qur'an.

49. Ibrahim, Anwar (b. 1947), As a thinker and political activist of Malaysia, he has consistently stressed justice, an integrated form of government, and excellence in education and economic production. He is influenced by such intellectuals as Naquib al-Attas, Ismail R. al-Faruqi, Yusuf al-Qardhawi, Hassan al-Turabi, Malek Bennabi and Muhammad Natsir. He believes in pluralism, democracy and parliamentary form of government, and is opposed to dictatorship monarchy and religious rigidity in jurisprudential issues. His thought and personal reflections may be seen in Morais, J. Victor, *Anwar Ibrahim: Resolute in Leadership*, Kuala Lumpur, 1983.

*****

# 2

# SOME MISPERCEPTIONS ABOUT ISLAMIC POLITICAL THEORY

What exactly is the nature of Islamic political system and its premier institutions? The question has been quite baffling to Muslim thinkers in the past and more so in the present when interest in discovering true Islamic principles of politics and modelling Muslim governments on them has been greatly intensified by a genuine desire to return to Islam in all walks of life. There is a lot of confusion about which interpretation is truly representative of Islam, as several doctrinal and dogmatic theses based on sectarian prejudices and predilections, claim exclusive religious credibility for themselves, branding all others as un-Islamic. The concept of the premier political institution of Islam, that is, the *khilāfah* or the *imāmah*, is itself debatable and controversial. Other key political institutions of the Islamic polity such as *shūrā* are also shrouded in great controversial statements.

There is also a great deal of confusion in Muslim political thought regarding foreign systems and their political terminology. This confusion is due to the researchers' insufficient knowledge of the foreign systems, on the one hand, and the inadequacy of their approach on the other. Islam and international relations is, perhaps, the most neglected field of research among Muslim scholars, because of the immense difficulties involved in reformulating the old concepts of Islamic Public Law to meet the new and substantially different conditions of the modern world.

The confusion is worse confounded if one turns to the writings of medieval theologians, political scientists and scholars on Islamic polity. There is much substance in the charge of the orientalists and other critics of Islam that medieval writers on the polity of Islam were interested in, rather guided by, factual politics of the Muslim rulers than the formulations of Islamic political science. Prominent political scientists of the medieval period like 'Abd al Hasan 'Alī Al-Māwardī (d. 1058 A.D.)[1] and several of his illustrious predecessors and successors such as al-Farabi (d. 905),[2] Nizām al Mulk Tūsī (d. 1091),[3] al-Ghazālī (d. 1111),[4] Ibn Jama'ah (d. 1393),[5] 'Adud al-Dīn al-Ījī (d. 1355),[6] Ibn Khaldūn (d. 1406)[7] and Shāh Walī Allāh Dehlavi (d. 1762)[8] were influenced by factual political developments in their respective periods of history and modelled their political schemes and principles of governance on them, justifying in most cases the actions of the Muslim rulers of their time.

## The Issue of Imamah

The writings of these medieval jurists on constitutional theory and law were stimulated by a political situation fraught with grave danger to the survival of the *ummah*, and they represent a significant blend of ideal theory and ugly political reality. These books were written in defence of the 'Abbāsid caliphate whose authority was threatened by effective political rulers, *amīrs* or *sultāns*. Their principal aim was to maintain disintegration due to the slipping away of effective of Islam's religious and political unity and the protector of the *Sharī'ah* throughout the Islamic empire. In this process the *Sharī'ah* became less and less of a reality, hence the greater need to preserve it as the ideal constitution and law of the *ummah*. The reforming zeal of Ibn Taymiyah (d. 1328 A.D.), long after the fall of the 'Abbāsid Caliphate in 1258 A.D., was aimed at full restoration of the *Sharī'ah* to secure the survival of Islam in its pristine purity in conformity with the *Sunnah* of the Prophet (SAW).[9]

On the other hand, political and religious sects of the Khawārji and the Shīah formulated their own ideas of Islamic polity, contradicting the formulations of the majority group. The Shi'ah held that the *imām* would not be chosen by the community. They called the *imām* the pillar of faith and the foundation stone of Islam and it was the duty of the Prophet (SAW) to nominate the *imām*, not to leave the choice to the community, while the Khawārji stood at the other extreme as against the Shī'ah. To them *khalifah* is dependent upon the free vote of Muslim community and is not restricted within the

Quraysh or the Arabs. According to them, the *khalīfah* is allowed to function till he observes the right path and practises justice and is to be deposed or assassinated when he acts contrary to it. The orientalists and their Muslim followers form a third group of political thinkers and writers on Islam and digressed from certain postulates of the Qur'an when political and practical expediencies of the hour demanded it. H.A.R. Gibb,[10] the most acclaimed writer on Islam in modern times, not only criticises, at places quite rightly, the approach and treatment of the subject by medieval Muslim writers but ventures to declare that Islamic political doctrines were never put into practice. Some hostile critics declare that there are no political laws and doctrines in Islam, and in case there are some, they are not applicable today, for they are not suited to the dictates of modern age. The first on this matter was Shaykh 'Alī 'Abd al-Rāziq[11] in a book entitled *Al-Islām* wa *Usūl al-Hukm* published in 1925 when he was a judge in the *Shari'ah* courts in Egypt. He claimed that the government of the Islamic State can be of any kind – it can be an autocracy or bureaucracy; a monarchy or republic; a dictatorship or constitutional or consultative government; it can be democratic, socialist or Bolshevik; that the Prophet (SAW) was nothing but a *rasūl* for a religious call, purely for the sake of religion, unblemished by any tendency to rule or call for the formation of a state; and that Islam is a religious unity, and the Prophet (SAW) called for that unity and had actually achieved it before his death, and that for the sake of that unity he struggled with his tongue and his sword and Allah's help and victory came to him. The author also says that it should be realized that *al-risālah* in itself required the Prophet (SAW) to acquire some form of leadership and power over his people. But this is very far from the leadership of kings and their power over their subjects. Hence one must not confuse the leadership of *al-risālah* with that of the king and that the rule of the Prophet (SAW) over Muslims was the rule of *al-risālah* which is untainted by any urge to rule. The ideas of the author were severely criticized by a number of scholars from Egypt and abroad. Shaykh Muhammad al-Khidr Husain, Shaykh Mohammad Bakhit al-Mut'ii, Shaykh Mohammad al-Taher b. Ashur, Prof. Abdul Hamid Mutawalli, Dr. Ziyauddin al-Rayes and others refuted the claims of 'Ali 'Abd al-Rāziq. They all agreed that Islam has laid down principles for a system of government in the verses of the Holy Qur'an which are related to constitutional rules. They also agree that these principles were further augmented by the application of these verses by the Prophet (SAW) who added his *Sunnah* to them which followed the same course in establishing the overall general rules concerning the system of government and the policy of the state.[12]

## Khilafat or Mulukiyat

In the Indian subcontinent (South Asia), several Muslim scholars like Mawlānā Sayyid Abul Ala Maududi (d. 1979), Mawlānā Ishaque Sandelvi and Prof. Mohammad Yasin Mazhar Siddiqui to name a few most prominent, tried to formulate the political laws and rules of governance on the basis of Qur'an, *Sunnah* of the Prophet (SAW) and the *āthār* (practices) of the *al-Khulafā al-Rāshidūn* (the Pious Caliphs) whose rule is generally regarded as a faithful representation of the Qur'an and the *Sunnah* and is termed as *al-Khilāfah 'ala-Minhāj al-Nubuwwah* (government on the lines of the *Sunnah* of the Prophet (SAW). But once again a great difficulty is faced by a student of Islamic polity when he finds that these scholars themselves are divided into two groups; one is of the view that the Islamic *khilāfah* started changing into temporal monarchy (*mulūkiyah*) from the second half of the reign of the third Caliph who had in the opinion of this group, digressed from the *Sunnah* of the Prophet (SAW) and his illustrious successors; while the second group maintains that the entire thirty-year-period of the Caliphate was based on the tenets of Islam. The third group, on the contrary, claimed that Islamic *khilāfah* did not change into *mulūkiyah* even when the Umayyads established their state on hereditary lines. According to these historians, the Umayyad Khilafah was the continuation and extension of the *Khilāfah Rāshidah* and it was not any other system different from the Islamic *khilāfah*. The Islamic capital was ofcourse, transferred from Madinah to Damascus and the power was transmitted from one group to the other. Both the groups were Islamic and the governments on Islamic pattern. The only difference between the two was that the first period was categorized by Ibn Taymiyah as the *Khilāfah Nubuwwah* because it was initiated just after the death of the Prophet (SAW) and was established by the best and noblest persons of the *ummah*, while the second period was of the *Khilāfah Rahmah* and the government was established by the holy *Companions* of second rank and their followers.[13] Neutral readers may find numerous shortcomings in the writings of these groups and demand to know the actual political teachings that are envisaged in the Qur'an, the *hadīth* and other sources of the Islamic Law. Unfortunately, in the past, no theoretical or speculative formulation of Islamic political science similar to law and jurisprudence, was ever attempted.

Of late, the domain of political thought among the Muslim writers represented a feeble effort to solve the so-called problem of religion and democracy. Without emphasising the real significance of Islam as a *dīn*, Muslim thinkers are either grouping in search of democracy in Islam or in their stretch of imagination seem to hit upon the novel idea of Islamic democracy or regard spiritual democracy as the ultimate aim of Islam. This is in consonance with the prevalent tendency to identify Islam with every form of the Western political theory, however, conflicting they may be in their nature and contents. On the other hand, it is equally misleading to contend that no part of the Western political thought corresponds with any aspect of the Islamic political theory. The confusion arises out of a misunderstanding of the true nature of the Islamic polity and a very wrong method of interpreting Islam through the medium of Western ideas, terminology and technique. The Syrian scholar Mustafa Al-Sibai[14] may be cited here. His main contribution to Islamic thought is regarded his book entitled the *Ishtirākiyah al-Islām* (The Socialism of Islam) in which he argued that Islam teaches a unique type of socialism, one distinct from its western materialistic variants emphasizing class struggle. He saw Islamic Socialism as conforming with human nature, based on the ownership. God is the ultimate owner of all, and man is deputized to make use of property through honest labour. The state plays a regulatory function through nationalization (*tā'mīm*) of essential public services, implementation of Islamic laws on mutual social responsibility (*al-takaful al-ijtima'ī*) and sanctions (*mu'ayyidāt*). This theory created an uproar because of its opposition to capitalism, its association of Islam with socialism; and its ostensible support of Naseer's ideology at a time when Egyptian Ikhwan were suppressed.[15]

Mawlānā Hifzur Rahman Seoharvi[16] (the famous scholar and political activist in South Asia), declaring the Islamic system of government contradictory to secular philosophy of Communism, thought it similar to some extent in its economic aspects. He held that while discussing the economic aspects only of communism and comparing it with other non-Islamic philosophies, we should have no fear or hesitation in saying that Islam and Communism are closer to each other in many aspects of their economic systems.[17] The renowned western scholar of Islam Prof. Arnold[18] tried to prove the system of government under the Prophet (SAW) as arbitrary and autocratic.[19]

## Westernization or Islamization

The confusion over the interpretation and understanding of the Islamic political concepts being influenced with the western thought and action may be traced back to the ferment and crisis in the minds of the modern Muslim intellectuals when the British and French colonial empires disappeared from Asia and Africa. The Islamists in most of the countries, and the achievement of freedom and independence from foreign rule, created the conditions necessary for the battle of minds that is to determine the character of the new Muslim society. The two main trends in this period were found; the '*ulamā*' and Islamically oriented people expected the purification of religion from superstitions to lead to an Islamic revival, whereas the westernized intellectuals, who formed the cadres of civil servants and officers, aimed at a reform of Islam itself in terms of western thought and institutions of western political organization and legal codes and courts.[20]

According to Rosenthal, the identification of the West with Christianity in modern times has contributed in three ways to the changing attitudes towards Islam. First there is the conservative or even reactionary group advocating and working for Islamic state on rigidly orthodox lines, in defence of Islam against an allegedly inimical Christian West, completely rejecting every thing western as anti-Islamic. Next there is the middle-of-the-road position, of advocating a coming to positive terms with western techniques and institutions on the basis of Islamic principles that are to guide state and society. This position contains within itself several shades, ranging from a full synthesis between East and West through a partial accommodation to a mere clothing of western institutions in Islamic words. Finally, at the other extreme, we find a complete severance of Islam as faith from the body politic: the separation of religion and politics. These principal divisions, as made by Rosenthal, have left the Muslim society in the mental, ideological and psychological conflicts. It is, therefore, all a matter of interpretation and largely depends upon what one understands by Islam:[21] secularist Islam, liberal Islam, nationalist Islam, Communist Islam, Western Islam or Islam in the texts of its own. "If the western political scientists and constitutional lawyers cannot easily apply their concepts and the terms that express them to things Islamic and Muslim, neither can they expect the contemporary Muslim thinker, statesman or administrator to deny his spiritual roots in and attachment to Islam and to bid farewell to his inherited concepts by accepting those of the West.'[22]

This is the true analysis of the situation. Islam must be studied and analysed from within. It must be viewed in its own context of basic tenets and history and in its own premises. As far as the western or non-Islamic terminologies are concerned, their use in Islamic context and with Islamic meanings may not be advisable. The Holy Qur'an has guided the Muslims not to speak such words that convey both the right and wrong meaning lest the enemies of Islam might benefit from the situation for their unholy interests:

> O ye of Faith! Say not (to the Apostle) (*rā'inā*) words of ambiguous import, but (*'unzurna*) words of respect; and hearken (to him): To those without faith is a grievous punishment.[23]

The background of these holy verses lies in the fact that whenever the Jews came to see the Holy Prophet (SAW) they showed every kind of respect for him, but inwardly they would try by every trick to slight and insult him. For instance, when during conversation, they wanted to draw his attention to a particular thing, they would say, "*rā'inā*" which apparently meant: "please show us concession, or pay attention to us", but this word implied some derogatory meaning also. Therefore, the Muslims were commanded not to use this word but instead say, "*unzurna*": "Pay attention to us please, or pause a little so that we understand the thing better."[24]

This was not a commandment specific to any particular age or personality. It is a general principle of Islam to avoid the use of such words and terminologies that may create misunderstandings.[25]

*****

## NOTES AND REFERENCES

1. Al-Māwardī (d. 1058), an Ash'arite thinker whose book entitled *'Al-Ahkām al-Sultāniyah* (The Ordinances of Government) is very famous in the history of Islamic political thought. The work was compiled to strengthen the authority of the 'Abbāsids against the Buwayhids who, in effective control of their state government and administration at all levels, were the principal concern of this book.
2. Al-Farabi (d. 950), the eminent philosopher and statesman wrote several books on politics. *Al-Madīnah al-Fādīlah, Al-Fusūl al-Madaniyah* and *Al-Siyāsah al-Madaniyah* are the most important ones. The theory of 'Ideal State' propounded by al-Farabi was compared with that of Greek philosophers. He was the first Muslim thinker who contributed to political thought either in the form of commentaries or in treatises of his own based mostly upon Plato. He gave the idea of a philosopher king who can secure complete happiness to man and this is the ultimate goal of the government.
3. Nizām al-Mulk Tūsi (d.1091), Chief Minister of the Saljuqids, the powerful statesman, who laid the foundation of Madrasah Nizāmiyah at Baghdad, wrote two books on politics; the *Siyāsat Nāmah* for Sultān Malik Shāh and the *Majma 'al-Wasayah wa Dastūr al-Wuzarā'* compiled mainly for his son Fakhr al-Mulk. His *Siyāsat nāmah* has been compared with Machiavelli's *The Prince* by many scholars.
4. Al-Ghazāli (d. 1111) besides discussing *imāmah* in his theological works wrote the *Fadā'ih al-Bātiniyah* at the request of the 'Abbāsid Caliph Al-Mustazhir to defend him against the Fātimid claims. In his book *Ihyā' al 'Ulūm* he bows to the actual power of the Saljuqids in his attempts to preserve the institutions of *khilāfah* as the symbol of the unity of the Muslim community.
5. Ibn Jama'ah (d. 1393), a Shāfi'ī jurist who adapted Sunnī theory of caliphate to the situation created by the destruction of the 'Abbāsid caliphate of Baghdad in 1258. His book on constitutional theory and administrative law namely *Tahrīr al-Ahkām fī Tadbīr Ahl al-Islām* deserves notice as a compendium of political statutes.
6. 'Adud al-Din al-Īj (d. 1355) theologian and philosopher author of various books, among which *al-Mawāqif fī 'Ilm al-Kalam* is the principal one.
7. Ibn Khaldūn (d. 1406), both a historian and statesman, tried to study the state and society in a scientific way. He propounded the theory of power state which transcended the opinions generally held in the Middle Ages. His political theory in his *Muqaddimah* is a part of his description of *'Umrān* (civilization) and politics as the part of government as apparent from his terminology, for *'Umrān* is synonymous with *Madīnah* or *Hādarah*, settled urban life (as distinct from *Badawah*, rural life). His empiricism is deeply rooted in the

traditional beliefs and convictions of Islam and steeped in the traditional sciences.

8. Shāh Walī Allāh Dehlavi (d. 1762), a revolutionary Indian thinker, attempted to reintegrate the socio-economic and religio-political structure of Islam. The reform movement outlined by him revolved round his concept of *Maslahah i.e.*, the establishment of a kind of welfare state based on the relationship of man's development with the creative forces of the universe. His famous book the *Hujjah Allah al-Bālighah* gives a complete picture of Islamic system and concentrates upon his theory of *Irtifāqāt*. His other works are the *Asrār al-Dīn, Tafhīmat Ilāhiyah*, and *Izālah al-Khifā' 'an Khilāfah al-Khulafā*.
9. E.I.J. Rosenthal, *Political Thought in Medieval Islam, An Introductory Outline*, Cambridge, 1962, Chapter "The Caliphate: Theory and Function": also see *Islam in the Modern National State*, Cambridge, 1965, pp. 12-27.
10. H.A.R. Gibb (*Studies on the Civilization of Islam,* Routledge and Kegal Paul Ltd. London, 1962) has claimed that "even in the Sunni Community there was no one universally accepted doctrine of the Caliphate", and that "the very basis of Sunni thought excludes the acceptance of any one theory as definitive and final" (p. 148). On the other side he admits that "the Sunni Islam lays down the principle, that Caliphate is that form of government which safeguards the ordinances of *Shari'āh* and sees that they are put into practice. So long as that principle is applied, there may be infinite diversity in the manner of its application". The scholar asserts that the Muslim thought "exerts a constant pressure, whose influence is to be seen in the unobtrusive reshaping of theory which, beneath an outward inflexibility, characterizes all branches of speculative activity in Islam, where Islam has remained a living organism" (p. 149).
11. 'Alī 'Abd al Rāziq (1888-1966), Egyptian Sharī'ah judge, controversial intellectual, was a member of a powerful land owning family from the village of Abu Jirj in al-Mina Province. A graduate of al-Azhar and Oxford Universities, he rose to the position of judge in the al-Mansura Shari'āh court. He, besides his *Al-Islām wa Usūl Al-Hukm* (Islam and the Bases of Political Authority), edited a study of the life and work of his brother, a rector of al-Azhar, entitled *Min Āthār Mustafā 'Abd al-Rāziq* (Cairo, 1975) and *Al-Ijmā fī al-Sharī'ah al-Islāmiyah*. His book on political system of Islam not only created a constitutional crisis in Egypt but it generated violent controversy throughout the Muslim world. The Egyptian Higher Council of Ulama brought him to trial and expelled him from both their ranks and his position as a Sharī'ah judge.
12. 'Alī 'Abd al-Rāziq, *Al-Islām wa Usūl al-Hukm,* Al-Hayat Library, Beirut, 1966, pp. 82, 83, 136, 141 and 142. Khalid Muhammad Khalid in his book entitled *Min Huna Nobda* supports Shaykh 'Alī 'Abd al-Rāziq's views in his own way (see pp. 149-184, 10th edition, Cairo), Khālid's

views were also refuted by Shaykh Muhammad al-Ghazāli in his work *Min Huna Na'lam* which was reprinted several times in Cairo.

13. Prof. Muhamad Yasin Mazhar Siddiqui, *Tārikh Tahzeeb Islāmi,* N. Delhi, 1998, Vol. II, pp. 97-112.
14. Mustafa Al-Sibai (1895-1964 A.D.) Syrian political thinker, educator, and founder of the Muslim Brotherhood in Syria. Born in Homs, Al-Sibai came from a prominent family of *'ulamā'*. His father's nurturance of him in Islamic learning included a strong sense of political activism that later put him on a collision course with the authorities of the French mandate. When he was eighteen years old, he travelled to Egypt. His studies at al-Azhar were accompanied by involvement in political activism, membership in the Egyptian al-Ikhwān al-Muslimūn, and close association with Hasan al-Banna. In 1934 al-Sibai was jailed for participating in anti-British demonstrations; in 1940 the British charged him with subversion and sent him to the Sarfad Camp in Palestine. After his release (1941) he returned to Homes to establish an organization called Shabab Mohammad. Soon he was arrested and jailed by the French for two and a half years. Despite his deteriorating health brought on by torture, al-Sibai's release from prison in 1943 ushered in two decades of dynamic activity as writer, teacher and leader of Syria's Islamic movement. By 1946 he forged a merger between different Islamic organizations to form the al-Ikhwan al-Muslimun, and was elected its *al-Muraqib al-'amm* (the general supervisor). Until the Ikwan's suppression by the Shishakli regime in 1952, he worked to strengthen this movement. He was also a distinguished educator and administrator at the University of Damascus. Because of his failing health, in 1857 he turned over leadwership of Ikhwan to Isām al-Attar, although he continued to write until his death. In addition to his book on Socialism, al-Sibai edited three journals, *Al-Manār, Al-Muslimūn,* and *Hadarah al-Islam* and began to compile an *Encyclopaedia of Islamic Law.* His other books were al-*Marah bayn al-Fiqh wa al-Qānūn* and *Hakadha Allamatni al-Hayah*.
15. See the article of R. Hrair Dekmejian, *The Oxford Encyclopaedia of the Modern Islamic World,* 1995, Vol. IV, pp. 71-72; Al-Sibai, *Ishtirākiyah al-Islam,* Muassasah al-Matabu'at al-'Arabiyah, Damascus, 1960.
16. Mawlānā Hifzur Rahman Seoharvi (d. 1962), a religious scholar, a political activist in the Indian subcontinent, founded Nadwatul Musannifin in Delhi for study and research in Islam. He was an active leader of Jameatul Ulama. He opposed the two-nation theory with Islamic arguments and supported the Indian National Congress in its struggle for independence. He wrote a number of books. His work *Qisas al-Qur'ān* (The stories of the *Qur'ān*) consists of four volumes. His main work is entitled *Islām kā Iqtisādī Nizām* (The Economic System of Islam).

17. Hifzur Rahman Seoharvi, *Islām kā Iqtisādī Nizām*, Delhi 1951, p. 386.
18. S.T.W. Arnold has also criticized the contribution of Muslim philosophers to Islamic political thought. According to him, the idea of Islamic *Imām* to these philosophers was an adaptation of the Platonic ideal of the Philosopher King. The adaptation was fully developed in later Persian and Arabic literature (*The Caliphate,* Routledge Kegan Paul Ltd., London 1965, Chapt. X). The author has claimed that step by step Islamic political theory ended up by divorcing the *Imāmah* from *Shari'ah* and the complete negation of the rule of law. For life and works of Arnold, see Bakhtiyar Hasan Siddiqui, "T.W. Arnold: Life and Works", *Iqbal*, Lahore, Vol. XVI, No. 3, January 1968, pp. 59-67.
19. S.T.W. Arnold, *The Caliphate, op.cit.*, p. 53.
20. H.A.R. Gibb, "The Search for an Islamic Democracy, being "Social Reform: Factor X", in *The Middel East in Transition*, ed. W.Z. Laqueur, London, 1958, p. 6.
21. Rosenthal, *Islam in the Modern National State, op.cit.*, pp. 5-6.
22. Ibid., p. XIX.
23. *The Holy Qur'an*, Eng. Tr. Yusuf Ali, Qatar ed., II: 104.
24. Sayyid Abul Ala Maududi, *The Holy Qur'ān Translation and Brief Notes with Text,* Trans. Muhammad Akbar Muradpuri and Abdul Aziz Kamal, Lahore, 1987, p. 25.
25. S.A.A. Maududi, *Tahrīk Āzādī Hind Awr Musalmān*, Lahore, 1987; Vol. I, p. 332.

*****

# 3

# ISLAMIZATION OF POLITICAL SCIENCE

The past decade has witnessed the resurgence of a widespread collective desire in the Muslim world to establish the supremacy of Islamic value in the conduct of public life. The process of revivalism has defied the expectation and logic of social scientists' notions regarding the change and development in the Third World. They have either sought to explain the resurgence of Islamic values as a manifestation of national identity crises such as the Islamization in North Africa, Turkey, Pakistan or Malaysia, or have seen it as essentially a reflection of socio-economic disequilibria merely expressed in Islamic terms.

Regarding Islamic awakening in the Arab Near East, the social scientists have presented another explanation. It is argued that with the fall of Baathism and Arab Socialism which culminated in one man rule in Iraq and Syria and promoted political instability in Libya and Egypt, an ideological vacuum was created in the Arab world that came to be filled by Islam because:

(i) the regime of Anwar al Sadat in Egypt actively encouraged the resuscitation of Islam,

(ii) the Arab's repeated defeats at the hands of Israel, a religion based state tended to refute the arguments of Arab socialists who saw scientific socialism and Arab nationalism as the progressive forces for a victorious future,

(iii) the feeling of unity and universalism which was created in the era of Pak-Arabism from 1954 to 1967, was encouraged and replaced by Islam, and

(iv) Islam became increasingly a factor in Arab politics.

A number of social scientists hold the view that Islamic revivalism often has no base other than echoing a major historical event. Others have argued that the Islamic resurgence is directly connected with the accumulation of oil in the hands of Arabs after 1973.

By and large, these approaches have focussed on the symptoms rather than the cause. Moreover, they have confused mechanisms which have been used by Islamic revivalism, or events which have helped a more rapid dissemination of Islamic sentiments with the cause of resurgence of Islam. The discussions continue to identify factors that catalyse the spread of Islamic revivalism but fail to discern why Islamic sentiments came to the fore in first place. This failure of the social scientists vis-à-vis Islam emanates from their liability to face squarely the presence of Islam in the process of change and development. The social scientists are, therefore, more eager to study Muslims than Islam. For the social scientists Islam is all that something about the lives of Muslims, and hence, they have a greater tendency to focus on what they believe to be that something about the life of Muslims, and to view Islam as a mere factor therein.

This penchant of the social sciences for side stepping Islam has created serious distortions in their outlook and various socio-political issues and crises which they associate with Islamic revivalism were exaggerated in an effort to endorse the legitimacy of their own conceptions and keeping Islam as a subject of analysis at bay. Hence, the socio-economic maladies leading to the revolution in Iran and cultural questions in Pakistan, Malaysia and Turkey have been accentuated with the objective of minimising the role of Islam as the independent actor initiator and harbinger of the process. They have reduced Islamic revivalism to a form of activist retrogression, an expression of anti-modern fanaticism, which, gradually encompasses all the hostilities of the West vis-à-vis Islam.

## The Western Methodology

In fact, the social sciences have generally viewed religion as either an impediment to its objectives or as irrelevant to the forces of change and development. This process has its roots in the historiography of Europe on the one hand and the tradition of orientalism on the other. The modern west emerged from the Medieval Ages against a background of conflict between the Catholic Church and proponents of enlightenment. With the successful institutionalisation of the precepts of the Renaissance, modernisation of Europe occurred hand in hand with religious reform and secularism. Hence, the tell-tale of development of Europe has been that, religion impeded the progress of change in Europe and shackled civilization in what has come to be known as the 'dark ages'. The obstructive power of religion was overcome when the rebellion of Martin Luther and his protestant successors loosened the grip of the church over the masses in Northern Europe. Thenceforth, development in Europe occurred in tandem with reformation of religion, and eventually privatization of faith and, hence, secularization of culture and society.

It needs no reiteration that Europe has viewed its own experience as the law of history, as the inevitable dialectics which every nation and country is bound to encounter. Not surprisingly, the West expects that the outcome of the process will resemble the European experience. It is for this reason that the social sciences have been caught dumb founded in the face of the revival of Islam. For, they surmised that decades of modernizing change in the Muslim world was calculated to metamorphose Turks, Iranians, Pakistanis, Arabs and Malaysians into secular societies instead of working as a fertile ground for the regeneration of their traditional faith and values.

Having adopted European history as the model for future developments in the Third World and as the immutable law of historical change, social scientists from Tonnies to Durkheim have sought to envisage the course in which modernization marginalized religion. The German thinker Max Weber's sociology began with his inquiry into the roots of capitalist development and, hence, modernization of Europe. He had pin pointed religion as the harbinger of the quintessential element of development, namely, capitalist economic growth. He had found religion as positively correlated with development. But, surprisingly, in the case of Islam, his attitude was totally biased.

For, the existing literature in that age was highly hostile, biased and negative towards Islam. Moreover, he was a practising and devout Protestant and, hence, his enraged conscience forbade him from accepting the authenticity and possibility of merit in other religions, such as Islam. In this regard Weber fell victim to the prevalent bias against it.

The French sociologist Emile Durkheim's main interest lays not in charting out the socio-political charge or discerning its roots and agents, but analysing social existence-community, to be exact. His analysis brought him to the concept of collective conscience which he saw at the root of all social affirmities. While he did not address the issue directly, it was clear that religion would be a primary agent in fostering the collective conscience, and that by implication, the resultant social affinity and harmony would serve as a pre-requisite for development.

It may be pointed out here that hardly any of these studies were based on indepth empirical investigations: they sprouted from the theoretical axioms and positions held on religion. Moreover, Muslim governments too were partly responsible for the social sciences apprehensions regarding Islam. The criticism of traditional Islam by Muslim modernists, being extensively propagated became a permanent part of social sciences' rejection of ideas on Islam. This bias was further aggravated by the onslaught of regimes such as those of Mustafa Kamal Ata Turk, Reza Shah Pahlavi, Gamal Abdel Nasser, Syrian Bath Party, Sukarno and Bourqibah against Islam, as the cause of Muslim backwardness and the primary obstacle to all developments.[1]

The main shortcoming lies in the social sciences' assumption that human behaviour can be investigated with exactitude and the laws of physical sciences can be applied in toto. Behaviouralism believes in the applicability of empirical and scientific methods to every field of knowledge.[2] It rejects every knowledge that is based on the supposition that there is some reality beyond worldly existence. This approach, become synonymous with the logical positivism values. By the beginning of the twentieth century, particularly under the impact of Weber's ideas, the social scientists had, in general, accepted as axiomatic that empirical research must be free of all political values and preconceived preferences.[3]

Thus, behaviouralism has been characterised by its attempt to liberate nature from religious outlook and to base its instruments of knowledge exclusively upon human reason and to enable man to discover laws of development inherent in non-religious world. It has made the moral and ethical questions irrelevant and attempted to make science of objective and value-free stating all phenomena, as Dahl observed, in terms of the observed and observable behaviour of men.[4] Consequently, research methodology was borrowed from the natural sciences and hence faced with increasing incidence of authoritarian rule and violation of even the moral conscience of the world in Lebanon, the Ghaza Strip and Afghanistan, society is in a state of decay and it was realized even by those who earlier advocated behavioural persuation in politics.[5]

## The Theocentric Islamic Methodology

This paradigm should be replaced with one which studies individual behaviour within the context of an entire social system. Islam, as a total civilization looks upon human life as on organic whole. From the concept of the unity of Allah (Tawhid) the unity of this creation follows as a logical necessity.[6] Creation is an integral whole because it is the work of the Creator whose orders and designs have infused every part of it. Cosmic order consists of the laws of nature. These operate throughout the universe and permeate every part and aspect of it. Allah has designed the nature and continues to operate and control it. He is eternally alive and active. Every being in the cosmos and every event that takes place does so by His command. The *Qur'ān* declares:

> Allah! There is no God but He-the Living, the Self-subsisting, Eternal. No slumber can seize Him nor sleep. His are all things in the Heavens and on earth. Who is there can intercede in His presence except as He permitteth? He knoweth what (appeareth to His creatures as) before or after or behind them. Nor shall they compass aught of His knowledge except as He willeth. His Throne

> doth extend over the heavens and the earth, and He feeleth no fatigue in guarding and preserving them or He is the Most High, the Supreme (in glory).[7]

Based on the Ayah al-Kursi and the like, methodology of Islamic political science can not but be theocentric which stands totally opposed to the Western concept of man and nature in all its details.

The western social science, as pointed by S.H. Nasr is reductionist, for it not only separates reason from revelation but rejects the latter as a means of knowledge.[8] Based upon Greco-Roman cultural tradition and rational philosophy, it accepts nothing which can not fit the scale of reason and human intellect, and abiding by the same standard, it considers nothing as moral if it fails to yield maximum returns in material terms.[9]

In contrast, the Islamic culture and civilization is deeply rooted in Divine revelation. Muslim scholars disentangled the various issues of revelation. They maintained the revelation's relations to reason in all their philosophical and theological debates because the revelation was a distinguishing feature of the methodology of Islamic research rather than posing a problem in the form of contrast between Divine Law and human reason as argued by Rosenthal[10], both have been complementary to each other in Islamic history. This is in accordance with the *Qur'ān*'s repeated exhortations to reason out and weigh rationally all matters to enable one to follow the right way.[11] If reason is the tool required to know the world about the man, to utilize it in satisfying his needs and in shouldering his responsibilities as a *Khalifah*, the revelation is meant to guide him towards the knowledge of the aims of righteousness, of the definition of its responsibilities and of ascertaining its components. Thus, both are complementary and essential for righteous life on the earth.[12]

## Value-based Social Science

There is no room for a neutral or value-free social science in Islam. The value neutral science based on research methods borrowed from mathematics, physics, biology and other similar natural sciences as advocated by behaviouralists, goes against the very spirit of goal-oriented Islam. According to the *Qur'ān* everything is created with a precise measure that assigns to it's nature, relations to other beings and the course of its relations to other beings and the course of its existence. The *Qur'ān* says:

> "He created all things and ordered them in due proportions[13]".

All things in the universe serve a purpose and all purposes are interrelated as a means and an end to one another, because Allah is ultimate end – the final purpose unto whom everything returns. The *Qur'ān* declares:

> "To Him belong the keys of the heavens and the earth and those who reject the signs of Allah-it is they who will be in loss[14]".

This aspect of Islamic faith makes the Muslims struggle continuously though their struggle may not yield fruit but this does not dishearten them nor deter them from exerting more effort. This owes to the nature of ultimate objective of human life as envisaged by the *Qur'ān* and to the logical consequences that follow. This ultimate object is Ibadah. The *Qur'ān* says:

> "I have only created *jinns* and men, that they may serve Me. No sustenance do I require of them, nor do I require that they should feed Me. For Allah is He who gives all sustenance, Lord of Power, Steadfast (for ever)[16]".

This is the end and everything else constitutes the means. Hence, it becomes imperative that all human activity be, directly or indirectly, conceived as means to this ultimate end. There would be a chain of sub-ends, no doubt, but the ultimate end must be the motivating force behind all human activity, generating and directing them.

Allah, who is to be served, is Omniscient and Omnipresent, observing our actions, reading our thoughts and knowing our intentions. It is ever so. Nowhere, in no walk of life, is an outside his surveillance. This belief makes the Muslims end-conscious and spiritually motivated. It is further reinforced by the doctrine of accountability on the Day of Judgement and of the Final Reckoning. Worldly life is short and fleeting, while the Hereafter is eternal and infinite. This consideration is significant and has far reaching consequences, on the conduct of life. It heightens man's end-consciousness and invests all his activities with a normative value content.

Moreover, Islam strikes a balance between the material and spiritual aspects of human life. According to the *Qur'ān*, when the material considerations get precedence the result is chaos and degeneration. Disillusionment and frustration gradually lead to disintegration of human personality. When the balance is tilted the other side, that is, when it is only the spiritual that matters, the result is a suppression of activity rarely conducive to progress and development, scientific discoveries and inventions, resulting ultimately in a loosening of the social bonds of life. The good among the men become indifferent to the temporal while the bad acquire, holding unchallenged sway over the polity and the economy.

An optimum combination of the material and the spiritual could avoid these dangers. This does not imply, however, that Islam conceives the temporal and the spiritual as two distinctive realms balanced against one another in the Islamic order of life. It is not that they are two separate departments of life in the functioning of which a sort of harmony is desired. Life is one and indivisible and it is as inalienable aspect of human activity that the material and the spiritual are conceived off. This is the total rejection of Western secular overtone which is based upon the theory of logical positivism.

The fact that the dichotomy between natural and social sciences necessitates the adoption of separate methodologies for each is admitted even by the staunch supporters of behavioural approach. This trend was based on the desire for increased social prestige, the achievement of scientific respectability, and the quest for social status at par with that of natural scientists.[17] The behavioural political scientists assumed not only the stance of the physical model but also its epistemology and its assumptions about the nature and means of knowledge. They considered human behaviour in an artificial manner, stripped the variables of their meaning in order to operationalize them, and tended to bend, reshape and distort the political map to fit the model they use to investigate it. As Deutscher puts it:

> "We concentrate on consistency without much concern with what it is we are being consistent about or whether we are consistently right or wrong. As a consequence, we may have been learning a great deal about how to pursue an incorrect course with a maximum of precision."[18]

It may be concluded from above analysis that political science must abandon claims to approximating natural science without ceasing to aspire to comprehensive knowledge.

## The *Qur'ānic* Concept of Knowledge

According to the *Qur'ān*, knowledge (*ilm*) is to be obtained through the absolute knowledge (*haqq al yaqeen*[19]), rationalism or inference based upon judgement and appraisal of evidence (*ilm al yaqeen*[20]), and through empiricism and perception that is by observation, experiment, historical reports, description of life-experiences and the like (*ayn al yaqeen*)[21]. Thus, the *Qur'ānic* way of knowing accords full freedom to experience and experiment and to rational and intellectual inquiry within the circumstances of revealed knowledge. It is indeed advisable to benefit from the best offered by one field for the better understanding of the other, but one must recognize the distinction between the two fields, which is in terms of research strategy and techniques.[22]

This *Qur'ānic* scheme of knowledge (*ilm al yaqeen, ayn al yaqeen and haqq al yaqeen*) has been described in other terms too. The *Qur'ān* describes *sama*, *basr* and *fuad* as the three basic sources of knowledge. Faud is the most important authentic source in Islam. Due to special divine favour some very highly developed *fuads* are enabled to grasp the ultimate principles and the Divine purposes more clearly and definitely.[23] This revelation or faud of haqq al yaqeen is the backbone of the Islamic methodology. The revelation must be supported by using the *sama* and *basr*, *i.e.*, the empirical methods. In this empiricism the principles of *jalb al manfaat* and *dafe mazarrat* (the achievement of general welfare of mankind and avoidance of harm in general) or *La zarar wala zerar* (Do not harm anyone nor tolerate it) is so important that the Prophet (SAW) himself suspended some of his judgements upon such a knowledge of facts about the social reality.[24]

Political Science, by virtue of its orientation to the model of natural sciences, has limited its scope to observable behaviour. Politics has been defined either in terms of "the study of influence and the influential", as Lasswell defined or the study of who gets, what 'when and how' as Desutch did, or "the authoritative allocation of values" as Easton described. Similarly, political association or state is conceived as an instrumental apparatus for the pursuit of contingently determined ends that can be calculated according to a strategic instrumentalist conception of rationality, *i.e.* expediency, gross national product and utilitarian considerations.

The idea of modern secular state is developed in its original cultural milieu, Europe, and its spread by force to every corner of the world. The central claim of the state today, as described by Andrew Vincent is that of its being a public power above both ruler and ruled which provides continuity and order to a polity. Among the other prerequisites of a modern state, is the possession of territory: a state exists primarily within a geographically definable territory over which it holds jurisdiction. Moreover, within its own territory, the state claims hegemony over all other associations, organizations and groups. However, the supremacy which the state exercises over other associations is legal in nature. And yet, the most salient formal feature of the modern state is its monopoly to use force. Consequently, the state has the maximum control of the resources of the violence. Tied to this privilege is also the claim of legitimacy: the force exercised by the state is recognized as de jure. Authority, then in the ensuring sense, is the legitimate use of force. Acting as the supreme legal authority within its territory, the modern state also lays claim to being sovereign. State sovereignty, however, is a concept notoriously difficult to define and in practice often entails the recognition of a state's territorial integrity as well as that of its status as a separate and independent political entity by other states.[25]

Against the backdrop of European political and intellectual history, Vincent discusses the 'Absolutist'. 'Ethical', 'Constitutional', 'class' and 'pluralist' theories of the state that are the legacy of the political thinkers in the West. It is indeed a most useful summary and though we may not share many of his ideas, we may, benefit enormously from the penetrative analysis. For instance, in the concluding chapter, 'Do we need theory of State?' there is the following admission:

> "We must bear in mind that the state is not primarily an empirical entity at all. We can not touch or see a state. It is nothing but a mental category, although it may be an extremely concrete one. We do not realise that the state is mode of being and a complex of values, as well as an institutional structure. The grasp of such a category is not primarily gained from history but from theory and philosophy."[26]

Obviously, the European idea of the state a continuous political entity that is above both ruler and ruled – is mythological. It has its own metaphysics, which generates its peculiar mystique, and it relates to the world of morals and ethics in its own perverted way.[27]

Ernst Cassirer, traces the geneology of the modern monster with great perception and poignancy and shows how 'the myth of the state' evolved from pre-historic times through Plato. Dame, Machiavelli, Carlyle and Hegel to pave the way for the modern totalitarian state. At heart a passioned plea for the subjugation of 'politics' to some higher, 'rational' not 'mythological' principle of morality Cassirer's work is a forceful indictment of the Machiavellian nature of modern statehood that has come to prevail since the time of renaissance.

With the advent of the modern secular state, notes Cassirer, universal morality applicable to all human activity is excluded from the canons of statecraft. His own biting criticism of Machiavellianism, which claimed the autonomy of politics from the 'shackles of religion' reads:

> "With Machiavelli we stand at the gateway of the modern world. The desired end is attained; the state has won its full autonomy. Yet this result has had to be bought dearly. The state is entirely independent; but at the same time it is completely isolated. The sharp knife of Machiavelli's thought has cut off all the threads by which in former generations the state was fastened to the organic whole of human existence. The political world has lost its

> connection not only with religion or metaphysics but with all other forms of man's ethical and cultural life. It stands alone in any empty space."[28]

## Islamic Concept of State

It may be concluded from the above discussions that the notion of the state, which is a 'fact' of modern consciousness and a 'given' of the international system, is ineluctably secular. It is totally antithetical to the moral idea of the sovereignty of Allah. It is a total rejection of Islamic concept of state which is conceived not as a means to ends that are separable from the state but as itself the locus of religio-cultural purposes. That is why the *Qur'ān* stresses the need for organization and authority for the realization of its goals. The *Qur'ān* declares:

> "We sent aforetime Our apostles with clear signs and sent down with them the Book and the Balance (of Right and Wrong) that man may stand forth in justice; and we sent down iron in which is (material for) mighty war, as well as many benefits for mankind, that Allah may test who it is that will help, unseen, Him and His apostles."[29]

The *Qur'ān* condemns disorder and anarchy and says:

> "When he (the non-believer) turns his back, his aim everywhere is to spread mischief through the earth and destroy crops and cattle but Allah loveth not mischief."[30]

> "Tumult and oppression are worse than slaughter."[31]

Imam Ibn Hanbal held the opinion that in the absence of an *Imam* anarchy and disorder would certainly ensure.[32] According to Mawardi, the existence of *Imam* is as necessary as the striving for truth and the acquisition of knowledge.[33] Razi has explained the reason for such a heavy emphasis on organized authority for he says that "without political social organization man can not reach his destiny.[34] To Ibn Taimiyah, "religion can not exist without it."[35] Maulana Maududi maintained that the ultimate goal of an Islamic state is neither to maintain peace and raise the standard of living of its inhabitants nor to defend its frontiers. Its ultimate purpose is "to enforce and implement with all the resources of its organised power that reformatory program which Islam has given for the betterment of mankind."[36] The Islamic state is an ideological state, its approach is universal and all embracing, and its mission is to establish virtue and justice in accordance with revealed knowledge. In short the state in Islam "is only an effort to realize the spiritual and human organization."[37]

While discussing Islamic methodology in social sciences it is essential to keep in mind the Islamic values clearly and explicitly. The Stockholm seminar of 1981 on "knowledge and values" identified ten concepts which generate the basic values of Islamic culture, *tawhid* (unity), *khilafah* (vicegerency), *ibadah* (worship), *ilm* (knowledge), *halal* (permissible) and *haram* (prohibited), *adl* (justice), *zulm* (tyranny), *istislah* (public interest) and *dhiya* (waste).[38]

These values are organically related to each other and impart a unique character to the epistemology of Islam. These values enshrined in the *Qur'ān* impart a universal character to Islam. This universality of Islamic values grants a universal status to a discipline subservient to the Islamic framework.

*****

## NOTES AND REFERENCES

1. See for detail: Nasr, Sayyed Vali Reza, Islam and the Social sciences, *Hamdard Islamicus*, Karachi, Vol. XIII, No. 2, 1990, pp. 83-92.
2. Eldersveld, S.I., Research in Political behaviour, In Ulmer, S. Sidney, 1961, *Introductory Reading to Political Behaviour,* Rand Me Nally & Co., Chicago, Dahl, R.A., The Behavioural Approach in Political Science, Epitaph for a Monument to a successful Protest, *The American Political Science Review,* Vol. 55, De. 1961; Easton, David, The Current Meaning of Behaviourism, in Charlesworth, J.C. *Contemporary Political Analysis*, Free Press, New York, 1967.
3. Easton, David, The Decline of Modern Political Theory, in James A. Gould and Vincent V. Thursby, 1979, *Contemporary Political Thought*, New York, p. 308.
4. Dahl, R.A., *The Behavioural Approach in Political Science, op.cit.*, p. 766.
5. Hass, Michael and Maried, Henry, S., *Approaches to Political Science,* Chandler Publishing Co. California, 1970.
6. *The Qur'ān*, 21:23.
7. *The Qur'ān*, 2:255.
8. Nasr, S.H., *Islam and the Plight of Modern Man*, Longman, London, 1975.
9. Nadwi, S.A.H.A., *Religion and Civilization,* Academy of Islamic Research, Lucknow, 1970, pp. 62-70.
10. Rosenthal, E.I.J., *Political Thought in Medieval Islam: An Introductory Outline*, Cambridge University Press, 1962, p. 16.
11. *The Qur'ān*, 59:2; 7:86.
12. Abu Sulayman, A., *Islamization of Knowledge: General Principles and Work Plan*, International Institute of Islamic Thought, U.S.A., 1989, pp. 51-52.
13. *The Qur'ān*, 25:2, see also 65:3, 36:30, 10:5, 80:19, 76:16, 73:20.
14. *The Qur'ān*, 39:63.
15. *The Qur'ān*, 11:123.
16. *The Qur'ān*, 51:56-58.
17. Clinard, Marshall B., The Sociologist's Quest for Respectability, *The Sociological Quarterly* 7, 1966, pp. 399-412.
18. Deutscher, Irwin, "Words and Deeds: Social Science and Social Policy", *Social Problems*, 13, 1966, p. 241.
19. *The Qur'ān*, 56:95, 69:51.
20. *The Qur'ān*, 4:157.
21. *The Qur'ān*, 27:22.
22. Moten, Rashid, Islamization of Knowledge, *The American Journal of Islamic Social Sciences*, Vol. 7, No. 2, 1990, pp. 164-165; see also Ali, A. Yousuf, *The Holy Qur'ān Text, Translation Copmmentary,* The Islamic Foundation, Leciester, p. 1603.

23. Ahmad, Irfan, The Islamic Method, *Islamic Thought*, Aligarh, Vol. VIII, No. 2, 1961, pp. 8-13.
24. Ibid., The learned researcher has produced a very interesting case in this regard. He has quoted a hadith as follows:

    From Judama, the daughter of Wahb that she said I saw the Prophet (SAW) amongst a number of persons. He was saying: I had made up my mind to forbid you from *Gheelah* (intercourse with wife during the period when child depends upon his mother's milk) and then I saw that Persians and Romans observe *Gheelah* but it does not harm their babies.

    This hadith, as discussed by the researcher, clearly shows that the permission for *Gheelah* is due to the knowledge of the fact that it does not harm the children, and that if the observation had been otherwise the Prophet (SAW) would have forbidden the act.

    He has quoted another case in which an experiment by the people made the Prophet (SAW) change his decision. The story goes that the Prophet (SAW) had prohibited his people from cross plantation of dates. Most probably it was due to the idea that this was a type of a superstition. Later on, when actual experiment proved otherwise he changed his views and said that it was amongst those purely technical matters which do not fall under superstition, etc.

    In both the cases experience is a factor in the final decision and it is the discovery of fresh experience which changes the decision.
25. Vincent, Andrew, *Theories of the State*, Blackwell, Oxford, 1987, p. 15.
26. Ibid., p. 219.
27. Manzoor, S. Pervez, Islamic State Between the Mystique of Khilafah and the Logic of *Mulk*, *Muslim World Book Review*, London, Vol. 9, No. 1, 1988, p. 5.
28. Cassirer, Ernst, *The Myth of the State*, Yale University Press, New Haven and London, (Reprint 1986), p. 140.
29. *The Qur'ān*, 57:25.
30. *The Qur'ān*, 2:205.
31. *The Qur'ān*, 12:191, See also 2:191, and 2:193, 217, 8:39, 73.
32. Ibn Abdul Barr, *Jame Bayan al Ilm Wa Fadhlih*, Al-Maktaba al Ilmiyah, Madinah, p. 62.
33. Al-Mawardi, Abdul Hasan Ali, *Al-Ahkam al Sultaniyah*, Isa al Babi al-Halbi, Cairo, 1960, p. 5.
34. Cited in Rosenthal, *Political Thought in Medieval Islam*, p. 14.
35. Khan, Qamaruddin, *The Political Thought of Ibn Taimiyah*, 1983, Lahore, Islamic Book Foundation, p. 29.
36. Maududi, S.A.A., *The Islamic law and Constitution,* tr. Khurshid Ahmad, Islamic Publications, Lahore, 1967, p. 248.

37. Iqbal, M. *The Reconstruction of Religious Thoughts in Islam*, p. 155.
38. Sardar, Ziauddin, *The Touch of Midas*, Manchester University Press, Manchester, 1984.

*****

# 4

# LIBERATION STRUGGLE OR ISLAM
## (REFLECTIONS ON THE MUJAHIDIN MOVEMENT OF INDIA)

### Introduction

The chapter basically provides a blue print of the *jihad* led by Sayyid Ahmad Shaheed and his remnant. This jihad movement targeted both the Sikhs and the British in order to establish truly Islamic State on the pattern of the prophethood modelled on *Khilafah Rashidah* after overthrowing the non-Islamic government, in the pursuit of which emancipation of the country from the foreign domination was a necessary step. It highlights the main objectives and ends of the freedom struggle initiated and the reformatory movement launched in Islamic perspective and in the light of original sources available.

### Sayyid Ahmad Shaheed

Sayyid Ahmad Shaheed (1786-1831 A.D.) the pious Islamic scholar and leader of Jihad was born in Rai Bareilly in the old Mughal province of Awadh in north India. He died in the battle of Bala Kot situated at the mountainous frontier of the Northwest. Three strands of experience in his life came together in this military endeavour. First, he was born into a family of Sayyids, known for their piety and learning but, like many of the educated and well-born, now impoverished and frustrated in finding employment in a princely court. Second, in Delhi from 1806 to 1811, he entered into the circle of the family of Shah Wali Allah with its program of the dissemination of scripturalist norms. Third, at about the age of twenty-five, he left Delhi to spend some seven years as a cavalryman for Amir Khan (1765-1834) in central India, immersing himself in the world of local state-building so characteristic of this period.

Back in Delhi, Sayyid Ahmad Shaheed rejected the reformist Ulama but glaringly distinguished himself by more far-reaching and stringent reforms, for example in opposing the Islamic Sufi practices and enjoining such aspects of family behaviour as the remarriage of widows. His thoughts and basic tendencies of reforms are reflected mainly in the *Sirat Mustaquim*[1] compiled by Maulana Shah Islamil Shaheed (1779-1831) and the *Taqwiyah al-Iman*[2] both circulated in the vernacular Urdu language. The texts identified practices derived from false Tasawwuf, Shiah doctrines and local customs. It is notable that Sufism as such was not opposed. He had rather taken the oath of allegiance on the hands of Shah Abdul Aziz (1746-1824) in 1804. The Shah guided his disciples, desirous of spiritual ascent on the path of Chishtiyah[3], Qadiriyah[4] or Naqshbandiyah[5] order, in accordance with the desire expressed by them Sayyid had learnt from his teacher all the three systems.[6]

With a sincere and devoted group of followers, Sayyid Ahmad Shaheed toured northern India in 1818-1819. In 1821 he undertook the *Hajj* as a prelude to *jihad*, travelling down river to Calcutta, preaching and collecting a band of some six hundred for a journey whose very practice had long been neglected. In 1823 he returned to Rai Barielly where he spent two years teaching and preparing for *jihad*.

Muslims regarded him as the *mujaddid* for the remarkable contributions he made in the field of reformation and renewal. The followers of the movement were prepared to abjure customs that had defined and given honour to personal and family status; many were prepared to leave their homes and even to die. The model of *jihad*, while seen as following prophetic precedent, took its shape from the quest for new states in the post-Mughal period.

In 1826 Sayyid Ahmad Shaheed left for the frontier, an area of Muslim population as precedent required, to launch warfare on Punjab, then under the Sikh rule (See Tables 1 & 2). He was trapped in Balakot with some six hundred followers and Killed in 1831. Ahmad Shaheed's example and teachings inspired the reformers, revivalists, freedom fighters long after his death.[7]

## Post-Balakot Clashes

After the battle of Balakot was won by the Sikhs and the Chief Lientenant of the leader Maulana Ismail Shaheed also fell in the same battle, the remnant numbering about 1000 escaped to the hills and were joined after some time by the Sayyid's nephew, Sayyid Wali Muhammad who, along with Maulawi Ruknuddin, had been sent by Sayyid Ahmad Shaheed to Kashmir on a special secret mission. After a long wondering the largest group of mujahidin alongwith the new leader left for Tonk, a princely state in Rajputana.

The mujahidin now split up into two sections. One of these devoted itself to the normal life of religious education and social reform in Bengal and elsewhere with extraordinary zeal like Maulawi Karamat Ali of Jaunpur[8] and others. The other group still continued to concentrate on jihad. It was led by two famous brothers Maulawi Wilayat Ali (d. 1852) and Maulawi Inayat Ali (d. 1858) who belonged to prestigious family of Sadiq Pur (Patna), which henceforward became the organizational headquarters of the movement – position formerly occupied by Delhi.[9] The two brothers between them were largely responsible for keeping the movement active against British imperialism. Their role was two-fold. In the frontier they directly led the mujahidin, while as in India they organized support for the movement by propagating the cause and by sending men, money and ammunitions to the mujahidin. Among the local leaders who waged jihad against imperialism were Maulawi Nasiruddin of Delhi, Mir Aulad Ali of Surjadh, Sayyid Wali Muhammad of Phulat, and Sayyid Abdur Rahim of Surat. After the death of Maulawi Inayat Ali in 1858, Mir Nasrullah and Mir Maqsud Ali led the movement for short periods. In 1862, however, Maulawi Abdullah, the son of Maulawi Wilayat Ali, became the leader and continued in that position for a long time right upto his death in 1902. Practically his whole life was spent in the Frontier.[10]

In 1853 occurred the first serious clash with the British. Mujahidin afforded some resistance to the hasanzais against whom British had undertaken an expedition because they had seized a fort at Kotla which is situated on the right bank of the

Indus and which belonged to a feudatory of the British, the Nawab of Amb. A British force was sent to deal with the situation. The mujahidin, whom the British chose to call "Hindustani fanatics", were forced to evacuate Kotla (See Table-3).

In 1857 came the great upheaval that shook the formation of British Rule in India. The mujahidin took a prominent part in this what is regarded to be the Ist war of independence. In Patna Maulawi Ahmadullah a prominent member of the family of Maulawi Inayat Ali, was closely associated with the movement, and on the Frontier Maulawi Inayat Ali himself was collaborating with the "mutineers" and was busy in preaching Jihad. He issued several proclamations exhorting the Yosufzais to rise and fight against the British.[11] Maulawi Liyaqat Ali of Allahabad, who was not only an Ahl-Hadith scholar but also a distinguished freedom fighter, played a key role in propagating Jihad against the British infidels. He himself joined the jihad movement and in order to mobilize the Muslims in his favour, he distributed two posters, one in provocative prose form and the other in poetic one.... The poster recites;

واسطے دین کے لڑنا نہ پئے طمع بلاد  اہل اسلام اسے شرع میں کہتے ہیں جہاد
جو مسلمان رہ حق میں لڑا لحظہ بھر  روضۂ خلد بریں ہوگیا واجب اس پر
جو رہ حق میں ہوئے ٹکڑے، نہیں مرتے ہیں  بلکہ وہ جیتے ہیں جنت میں خوشی کرتے ہیں
گر رہے جیتے تو گھر بار میں پھر آؤگے  اور گئے مارے تو جنت میں چلے جاؤگے

(Fight in order to defend the religion; not for the sake of land or territory. The people of Islam call it jihad in terms of Shariah!
A Muslim who fought in the way of right and truth though for a moment, the Garden of eternal paradise becomes due to him!
Those who are made into pieces in the right path, are not killed. They are everlasting and enjoy with the Paradise!
If you remain alive, would come back to your home; if you are killed, would enter Paradise!)

W.W. Hunter has quoted the popular song of Muslim freedom fighters whom he has called the 'Indian Wahabis'. The song breathed the same spirit of jihad. 'The rebels', as he narrated, in the camp on our Frontier were drilled morning and evening to the sound of its solemn strains, and the companies of recruits who passed northwards from the heart of our territory chanted its stanzas along the British high roads:

> 'First I glorify God, who is beyond all praise, I laud His Prophet and write a song on Holy War:
> Holy war is a war carried on for religion, without any lust of power. In the sacred scriptures its glories are related; I mention a few.
> War against the infidel is incumbent on all Musalmaans, make provision for it before all things.
> He who from his hearts gives one farthing to the cause, shall hereafter receive seven hundred fold;
> And he who both gives and joins in the fight, shall receive seven thousand fold from God.
> He who shall equip a warrior in the cause of God shall obtain a martyr's reward;
> His children dread not the trouble of the grave; nor the last triumph; nor the Day of Judgement.
> Cease to be cowards; join the divine leader and smite the infidel.
> I give thanks to God that a great leader has been in the thirteenth century of the Hijra.
> Oh friend, since you must sometime die, is it not better to offer up your life in the service of the Lord?
> Thousands go to war and come back unhurt; thousands remain at home and die.
> You are filled with worldly care and have forgotten your Maker in thinking of your wives and children.
> How long will you be able to remain with your wives and children? How long to escape death?
> If you give up this world for the sake of God, you enjoy the pleasures of Heaven for ever.
> Fill the uttermost ends of India with Islam, so that no sounds may be heard but "Allah!" "Allah"![13]

According to the same writer, any attempt at even the briefest epitome of the Wahabi Treatises in prose and verse on the duty to wage war against the English would fill a volume. The sect has developed a copious literature filled with prophecies of the downfall of the British Power and devoted to the duty of Religious Rebellion. The mere titles of its favourite works suffice to show their almost uniformly treasonable character.[14] Hunter admits that 'some of these books are of so flagrant a character as to require to be secretly passed from hand to hand in manuscript others are widely circulated. The poison, however, is not confined to their readers alone, but is carried into every district of Bengal by a swarm of preachers. Every one of whom is carefully nurtured in treason before he goes forth on his proselytizing work'.[15]

## Ulama of Sadiq Pur

The role of the Ulama of Sadiq Pur (Patna) in the Jihad movement was well appreciated even by Hunter when he declared, 'They (the leaders of Patna Propaganda) enlisted the more certain and more permanent hatred which the Indian Muhammadans feel towards the English. They thus transferred the basis of their teaching from the noblest capabilities of the Musalmaan heart to the fanatical fury of the populace... They converted the Patna Propaganda into a caravan-serai for rebels and traitors'.[16]

The author goes on admiring the sound and uncompromising character of Wahabi mujahidin. He says : 'I find it impossible to speak them without respect, most of them start life as youths of enthusiastic piety; many of them retain their zeal for religion to the end, with singularly little tincture of the poisonous doctrines in the Patna preachers have trained them the civilized man, cribbed within cities, and only permitted to move about this world clogged with luggage, and in the ceaseless society of fellow-travellers, can with difficulty realise the unencumbered life and isolated wanderings of the Wahabi Missionary. ... Certain it is that the Wahabi Missionary furnishes, so far as my experience goes, the most spiritual, the least selfish type of the sect'.[17]

Hunter has also pointed that the District Centres of treason in Bengal kept up a regular correspondence with the Central Propaganda at Patna and each had its own machinery for raising money and recruits complete within itself. The author has provided an interesting example of Maulawi Ahmadullah who was convicted of treason, and sentenced by the Sessions Court at Patna to death and his property to be forfeited. The capital part of his sentence, however, was afterwards mitigated to transportation for life. Inspite of this warning, Maulawi Ahmadullah continued his levies of money and men for the

Frontier War; openly went from village to village preaching rebellion; and in 1868 when he found the liberality of his people slackening, brought down the son of Patna Khalifa to assist him in reviving their zeal. His jurisdiction extended over three separate Districts; and for several days' journey down the Ganges the ignorant Musalmaan peasantry on both banks, and on the islands which the river has thrown up in its bed, owned his control. The number of recruits whom he sent to the Frontier Camp can never be ascertained; but at a single one of the Traitor outposts on our Frontier, containing 430 fighting men, more than 10 per cent had been supplied from his jurisdiction.[18]

Maulawi Yahya Ali, one of the champions of jihad against British Empire is reported by Hunter as the 'Chief Priest and Khalifah' of the Patna Propaganda who ruled over the headquarters with a firm but gentle hand. The recruits whom the itinerant missionaries sent up in flocks from the Districts of Lower Bengal were kindly received at the hospice. The better part of them he carefully trained up as preachers while those destined immediately for the Rebel Camp were handed over to a lay brother, Abdul Ghaffar who fanned their zeal for the conflict without troubling them very much with matters of doctrine.[19]

Maulawi Yahya Ali in the Propaganda Centre had many duties. He corresponded with the itinerant preachers as Spiritual Director of the sect in India. He organized and personally worked a complicated system of drafts in a secret language, by which large sums were safely transmitted from the center of the Empire to the Rebel camp beyond the Frontier. He conducted the public ministrations in the mosque. He examined and passed the riffles for the Fanatic Host, delivered a course of divinity lectures to the students, and by private study acquired an intimate acquaintance with the Arabic Fathers.[20] Seldom have more impressive words been uttered in a Court of Justice than those in which Sir Herbert Edwards passed sentence of death upon this man:

> 'It is proved, he said, 'against the prisoner Yahya Ali, that he has been the mainspring of the great treason of this trial has laid bare. He has been the religious preacher spreading from his mosque at Patna, under the most

solemn sanctions, the hateful principles of the Crescentade. He has enlisted subordinate agents to collect money and preach the Moslem Jihad (war against the Infidel). He has deluded hundreds and thousands of this countrymen into treason and rebellion. He has plunged the Government of British India, by his intrigues, into a Frontier War, which has cost hundreds of lives. He is highly educated man, who can plead no excuse of ignorance. What he has done, he has done with fore thought, resolution, and the bitterest treason. He belongs to a hereditary disloyal and fanatical family. He aspires to the merit of a religious reformer; but instead of appearing to reason and to conscience, like his Hindu fellow-countrymen in Bengal, of the Brahmo Samaj, he seeks his end in political revolution, and madly plots against the Government, which probably saved the Muhammadans of India from extinction, and certainly brought in religious freedom'.[21]

## The Wahabi Trials

The five great State Trials in British India after the break up of 1857 freedom movement are known as the 'Wahabi Trials'. These judicial proceedings were carried out to punish the 'mutineers' and suppress and crush the freedom fighters with an iron hand. The first of these judicial proceedings is known as the Ambala Trial 1864. In that process the accused were tortured, the witnesses were tutored and the judges were bent upon laying the blame on the 'Muhammadan fanatics' whose fanaticism and bigotry was, in the eyes of their rulers, 'the characteristic of the race'. Of the 11 persons arrested and put on trial were Maulawi Yahya Ali, Maulawi Muhammad Jafar Thanesari, Maulawi Abdur Rahim, Qazi Mian Jan of Comercolly, Abdul Ghaffar, Elahi Bakhsh of Patna, Husaini of Thanesar their servants Abdul Ghafoor and Husaini, Muhammad Shafi a contractor and his servant Abdul Karim. They were charged under Section 121 of Indian Penal Code for waging war against the Queen. Some of them were sentenced to death and their property was confiscated. Some were transported for life and their property was confiscated. This was the first caravan of Wahabi mujadihin that was taken from Ambala to Lahore on foot laden with heavy chains and from there transferred to Karachi in a close compartment, chained together and tied to a wooden plank.

Ultimately the caravan reached Andaman Islands on 11th January 1866.[22]

That was followed by the second judicial proceeding known as the Patna Trial of 1865. The main accused mujahid was Maulawi Ahmadullah the elder brother of Maulawi Yahya Ali. He was arrested in November\ 1864 and charged on the 16th January 1865 with waging war against the Queen. The Session Court sentenced him to death and ordered for the confiscation of his property on the evidence of only one prosecution witness namely Ilahi Bux. The High Court also confirmed the sentence but directed that he should be transported for life. He was thus first to reach Port Blair in Andaman Islands where he arrived in June 1865 about seven months ahead of his brother.[23]

The Maldah trial of September\ 1870 under O'Kinealy then Officiating Magistrate obtained depositions of sixteen mujahidin and arrested eight suspects including Nazir Sardar of Kazeegram who realized contributions from the Muslims of the locality for the jihad. The judiciary also implicated Ibrahim Mandal as the head of the center who received the funds from Nazir Sardar. He was also brought to trial. Maulawi Amiruddin of Sundipa Narainpur was also accused of preaching sedition and sending recruits to join the jihad across the Frontier. The last two mujahids were prosecuted and sentenced to transportation for life.[24]

The Rajmahal Trial of October 1870 accused the districts of Dinajpur Maldah, Rajshahi, Murshidabad, Nadia, Burdwan, Jessore, Calcutta and 24 Parganas as the centers of rebellion and dens of jihad activities. In these districts a net work of compact organization was found that recruited fighters and collected subscription for the jihad in the North-West Frontiers. Under special trial these mujahidin were transported to life and their property was confiscated.

The fifth trial of Patna in 1871 which is known as the 'Great Trial'[25] discussed in detail the missionary and rebellious activities of seven fighters namely Haji Din Muhammad of Dinajpur, Pir Muhammad, father-in-law of Tabarak Ali son of Mubarak Ali both were the prominent members of jihad movement and were arrested, Amir Khan, Hashmatdad Khan and Aminuddin. Under Preamble of Bengal Regulations III of 1818, the persons placed under personal restraint, otherwise than in pursuance of some judicial proceedings, were required to be informed of the grounds of such detention, but the persons arrested in this case were not afforded this opportunity for more than six months, nor was the Viceroy informed of the detentions as required by the law.[26] The Habeas Corpus petitions of Amir Khan and Hashmatdad Khan were also rejected. Ultimately Hashmatdad Khan and Pir Muhammad were acquitted on 4th July 1871, while the remaining persons were sentenced to transportation for life and confiscation of their immovable properties.[27]

In the struggle of freedom made during the period from 1831 to 1934 A.D., most of the leaders and martyrs were originally associated with the first jihad movement led by Sayyid Ahmad Shaheed and Shah Islamil Shaheed, and a huge majority of them were Wahabis (Ahl-e-Hadith) whose selfless sacrifices and exemplary efforts resulted later on into the national movement of the country that made India free of English dominance.[28] This has been recognized by W.W. Hunter also who has clearly written that 'the Rebel Camp on the Punjab Frontier owes its origin to Sayyid Ahmad , of those bold spirits whom our extermination of the Pindari Power scattered over India half a century age.'[29]

## Main Objectives of Jihad

Now the most striking question that agitates the mind of a student of Islamic Political thought, is that what was the ultimate goal of the jihad movement? Whether Sayyid Ahmad Shaheed had directed jihad against the Sikhs and not the British, as was advocated by Sir Syed Ahmad Khan[30] and some others? Or was the exclusive objective of this jihad the emancipation of India for a comprehensive social and economic reform and nothing else, as discussed in detail by Maulana Sayyid Muhammad Mian[31]? Did Sayyid intend to resuscitate the crumbling empire of Delhi as is presented by Maulana Ubaidullah Sindhi?[32]

Sayyid Ahmad Shahid was not a political thinker to lay down the blue prints of his thought, yet his letters bear out the conceptual model of the state he desired to establish after emancipating country from the alien rule. The basic objective of his jihad was the Islamization of the society and the establishment of an Islamic state.[33] This ultimate objective is very clear in the letter written by him to Raja Hindu Rao, a minister of Gwalior. The letter reads:

ایں فقیر باچندے ازبندگان رب قدیر درحوالی پشاور
بخدمت گزاری اسلام وتائید ملت سید الانام مشغول
است وثمرۂ ایں مساعی جمیله از درگاه واہب العطایا
ماحول بر رائے سامی روشن و مبرہن است که بیگانگان
بعیدالوطن ،ملوك زمین وزمن گردیده اندوتاجران متاع
فروش بپایۂ سلطنت رسیده، امارت امراء کبار وریاست
رئوسائے عالی مقدار بر پا نموده اند وعزت واعتبار
ایشان بالکل ربوده چوں اہل ریاست وسیاست د رزاویۂ
خمول نشسته اند ناچار چندے از اہل فقر ومسکنت کمر
ہمت بسته این جماعه ضعفاء محض بنا بر خدمت دین
رب العالمین بر خیستند، ہرگز ہرگزاز دنیا داران چاه
طلب نیستند، محض بنا بر خدمت دین رب ذوالجلال
برخاسته اند نه بنا بر طمع مال ومنال، وقتیکه میدان
ہندوستان از بیگانگان دشمنان خالی گردیده و تیرسعی
ایشان بر ہدف مراد رسیده آئند مناصب ریاست
وسیاست بطالبین آں مسلم باد(34)

This humble man along with some other slaves of Powerful Lord is engaged in kirts of Pewshawar in the service of Islam and for the deliverance of the peoples of the Prophet. The result of these pious efforts on behalf of the Bestower of achievements and gifts has become very clear. It is now, by the Grace of God, approved that the strangers of remote home have become the rulers of the land and our country; these merchants have founded their empire! The power of great national rulers and the authority of dignified sovereigns is degraded and the honour and hegemony of these majesties are debased. Since the masters of domains are fast asleep in the corners of lethargy these few poor and ill-equipped men like us do dare to stand up and rise in the way of Allah. This weak group for the sake of serving the religion of the Lord only has got up. These bondsmen of God desire neither name nor fame nor temporal power. In order to defend the religion of His Majesty this group has come forward. They have no ambition to worldly temptation. They covet not the wealth and riches. Whenever India is evacuated of these strange enemies and we succeed in our efforts, the ranks of honour, rulership and governance shall be assigned to those who covet these and then they shall enjoy the real power and glory on a mere firm foundation.."

In his letter to Ghulam Haider Khan, Sayyid Ahmad Shaheed clearly stated that he intended to emancipate India from foreign domination:

اکثر بلاد ہندوستان بدست بیگانان افتادہ و ایشان ہر
جا بنیاد آئین جور وظلم نہادہ ریاست رئوسائے
ہندوستان برباد رفتہ، کسے تاب مقاربت ایشاں نمی
دارد، بلکہ ہر کس ایشاں را بجائے آقائے خودمی شمارد
و چوں رئوسائے کبار از مقابلۂ ایشاں نشستند لاچار
چندے از ضعفائے بے مقدار کمر ہمت بستند، پس دریں
صورت رئوسائے عالی مقدار لازم چناں چہ برمسند
ریاست سالہا سال متمکن ماندہ اند بالفعل درا عانت
ضعفائے مذکورین مساعی بلیغہ بجا آرند(35)

Most of the parts of India have passed into the hands of foreigners who have let loose a reign of injustice and oppression everywhere by their supremacy and dominance. The dominions of Indian potentates have been wrecked; none has courage to face them, instead everyone has recognized their overlordship. Since the great Indian rulers have abandoned all hopes to stand up against them, some of us, poor and paltry have now risen up. In that situation, it is incumbent upon those dignified rulers who have been gracing the thrown for a long period, to make serious efforts in order to assist these poor men like us.

Some selective portions from his lengthy letter addressed to the King of Bukhara, as quoted below reveal the same message. He was equally criticized by both the local pagans and the foreigner Christians who had established their rule of injustice and tyranny. The letter explains:

از مدت چند سال بتقدیر قادر فعال حال حکومت
وسلطنت ایں ممالک بریں منوال گردیده که نصارائے
نکوہیده خصال ومشرکین بدمآل براکثر بلاد ہندوستان
ازلب دریائے اباسین تاساحل شور که تخمیناً ششماہه
باشد تسلط یافتند ودام تشکیک وتزویر بنا بر اضمحال
دین رب خبیر بر بافتند آں اقطار را بظلمات کفر وظلم
مشحون گردانیدند وعزت رئوسائے کبار را بانواع
تکالیف رنجانیدند و به مساجد ومعابد اہل اسلام دست
تعدی رسانیدند ودر مقدمات ریاست وسیاست
ومعاملات قضا وعدالت قوانین شرع را برباد داوه
و آئین کفر را بنیادنہاده(36)

(Since the last few years, by the fate of the Divine Powerful Actor, the governance and rulership in these parts has become so worse that on most of the lands of India from the river Abasīn till the bank of Indian Ocean whose distance is of six months journey approximately, the Christians of tyrannizing habits and polytheists of cruel nature have dominated. The doubts, suspicions and fabrications are netted over the true religion of God. Those parts of the country are filled up with the darknesses of infidelity and tyranny. The honour of local respectable chiefs is smashed. The mosques and pious shrines of the Muslims are encroached and in all the spheres of politics and governance, court and judiciary laws of shariah are replaced and the laws and customs of infidelity do prevail.)

And again,

بناءً علیه احوال نکبت مآل تجبر کفره فرنگ وتعدی
مشرکین ہند بسمع مبارك رسانیده باشد تاغیرت ایمانی
که موروث از اسلاف کرام راست بجوش آید واساس اہل
کفر وضلال را از پا براند از دو جمعیة جنود ابلیس لعین
را برہم زند ورونق باز اراہل کفر وشرك بشکند(37)

(That is why the humiliating situation (for Islam and Muslims), the coercion of British infidels and the prosecutions of the pagans in India are briefly reported to your majesty in order to provoke your faithly zeal and spiritual enthusiasm which is surely inherited from your ancestors, so that the foundation of infidelity and deviation is demolished, the troops and recruits of the cursed Satan are scattered and the glory and terror of the people of infidelity and polytheism are replaced.)

And the following quotations from the same letter are also very important.

کفار فرنگ که به تسلط یافته اند نهایت تجربه
کار وہوشیار اند وحیله ساز ومکار(38)

(The British infidels who dominated the whole land are very experienced masters, tactfully dealers and crafty and cunning people.)

کفرہ ہند وفرنگ بالفعل برآں (ہندوستان) مسلط
گردیدہ۔پس استخلاص بلاد مذکورہ از دست آنہا
برذمہ جماہیر اہل اسلام عموماً و مشاہیر حکام
خصوصاً واجب(39)

(The non-believers of India and the British have prevailed over the country in fact. To evacuate these parts of the country from the hands of these elements is obligatory upon all the Muslims in general and the prominent rulers in particular.)

The above quoted few sentences from the letters of Sayyid Ahmad Shaheed suffice to prove that the Sikh government was the first and immediate target of the Jihad. It planned to attack the British and emancipate the country from their dominance later on. Tht is the reason why the Sayyid had criticized *Kuffar Farang, Nasara Nikohidah Khisal, Begangan Baeed ul Watan*, and *Tajiran mata'e Farosh* again and again. In the light of these statements can any one think that the aim of the jihad movement was to combat with the Sikh rulers? The real objective of the Mujahidin, instead was to fight against both the British infidels and Sikhs, as rightly pointed out by Muhammad Ayub Qadri. [40] Due to oppressive and dictatorial attitude and policies of the British towards the first freedom movement of the sub-continent, the original image of the Mujahidin movement could not be portrayed. In the earlier phase of the movement the source material published was either incomplete or allegorical. Sometimes the style of the writers turned into superstitious, supernatural and miraculous. Due to terror and horror some writings were even distorted and replaced. Some towering personalities who were not fully convinced with the jihad movement, interpreted the whole story according to their pre-designed thoughts that consequently turned the facts into fiction, or disfigured the true image of the movement.[41]

## Establishing Islamic State

The objective of the jihad movement was not confined to the emancipation of the country from the foreign or infidelity's domination. Its basic aim was to establish the Islamic state. Cooperation with Hindus was never ruled out; on the contrary, Sayyid sought their support and cooperation to fight the common enemy and was prepared to let them rule over the dominions in their possession. Still he was candid enough to inform almost every one whom he sent letters to join the jihad that he had wielded to sword to combat all that neglected the truth.[42]

آنچه داعیه جهاد وعزم ازالۂ کفر وفساد که درخاطر فقیر
ریخته اصلاً ومطلقاً بکدورت طلب ومال وعزت وجاه و
حشمت و امارت وسلطنت ونام ونشان وترفع براخوان
وافزان ہرگز مخروج ومخلوط نیست وانچه دعوت
مسلمین و ترغیب معرضین بسوئے اقامت ایں رکن
رکین از فقیر صادرمی گردد بجز ہدایت ایشاں بسوئے
رضامندی حضرت رب العالمین واتباع سید المرسلین
علیه افضل الصلوات والتسلیم ہیچ غرضے از اغراض
خسیسه دنیاویه درمیان نه(43)

(The incentive of fighting against and replacing the infidelity and corruption in the mind of this humble man must not be entirely and absolutely mixed with the impurity of any demand, wealth or riches, honour or dignity, post or power, horror or terror, rulership or governance, name or fame, or superiority or domination upon the others. I have invited the Muslims, and persuaded the opponents to establish this important but neglected institution (jihad). For the sake of God alone and inorder to follow sincerely the last Prophet (SAW) and to show these people the right path I have called the people for jihad. We have no temptation for the mean temporal objectives.)

تمام ایں معرکه آرائی وعربده آرائی غیرازعلائے کلمۂ
رب العالمین واحیائے سنت سیدالمرسلین واستیصال
کفرۂ متمرّدین واستخلاص بلاد مومنین از دست بغاة
مفسدین چیزے دیگر مقصود نیست(44)

(In the process of all these fightings, violent conflicts, and militancies there is nothing required except the domination of the word of God, the revival of the way of the Prophet (SAW), the extermination of transgressing infidels, and the emancipation of the Muslim Lands from the possession of vitiating tyrants.)

The jihad movement did never aim at reviving the glorious past of the Mughals or resusciating the crumbling empire of Delhi. The Sayyid had removed this confusion from the minds of his followers in a number of letters. He had declared to his disciples during one of his missionary tours: the "Kingship of Delhi consists merely of protocols and stately ceremonials, devoid of all power and authority."[45] The Sayyid clarified in his writings as follows:

محض لوجه الله علم جهاد برافراشتیم از طلب مال
ومنال و جاه وجلال وامارت وریاست و حکومت
وسیاست خیستیم وطالب غیر حق نیستیم، مائیم ہر
چند عاجز وخاکسار، ذرۂ بے مقدار امابلاشک ،بمحبت
حضرت حق مست و سرشار از محبت غیرحق بالکل
دست بردار ،نه باکسے از امرائے مسلمین منازعه دارم نه
باکسے ازرئوسائے معرضین مخالفه باکفار لئام مقابله
دارم نه بامدعیان اسلام نه دراز مویان بلکه باسائر کفر
خویان مقابله خواہم نه باکلمه گو یان اسلام واسلام
جویان این معنی معلوم ہرخاص وعام است(46)

(To seek the pleasure of God only, we have raised the flag of jihad. We do not covet the wealth and riches. We do not require the glory and dignity. We do not intend any governance or rulership nor any state and authority. We are nothing except the seekers of truth. We – the few poors and baseless particles without any weight – enjoy and rejoice with the love of God. We withdraw from any link with any thing else. We have no conflict with the Muslim emirs, no tussle with the opponent chiefs. We intend, as such no struggle against the sordid infidels nor with the claimants of Islam. We do not threat as such the people of long hairs nor the entire non-believers. We do not target the so called Muslims also. It is very clear to all the nobles and laymen.)

It is, however, noteworthy that the mujahidin's struggle first against Ranjit Singh of Punjab, and then against the British rule in India did not give rise to any conflict of communal interests. The voluminous mass of letters written by Sayyid and Shah Ismail Shaheed do not contain even a hostile reference towards the Hindus whose sympathy and, sometimes active support, was enjoyed by the jihad movement.[47]

*****

## NOTES AND REFERENCES

1. Sirāt Mustaqim is basically the Sayyid's discourses compiled by Shah Ismail Shaheed. It was completed in 1818, three years before he went for the pilgrimage. The book demonstrates the way of social and moral reform to the Indian Muslims and clearly denounces the non-Islamic elements penetrated in Tasawwuf.
2. Taqwiyah al-Iman (Strengthening the Faith) is treated as the classical book compiled by Shah Muhammad Ismail Shaheed to nullify the religious innovations crept in the Muslim Society. There is no academic work in the contemporary world so appealing, argumentative and serious both in style and content. According to a research made by Maulana Noorul Hassan Rashid Kandhlavi, just after the compilation of the book in 1232-33 A.H., it was widely published, studied and copied to the extent that at least eleven copies prepared during the life time of the author himself are still preserved in the various personal libraries and the copies made in between 1274 and 1276 A.H. are numbered in 20-25. It was first published in 1242 A.H. by Sayyid Abdullah bin Sayyid Bahadur Ali from Matba' Ahmadi Delhi. Till date more than hundred editions are printed from various parts of the country. (*Al-Furqan* Monthly, Lucknow, July, 1993, p. 32; August-September 1993, pp. 67-68.). For English version of the book see, Muhammad Ismail, "Translation of the *Takwiyat ul Iman*, preceded by a Notice of the Author, Maulavi Ismail Hajji", Translated by Mr. Shahamat Ali in *Journal of the Royal Asiatic Society* 13 (1832); 479-498. The author has categorized polytheism (*Shirk*) in to four: association with Allah in the knowledge, association with Allah in the authorities, association with Allah in the prayers and Association with Allah in the customs and routine life *e.g. Ishrak fi al-Ilm, Ishrak fi al-Tasarruf, Ishrak fi al-Ibadat* and *Ishrak fi al-Adat*. He has criticized all kinds of superstitions, religious innovations and non-Islamic practices in detail. Shah Muhammad Ismail, in his another work *Tazkir al-Ikhwan* a compendium to *Taqwiyah al-Iman*, has nullified all the sects and orders like *Tafziliyah, Chishtiyah, Qadriyah, Naqshbandiyah, Suhrwardiyah, Rifayiah, Madariyah Jalaliyah* etc.
3. One of the main Sufi brotherhoods of South Asia, Chishtiyah takes its name from the village of Chist, near heart in Western Afghanistan, where it is said to have originated. Its supposed founder in India, Muinuddin Chishti (d. 1236) is a shadowy figure surrounded by many legends. The brotherhood has spread throughout present-day India, Pakistan and Bangladesh; it is characterized by its extreme enthusiasm for ecstatic listening (*simá*) to music and poetry. It has continued to play an important role in harmonizing Islam with indigenous Indian culture. New perspectives were brought by an important figure, Abdul Quddus of Gangoh in Uttar Pradesh, who was a vigorous advocate of *Ibn Arabi's Wahdatul Wajud* and *al-Insan al-Kamil*. He departed from his

predecessors' insistence on accepting only non-recurrent gifts rather than permanent grants from rulers, and he adopted Hindu techniques of meditation and breadth control. He was also the most fervent defender of the famous Chishti practice of worshiping upside down while hanging suspended by a rope tied around the ankles. At the shrines Chishtis have a flourishing and well-developed musical culture designated by the term *qawwali*, meaning a group song genre of Hindustani light classical music which presents mystical poetry in Persian, Hindi and Urdu; it is performed in Sufi assemblies in order to produce religious emotion and ecstasy.

4. Among the better known names in Islamic Sufism is that of Abdul Qadir Jilani (470-561 A.H.) who came from the Persian province of Gilan as a student to Baghdad where he spent most of the years of his life. He was a Hanbali jurist a part-time mufti, a public preacher and a practicing Sufi as in his authentic writing *Al-Ghunyah li talib'i tariq al-Haqq* is manifested when he describes the relations of Sufi students (murids) and their Shaykhs or murshids. Shaykh Abdul Haqq Muhaddith of Delhi (1551-1642) the most distinguished theologian is a prominent name in this order. In the mid-seventeenth century another Qadiri figure, Mulla Shah Badakhshi initiated the Mughal prince Dara Shukuh into the order who was executed for heresy in 1659. During the eighteenth and nineteenth centuries the Indian Qadiriyah continued to flourish in the sub-continent and exists in whole India and Pakistan today.
5. One of the most widespread and vigorous of the Sufi orders, the *Naqshbandiyah* is found in most regions of Muslim Asia as well as in Turkey, Bosnia-Herzigovina and the Volga-Ural region. Orginating in Bukhara in the late fourteenth century, it began to spread to contiguous areas of the Muslim world within a hundred years. New impetus was given to its expansion by the rise of the Mujaddidi branch, named after Shaykh Ahmad Sirhindi Mujaddid-i-Alf Thani (d.1624), which by the close of the eighteenth century was virtually synonymous with the order as a whole throughout South Asia, the Ottoman Lands, and most of Central Asia. The leading characteristics of the *Naqshbandiyah* are strict adherence to the *Shariah*, a sobriety in devodance and a preference for silent *dhikr* and a frequent tendency to political involvement.
6. Ahmad, Mohiuddin, *Saiyid Ahmad Shaheed: His Life and Mission*, Lucknow, 1975, p. 36. It is very interesting to note that Shah Abdul Aziz instructed him to practice *muraqabah* or concentrated contemplation on the image of his Shaykh but was refused by the student. Later on Sayyid Shaheed explained why it was dangerous to practice the *muraqabah* although it informed an essential tenet in several mystical orders. To him, it was an innovation in the religion because of its resemblance to the worship of idols and that the practice to inanimate images and symbols which was considered heretical by Islam. See his book *Sirāt Mustaqim* (Discourses edited by Shah Muhammad Ismail Shaheed, Tr. Abdul Jabbar, Calcutta) 1856, pp. 388-391.

7. Metcalf, Barbara, D., Barelwi, Sayyid Ahmad, in *The Oxford Encyclopaedia of the Modern Islamic World*, ed. John L. Esposito, Oxford, 1995, Vol. 1. p. 200.
8. Maulawi Karamat Ali of Jaunpur turned later on into the passive supporter of British empire. Hunter has quoted him along with Sheikh Ahmad Effendi al-Ansari, Maulawi Abdul Hakim and Maulawi Abdul Latif Khan Bahadur to whom "it will be a comfortable that so respectable a body as the Muhammadan Society of Calcutta has formally declared, by the mouths of eminent doctors of Law, that India is still a country of the Faithful, and that rebellion is therefore incalled for." Hunter, W.W. *The Indian Musalmaans*, Reprint from the third edition, Calcutta, 1945, p. 124. This Karamat Ali of Kajgaon, Jaunpur was a Shii follower of the Sayyid, the most popular Karamat Ali of Jaunpur, the spiritual successor (Khalifah) to the Sayyid was a different man who was appointed to carry on missionary activities in East Bengal. The Latter saved the lives of two English women during the uprising of 1857 at Jaunpur but declined to accept any reward in this regard. He was a Hanafi Sunni Scholar. See for detail, Ahmad, Mohiuddin, *op.cit.*, p. 128, Note No. 2.
9. See for a detailed study of the two brothers, the standard works dealing with the movement in general and centring on the personality of the Sayyid Shaheed such as, Thanesari, Muhammad Jafar, *Sawānih Ahmadi* (1890); Nadvi, Sayyid Abul Hasan Ali, *Sirat Sayyid Ahmad Shaheed* (1939); and Mahr, Ghulam Rasul, *Sayyid Ahmad Shaheed* (1955). For a good account of their lives, the works as Abdur Rahim, Maulavi, Tazkirah Sādiqah (1901) and Nadvi, Mas'ud Alam, Hindustan Ki Pahli Islami Tahrik may also be consulted.
10. For an authentic history of the Mujahidin movement, see Mahmud Husain, The successor's of Sayyid Ahmad Shahid: Jihad on the North – Western Frontier in. *A History of the Freedom Movement*, Pakistan Historical Society, Karachi, 1960, Vol. II, pp. 145-169.
11. *Ibid.*, p. 150.
12. Rahmani, Nazir Ahmad, *Ahl Hadith Aur Siyasat*, p. 179.
13. Hunter, W.W., *op. cit.*, pp. 57-58.
14. *Ibid.*, p. 60. The author ahs provided a list of thirteen books that provoked the Muslims to wage jihad against the English Empire. The list reads:
    1. Sirat e Mustaqim by Sayyid Ahmad Shaheed.
    2. Qasidah of Maulawi Karamat Ali.
    3. Sharh Wiqayah
    4. Naat by Maulawi Nimatullah
    5. Tawarikh Qaisar Rum
    6. Asrar Mahshar by Maulawi Muhammad Ali
    7. Taqwiyatul Iman by Shah Ismail Shaheed
    8. Tazakir al-Ikhwan by the same author
    9. Nasihatul Muslimin by Maulawi Karamat Ali

10. Hidaya tul Muminin by Awlad Husain
11. Tanwir ul Ainain
12. Tanbih ul Ghafilin
13. Chahl Hadith (*Ibid.* pp. 58-60. Fotnote No. 3)

15. *Ibid.* pp. 59-60.
16. *Ibid.* p. 61.
17. *Ibid.* p. 63.
18. *Ibid.* pp. 72-73.
19. *Ibid.* p. 83.
20. *Ibid.* p. 84. The success of Maulawi Yahya Ali in despatching the newly trained mujahids to various parts of the country in order to wage war against the British Government, depended to some extent upon an ingenious system of aliases, and upon the secret language they used. For example a battle is called a Lawsuit; God, the Law Agent; Gold Muhars are called large red rubies, large Delhi gold – embroidered shoes, or large red birds; remittances in Gold, Muhars are spoken of as rosaries of red beads, and remittances in money as the price of books and merchandisc; drafts or moneyorders are called white stones, the amount being intimated by the number of white beads as on a rosary, Hunter, *op. cit.*, p. 90 Notes No. 4.
21. *Ibid.* p. 85.
22. Jafar Thanesari, Muhammad, *Tawarikh Ajib* or *Kala Pani,* Ambala, 1302 A.H. pp. 52-55.
23. Mahr, Chaudhary Ghulam Rasul, *Sarguzashat Mujahidin*, Lahore, 1956, pp. 404-405.
24. Ahmad, Mohiuddin, *Sayyid Ahmad Shahid*: His Life and Mission, Lucknow, 1975, pp. 369-373.
25. Hunter, *op. cit.*, p. 97.
26. Hardy, P. Dr., *The Muslims of British India*, Cambridge, 1972, p. 84.
27. Ahmad, Mohiuddin, *op. cit.*, p. 372.
28. Bhutti, Muhammad Ishaq in *Yadgar Majallah Ahl e Hadith*, *A Historical Document on the Academic, Dawah, Organizational, Missionary and Welfare Contributions* (Urdu), ed. Asghar Ali Imam Mahdi Salafi and Khalid Hanif Siddiqui Falahi (co-editor), Delhi, 2004, pp. 209-210. According to Bhutti, These details are well documented in the remarkable work of Ghulam Rasul Mahr, *op. cit.*, without identifying the jurisprudential affiliation of any freedom fighter.
29. Hunter, *op. cit.*, p. 3.
30. Sir Syed Ahmad Khan wrote a series of letters which were published in the Pioneer to refute the inimical and highly coloured account of the Wahabi activity by Hunter. These letters were collected by a certain Muslim advocate some time in 1872-73 and published by Henry S. King & Co. London under the title *Sayyid Ahmad's Review on Hunter's Indian Musalmans*. The same view was established by Mirza Hairat Dehlavi in the biography of Shah Ismail entitled *Hayat Tayyibah* (Lahore, 1958); and Aziz Ahmad in his *Islamic Modernism in India and*

*Pakistan* (London, 1967, p. 20). The competent scholars, such as Muhammad Mujeeb (*The Indian Muslims*, London, 1867, pp. 395-98), Ishtiaq Husain Quraishi (*The Muslim Community in Indo-Pak Subcontinent*, Haugue, 1962, p. 200), Shan Muhammad (*Syed Ahmad Khan: A Political Review*, Meerut, 1969, p. 128), Basheer Ahmad Dar (*Religious Thought of Sayyid Ahmad Khan*, Lahore, 1957, p. 79) and Dr. Hardy (*The Muslims of British India*, *op. cit.*, p. 58), however, are agreed that this jihad was directed not against the Sikhs alone but also against the British.

31. Mian, Muhammad, Maulana Sayyid, *Ulama-e-Hind Ka Shandar Mazi*, Delhi, 1957, Vol. II, p. 101. The learned author has ignored the primary objective of revivalist movement of Sayyid Ahmad, of which jihad was only a means, that is, the restoration of a truly Islamic rule in India – an ideal never conceived in the past in India so lucidly and with such clarity of vision. Nadwi, S. Abdul Hasan Ali, *Sirat Sayyid Ahmad Shahid*, Lahore, 1958, Vol. I, pp. 370-75.
32. Sindhi, Maulana Ubaidullah, *Shah Waliullah Awr Unki Siyasi Tahrik*, n.d. p. 75.
33. For a clear perception of Islam and Islamic society as perceived by the Mujahidin Movement see, Fahad, Obaidullah, Dr., Tahrik Shahidayn Ka Tasawwur Islam, *Majallah Al-Furqan*, Sidhdharth Nagar, Vol. II, No. 4, July-August 1998, pp. 32-43.
34. *Makatib Sayyid Ahmad Shaheed*, Lahore, Maktabah Rasheediyah, 1395 A.H./1975 A.D., pp. 79-79(a), These letters were first copied by Maulana Obaidullah Ghulam Husain in 1301 A.H. after 55 years of the martyrdom of the auther, and was edited and published by Sayyid Ahmad Shaheed Academy from Lahore.
35. *Ibid.*, p. 80.
36. *Ibid.*, pp. 25-25(a).
37. *Ibid.*, p. 27(a).
38. *Ibid.*, p. 28.
39. *Ibid.*, p. 28(a).
40. *Ibid.*, Preface, p. 38.
41. *Ibid.*, p. 39.
42. Ahmad, Mohiuddin, *op. cit.*, p. 131.
43. Makatib Sayyid Ahmad Shaheed, *op. cit.*, p. 13(a).
44. *Ibid.*, pp. 19, 26(a).
45. Sirāt Mustaqim, *op. cit.*, p. 178.
46. Makatib Sayyid Ahmad Shaheed, *op. cit.*, p. 9(a).
47. Ahmad, Mohiuddin, *op. cit.*, p. 387.

*****

**Table 1: List of Commanders/Emirs Under Mujahidin**

In India for the first time in its history Islamic jihād in its true sense was initiated by Sayyid Ahmad Shaheed in 1242 A.H. and continued till 1857/1367 A.H. A list of the commanders of these fightings is given below:

| S. No. | Amīr/ Commander of Mujahidin | Date of emirate/ Command | Duration | Central place/ Head quarter |
|---|---|---|---|---|
| 1. | Sayyid Ahmad Shaheed (amir) | 1233-1246 AH | 13 Years | Rai Barrielly, Panjtar |
| 2. | Mohmmad Ismail Shaheed (Commander-in-chief) | 1233-1246 AH | 13 Years | Rai Barrielly, Panjtar |
| 3. | Shahykh Wali Muhammad of Phulat (emir) | 1246-1253 AH | 7 Years | Panjtar, Jassi Koat, Asthana |
| 4. | Maulavi Nasiruddin Manglori (Commander then emir) | 1246-1254 AH | 8 Years | Do |
| 5. | Mir Aulad Ali Azimabadi (Ist term, Emir and Commander) | 1254-1255 AH | 01 Year | Asthana |
| 6. | Syed Nasiruddin Dehlavi (Emir and Commander) | 1255-1256 AH | 01 Year | Asthana |
| 7. | Mir Aulad Ali (IInd term as emir& commander) | 1256-1261 AH | 5 Years | Asthana |
| 8. | Maulavi Enayat Ali Azimabadi (Ist term as emir and Commander ) | 1261-1262 AH | 1 Year | Balakot, FathGarh |
| 9. | Maulavi Wilayat Ali Azimabadi (Ist Term as emir & Commander ) | 1262-1263 AH | 01 Years | Fath Garh |
| 10. | Mir Aulad Ali (IIIrd term as emir and Commander ) | 1263-1267 AH | 4 Years | Asthana |
| 11. | Maulavi Enayat Ali (IInd term as emir and Commander) | 1267-1269 Ah | 3 Years | do |
| 12. | Maulavi Enayat Ali (IInd term as emir & Commander) | 1269-1274 AH. | 5 Years | Asthana, Mangal thana, Naranji |
| 13. | Shaykh Nurullah, Shah Ikramullah, Mir Taqi (Council of emirate) | 1274-1275 AH | 01 Year | Malakka |
| 14. | Maulavi Maqsud Ali Azimabadi (emir & Commander ) | 1275-1278 AH | 3 Years | Malakka |
| 15. | Maulavi Abdullah Azimabadi (emir & Commander ) | 1278-1320 Ah | 42 Years | Malakka, Golonobari, Paluli, Telwai |
| 16. | Malavi Abdul Karim Azimabadi (emir & Commander) | 1320-1332 AH | 13 Years | Usmist |

| | | | | |
|---|---|---|---|---|
| 17. | Maulavi Nimatullah Azimabadi (emir & Commander) | 1333-1339 AH | 6 Years | do |
| 18. | Maulavi Rahmatullah Azimabadi (emir & Commander) | 1339-1367 A.H. | 29 Years | do |
| 19. | Maulavi Muhmnmad Bashir (Commander) | 1334-1353 A.H. | 20 years | Chamar Kund |
| 20. | Maulavi Fazl Ilahi Wazirabadi (Commander) | 1353-1367 A.H. | 14 years | do |

**Table 2: List of the Fightings Led by Mujahidin**
(Under Sayyid Ahmad Shaheed)

| S. No. | Fightings | Commander | Date | No. of Mujahidin | No. of enemy | Result |
|---|---|---|---|---|---|---|
| 1. | Akorah Fighting | Allah Bakhsh Khan Muranavi | Jumada al-Ula 1242 A.H./20 Dec. 1826. | 900 | 9000 | 700 Sikhs & 82 Mujahidis were killed |
| 2. | Bazar Battle | Syed Anwar Shah Amritsari | do | 100 | | Aggressive Sikhs were pushed back. |
| 3. | Shidu Battle | Shah Ismail Shaheed | 1224 A.H./1827 A.D. | | | The Durrani Chief Yar Muhammad rebelled. The Muslim conquest turned into defeat. |
| 4. | Attack on Damgallah | Syed Muhammad Muqim Rampuri | Oct. 1827 | 400 | 6000 | 300 Sikhs killed, few mujahids martyred |
| 5. | Shan Kiari Battle | Shah Islamil Shaheed | do | 40 | | 250 Skihs killed the remnant escaped. |
| 6. | Utman Zai Battle | Sayyid Ahmad & Shah Ismail | Zuqadah 1243/1828 | | 4000 | Guerrilla attack succeeded |
| 7. | Defence at Panjtar | Maulavi Khayruddin Sher Koti | 1244 A.H. | 300 | | Sikh regiment attacked unsuccessfully |
| 8. | Do | Sayyid Ahmad Shaheed | Zuqadah 1244/1829 | 2500 | 10000 | Do |
| 9. | Hund Battle | Shah Ismail Shaheed | 7 Sfar 1245/18 Aug. 1829 | 350 | | The mujahids captured the Hund fort. |
| 10. | Defence at Hund | do | do | | | Every attack in vein |
| 11. | Zidah Battle | do | 5 Rabi al-Awwal 1245/4 Sep.1829 A.D. | | | 300 Sikhs killed, 02 mujahids also were martyred. A lot of booty was captured. |
| 12. | Tarbillah Battle | Sayyid Ahmad Shaheed | 1245 A.H./1829 A.D. | | | Various clashes. Sikhs suffered a lot. |

| | | | | | | |
|---|---|---|---|---|---|---|
| 13. | **Enemy's attack on** Hund | **Akhund Zahur ullah** | 1245 A.H./ 1829 A.D. | 60 | | **Sikhs arrested mujahidin treacherously who escaped safely.** |
| 14. | Fightings at Ashrah & Amb | Shah Ismail Shaheed | Shawwal 1245/March 1830 A.D. | | | Mujahids captured Ashrah, Kotlah and Amb |
| 15. | Phoollarah Battle | Sayyed Ahmad Ali | Zuq'adah 1245 A.H. | | | Sikhs attacked in the night. Both suffered at lot. |
| 16. | Attack on Khulla Batt | Qazi Sayyid Hibban | 1830 A.D. | | | The entire region surrendered after few clashes. |
| 17. | Attack on Hund | Abdul Hamid Khan (risāldār) | | 300 | 700 | Sikhs evacuated the fort |
| 18. | Tlui Battle | Qazi Sayyid Hibban | 1830 A.D. | | 900 | Mijahids captured the fortress |
| 19 | Mardan Battle | Shah Ismail Shaheed | 1830 A.D. | | | Mujahids captured after a heavy clash. |
| 20. | Mayar Battle | Sayyid Ahmad Shaheed | 1830 A.D. | 3500 | 12000 | Durranis escaped defeatedly |
| 21. | March toward Peshawar | do | do | | | Durranis surrendered to peace. |
| 22. | Massacre of muijahids | Do | Nov. & Dec. 1830 A.D. | | | The natives of Summah plotted against the movement and massacred the unorganized mujahids. |
| 23. | Muzaffarabad Battle | Maulavi Khayruddin Sher Koti | Ziqadah 1246 A.H. | 300 | | Clash with the Sikhs |
| 24. | Balakot Battle | Sayyid Ahmad Shaheed & Shah Ismail Shaheed | 24 Ziqadah 1246 A.H. | | 600 | Sayyid Ahmad, Shah Ismail and several mujahids were martyred. |

**Table 3: 125 Years Continuous Jihad**

The jihad movement launched by Sayyid Ahmad Shaheed collapsed in Balakot on 24th Ziqadah 1246 A.H. The struggle, however lasted and concluded finally in the revolt of 1857, the first independence movement of India.

**The Term of Maulavi Nasiruddin Manglori, Shaykh Wali Muhammad Phulati 1246 A.H., 1254 A.H.**

| S. No. | Fightings | Commander | Date | No. of Mujahidins | No. of enemy |
|---|---|---|---|---|---|
| 1. | Fighting in Konush Vallay | Muhammad Bashir | 1831 A.D. | | |
| 2. | Attack on Bughah | Muhammad Hasan | Sep. 1831 A.D. | 200/60 | |
| 3. | Attack on Habburi | | 1832 | 100 | |
| 4. | Attack on Baliming | Maulvi Nasiruddin Manglori | 1832 | 200 | 700 |
| 5. | Attack on the fort of Birkhund | Paindah Khan, Maulavi Nasiruddin | | 230/150 | 4000 |
| 6. | Mallikpur Battle | Amanullah Khan Lucknavi | | 200/50 | 4000 |
| 7. | Fighting of Deshis | Maulavi Nasiruddin | | 400 | 4000 |
| 8. | Attack on Gajboori | do | | 200 | 9000 |
| 9. | Attack of Illais | do | | 400 | 9000 |
| 10. | Clash in Sichchun | do | | Few/125 | 3000 |
| 11. | Panjool | Muqim Khan r/o Kala Bagh | | | |
| 12. | Achcharyan | do | | 150 | 900 |
| 13. | Attack of Deshis | Maulavi Nasiruddin Mahanda, Jam'adar | | | |
| 14. | Guerrilla attack on Sikhs near Phagora | Abdul Ghaffar Khan | | | |
| 15. | Attack on Buland Kot | Maulavi Nasiruddin | | | |
| 16. | Attack on Gajboori | Sayyid Mir Khan | | 60 | 2000 |
| 17. | Attack on Jibbirh | Muqim Khan | | 200 | |
| 18. | Attack on Chahle | Mulla Lal Muhammad Qandhari | | 250 | 9000 |
| 19. | Attack of Sikhs on Mujahids of Kot | Muqim Khan | | 120 | |
| 20. | Batloon fighting | Maulavi Nasiruddin | 1834 A.D. | 400 | 5000 |
| 21. | Two attacks on Illais | Muqim Khan | 1834 A.D. | 400 | 5000 |
| 22. | Manarah watopi fighting | Maulavi Nasiruddin | 1834 A.D. | | × |

**Sayyid Nasiruddin Dehlavi**
Against Sikh and British in Sindh & Afghanistan
(1253-1263 A.H.)

| | | | | | |
|---|---|---|---|---|---|
| 23. | Roojhan fighting | Sayyid Nasiruddin Dehlavi | Nov. 1837/Shaban 1353 A.H. | | |
| 24. | Kann fighting | Do | Do | | |
| 25. | Pursuance in Bhammak | Do | Dec. 1837/Ramadan 1253 A.H. | | |
| 26. | Participation in Ghazni Battle inorder to help Emir Dost Muhammad Khan | | July 1839 | 1000 | |

**The Term of Maulavi Wilayat Ali, Maulavi Enayat Ali, Maulavi Abdullah and Maulavi Abdul Karim**
(1267-1333 A.H.)

| | | | | | |
|---|---|---|---|---|---|
| 27. | Balakot | Maulavi Enayat Ali | Zul Hijjah 1261 A.H./Dec. 1845 A.D. | | |
| 28. | Habibullah Khan Fortress | Do | Muharram 1262 A.H. | | |
| 29. | Muzaffarabad | Maulavi Mansur Ali | 1262 A.H. | 250 | |
| 30. | Fath Garh | Maulavi Enayat Ali | Rabi al-Awwal 1262 A.H. | | 6000 |
| 31. | Nawan Shahr | Do | 1262 A.H. | | |
| 32. | Shankiyari | Do | Do | | |
| 33. | Birkhund | Do | Do | | |
| 34. | Fighting in Dab Valley | Maulavi Wilayat Ali | January 1847 | | 1200 • approx imately |
| 35. | Attacks on Ashrah and Kotlah | Maulavi Enayat Ali | 20th Zul Hijjah 1261 A.H./3rd Dec. 1852 | | |
| 36. | Attack on Amb | Turrah Baz Khan | 24 Dec. 1852 A.D. | | × |
| 37. | Second attack on Amb | Maulavi Enayat Ali | January 1853 | 250 | • |
| 38. | Attack in night on Summah | Do | 2nd July 1857 | | |
| 39. | Attacks on Shaykh Jana & Shewah | Shafi Muhammad | 1857 A.D. | 40 | |
| 40. | Defencive fighting in Shaykh Jana & Nawakalai | Mirza Muhammad Risaldar Afridi | 1857 A.D. | 320 | • |
| 41. | Defence of Naranji | Maulavi Enayat Ali | 1273 A.H./21, July 1857 | 1273 | • |
| 42. | Do (Second time) | Do | Ist Aug. 1857 | | |
| 43. | Attack on Shaykh Jana | Maulavi Shariatullah | Oct. 1857 | | |

| | | | | | |
|---|---|---|---|---|---|
| 44. | Fighting in Shahnoor Lashi | Shah Ikramullah | | 60 mujahidis and few locals | 1050 • |
| 45. | Attack on chankalai | | 1863 A.D. | | |
| 46. | Ambella war (8 clashes) | Maulavi Abdullah as emir of Mujahids, Prince Mubarak Shah, Naser Muhammad & Kalimuddin | | 75000 as the total strength of both the parties | • |
| 47. | Campaign in Black Hills (i) | Emir Abdullah | Oct. 1867 | Mujahids and tribals | 1070 |
| 48. | Do (ii) | Do | Oct. 1888 | Tribals: 120 | 12000 • |
| 49. | Do (iii) | Do | March 1891 | Do | 6300 • |
| 50 | Ghazikot | Do | Do | | • |
| 51. | Mujjakot | Maulavi Abdullah | Do | | × |
| 52. | Mallakund | Emir Abdullah | 1897 | Tribals 1500 mujahids 100 | More than 2000 |

**The terms of Emir Nimatullah, Emir Rahmatullah, Maulavi Muhammad Bashir and Maulavi Fazl Ilahi Wazirabadi (1333-1367 A.H.) (Up-down of War and Peace)**

| | | | | | |
|---|---|---|---|---|---|
| 53. | Attack on Rustam Camp | | Aug. 1915 | | |
| 54. | Second attack | | Do | | |
| 55. | Third attack | | Do | | |
| 56. | Fourth attack | | Do | | 5000 |
| 57. | Attack on Nathiagali | | 1917 | | |
| 58. | Jihad in Kashmir | Emir Rahmatullah Maulavi Fazl Ilahi Wazirabadi | 1947-1948 | | |

***Note***: The battles and clashes in the table (3) marking no sign in the last column were won by the mujahids, the mark (×) signifies the non-deciding situation in favour of any group while the mark (•) means the success of the enemy and the loss-major or minor-of the mujahids.

[Courtesy for all the three tables: Majallah al-Jamia al-Salafiyah ka Mutamar al-Dawah wa al-Talim Number, Varanasi, Oc t. 1981, pp. 309-319].

*****

# 5

# ARAB NATIONALISM
## (A Study of Modern Arabic Poetry)

### Defining Nationalism

Nationalism, today is an ideology that prevails the whole world whether in the meaning of 'Love and sacrifice' for a nation or in a persons of 'peaceful co-existence' of different cultures or as 'an inevitable necessity' albeit evil and disgusting. It is a vague and ambiguous term [(1)] used by the different scholars to connote different meanings. Fredrick Hertz, while pointing out its vague aspect, narrates "Anyhow the lack of a clear and stable terminology greatly contributes to the confusion of ideas. Powerful groups, moreover have an interest in the vagueness of language, and the nationalists, in particular, must wish to maintain a certain obscurity about their aims." [(2)]

Nationalism, however, may be defined as a 'state of mind in which the individual feels that he owes his supreme secular loyalty to the nation-state'. [(3)] Dr. Tara Chand has described the three aspects – cognitive, affective and conative- essential for the national consciousness. It is cognitive because 'it is the recognition of group as the individual's social self'. It is affective because, 'it is an evocative feeling of love and sympathetic association with the place of birth, growth and death, the call of memories of fellowship and mutual dependence'. Lastly it is conative because, 'it is the will to Love, to perpetuate the larger self, to immortalize the universal in man'. [(4)]

Nationalism is also described as a political creed that 'underlines the cohesion of modern societies and legitimizes their claims to authority'. Nationalism centers the supreme loyalty of the overwhelming majority of the people upon the nation-state, either existing or desired'. [(5)]. It is also referred as 'a sentiment based on common cultural characteristic that binds a population and often produces a policy of national independence or separatism'. (6)

Nationalism has been defined by a few scholars also in terms of the objective factors like language, race, decent etc. It is also discussed as a ' policy actuated by national egoism, or as a mistaken, narrow-minded view of national interest'. (7) Since the interests of a particular nation are central figure to nationalism, it is commonly treated as opposed to universalism. It is, therefore criticized that ' a nation is by definition only a part of humanity not the whole. Nationalism is therefore something less than universal in scope and as such generates conflicts'. (8)

## Origin and Development

Scholars differed on the point of the exact origin of nationalism. It is, however, commonly agreed that the ' roots of nationalism sprang from the same soil as western civilization from the ancient Hebrews and the ancient Greeks. Both peoples had a clearly defined consciousness of being different from other peoples: the Hebrews, Gentiles, the Greeks from the Barbarians'. (9) According to the modern concept of the term, these ethnic groups of the past were extremely limited. " The word 'nation', basically 'would seem in its contemporary use to convey an idea of a unit larger than the city-state in which certain closeness of contact has been attained between the central government and its subjects as well as between the individual citizens'. (10)

Modern nationalism was the child of the deadly clash between the papacy and the Roman Empire. The imperial powers claimed for the 'Divine right of King' on the one hand, and the Papacy asserted its absolute sovereignty over the Empire on the other. Neither of them emerged victorious. The nation-state rather emerged as an outcome of these hostile interactions between the two.

By the 14th century, the Kings of the rising national states consolidated their Royal power. France in this regard led other nation-states. When Pope Bonafice endeavoured to prevent the French King from taxing ecclesiastical property, the King defied the Pope and was able to transfer the Papacy from Rome to

Avignon and to bring it under the French control. It weakened the position of the Pope who realized his utter failure before the rising nation-state. (11) Tout, therefore, comments, 'The conflict of the Papacy and Empire impaired the efficiency of both and made possible the growth of the great national states of the 13th century, from which the ultimate salvation of Europe was to come'. (12)

The writings of Dante Alighieri (1265-1321), Marislius of Padua (1270-1340), William of Ockham, Pierre Dubois, Wycliff and others also contributed to the cause of the nation-state to some extent (13). The tragic end of the Medieval history is thus summed up by Bowle: ' It was a considerable tragedy, the Medieval view of the European order had become involved with rigid and limited ideas and theocratic claims of a discredited Papacy. All the new ideas and the scientific outlook of the Renaissance were bound to be against it. Political wisdom seemed to point to the absolute prince as the only way out, Mechiavelli, Bodin, Becon and Richelieu, all the practical men, were bound to take this view, and by their lights they were right. But the sovereign national state brought its own enemies…the national Leviathan, which engulfs the smaller communities within the state and which, in relation to its own kind, lives in a 'posture of warre'. (14)

Nationalism, thus evolved and 'became more pronounced in 15th and 16th centuries. Strong monarchies were created in Spain by Philip II, in England by the Tudors and in France by the Bourbous'. (15) Gradually all the countries of the Europe and America declared themselves sovereign national states. Asia and Africa could feel the impact of the nationalism only in the 19th century. The Ottoman Empire collapsed in 1924 and all the states of the Empire were disintegrated and became independent territorial and secular states. Nationalism, thus, in the 19th and 20th centuries, became the most profound political ideology that dominated the entire world. (16)

## Arab Nationalism

Like other strands of the Third World nationalism, *qawmiyah arabiyah* or Arab nationalism cannot be understood apart from its anti colonial ethos and its glorification of the collectivity's origin and history in the face of western dominance. These general components of nationalist doctrine raise, however, important issues in the case of Arab nationalism. For example, anti colonial movements based on Islamic reformist thoughts of al-Afghani [17], Abduh [18] and Rida [19] or regional empire builders like those of Muhammad Ali [20] and his son Ibrahim[21], can not be considered precursors of the doctrine. Some scholars have looked even further back to emphasize the role of Salafia Islamic Movement led by Muhammad bin Abdul Wahhab [22] who preached a pure uncompromising Islam.

Arab nationalism, however, as a political movement as opposed to the concept of Islamic Ummah, is essentially a 20th century product. Its bases and components may originate with the presence of the Arabic language itself, or with the Arab's social, intellectual and political culture. This has been centered on 'Arabness' and hence on the question 'who is an Arab'. At present there is consensus around the view of Sāti 'al-Husri (1882-1962). [23]

## Sāti al-Husri

Al-Husri [24], in both the Ottoman and Arab phases of his carrier consistently worked for secular educational reform as a means of instilling patriotism in youth. Until 1919, he advocated secular Ottoman patriotism, with people of all religions, languages and ethnic groups joining as equal citizens. Later on due to various factors, Husri converted himself to Arab nationalism. He then admitted the force of linguistic bonds, which he had earlier denied and publicly opposed in case of Turkish nationalism and had clashed with Zia Gokalp. [25] Language and common history became the active ingredients of his theory of Arab nationalism. He believed that despite their fragmentation under western colonial regime, Arabic speakers from Morocco to Iraq and from Syria to Sudan constituted a single nation (Ummah). [26]

Al-Husri's emphasis on language and history, led him to refute writers who made religion, race, will (as argued by Renan) [27] economic circumstances, or geography the key determinants of national identity. Unlike his Iraqi contemporary Sāmī

Shawkat, al-Husri had no use of German racial theories.[28] Roaming freely through modern history, he selected examples to prove his points.[29]

For al-Husri, religion can help to create a kind of unity in the feelings of individuals. Religion has an essential relationship with a specific language, through its preaching, its sacred books and rites; it can only spread through the medium of that language, and it only spreads so far as the nation which speaks the language has a national interest in speaking it. National feelings use religion as a way asserting itself. Al-Husri provides examples from the world history and finally concludes that, " these examples, I believe suffice to show the force of national differences as against religious ties, and to prove that even universal religions can not efface national differences". al-Husri, thus is equally opposed to the Islamists who claim that the Arab's have the political loyalty to the whole Islamic Ummah whether Arabic-speaking or not, and to the regionalists who believe that there are distinct nations inside the Arabic speaking world.[30]

## Ibrahim al-Yaziji

In almost all the Arab writers in the modern times there is an element of *arūbah* (Arabness). All of them are conscious of tie of a language, which should bind together those who differ in inherited religious belief; they are proud of the culture expressed through the language, and their writings communicate this pride to those who read them. Ibrahim al-Yaziji called on the Arabs to remember their past greatness and awake, in a famous ode; and the secret society of 1875 of which he was himself a member, spoke in its proclamations of the ' Arab pride' of the people of the Syria and rejected the Sultan's claim to be Caliph as an usurpation of Arab rights.[31] In his famous ode, Yaziji addresses the Arabs; reminds them of their glorious past; and invites them to think over their grieving present as the Turks were humiliating them:

كم تظلمون ولستم تشتكون وكم

تستغضبون فلا يبدو لكم غضب

لانتم الفئة الكثرى وكم فئة

قليلة تم ء اذ اضمت لها الغلب

(How much you would be oppressed and you make no complaints? How much you would be provocated and you demonstrate no response against it?
You certainly are in huge majority. So many minority groups are there who dominated and were victorious as they were united).

Further he says:

بالله يا قومنا هبوا لشانكم

فكم تناديكم الاسفار والخطب

الستم من سطوا في الارض واقتحموا

شرقا وغربا وعزوا اينما ذهبوا

فما لكم ويلكم اصبحتم هملا

ووجه عزكم بالهون منتقب

لا دولة لكم يشتد ازركم

بها ولا ناصر للخطب ينتدب

اقداركم في عيون الترك نازلة

وحقكم بين ايدى الترك مغتصب

(I swear by God, O my people! Rise up for your dignity! How much do sermons and documents call upon you?
Are you not that people who had over-come the earth and penetrated the east and west and succeeded wherever they marched?
Woe to you! You are now neglected; the face of your honour is veiled with disgrace.
For you there is no Empire that may empower you and there is now responding voice favouring your calls!
Your values, in the eyes of the Turks are baseless and the Turks confiscate your rights! )

This western model of nationalism was advocated earlier by al-Kawākibi who attacked Ottomans and declared them despotic and hence not suitable for ruler-ship.

## Al-Kawākibi

Abd al Rahman al-Kawākibi (1894-1930) [33] in two of his remarkable works namely *Umm al-Qura* (Mother of the Cities) and *Tabāi' al-Istibdād* (The Characteristics of Tyranny), criticized despotic attitude of Ottoman Empire and declared it as opposed to the spirit of Islam. He regards despotism and tyranny as a central cause to the decay of Muslims. These were the despotic rulers who misused the religion and supported its distorted teachings. Despotism as such corrupts the whole society. The just state is that one in which the individual is free and freely serves the community, and in which the government watches over this freedom, but is itself controlled by the people; this is what the true Islamic state was. The despotic state is just the opposite: it encroaches upon the rights of its citizens, keeps them ignorant to keep them passive, denies their rights to take an active part in human life. In the end it destroys the moral relationship of the rulers with ruled and citizens with each other; it distorts the moral structure of the individual, destroying the courage, integrity, and the sense of belonging, both religious and national. Al-Kawākibi asserts that the balance of power inside the Ummah must be shifted from the Turks back to the Arabs. Only Arabs can save Islam from decay: because of the central position of the Arabian peninsula in the Umamh and Arabic language in the Islamic thought but also for the other reasons- Arabian Islam is comparatively free from modern corruptions and the beduins are free from moral decay and passivity of despotism. [34]

Among the poets who outlawed the Ottomans and developed the sense of Arab nationalism being badly influenced with the propaganda and ideologies of the western powers, are Maruf al-Rusafi, Jameel Sidqui Zahawi, Fuad Khatib and others. Al-Rusafi's [35] adverse remarks of Ottomans may be seen in the following ode:

حتام نبقى لعبة لحكومة

دامت تجرعنا نقيع الحنظل

تنحو بنا طرق البوار تحيفا

وتسومنا سوء العزاب الاهول

مابالنا منها نخاف القتل ان

قمنا اما سنموت ان لم نقتل (36)

(How much do we remain a toy for such a government
that is continuously offering the bitter fruits of hanzal?
That is leading us injustly to the ways of decay and destruction, and imposing upon us the worst terrible torture.
Why do we fear from the killing of the government if we are not killed we are naturally to die! ).

Zahawi, himself considered the rule of Ottomans as that of darkness, terror and suppression. It is evident from his ode composed at the time when the reform movement had compelled Abd al-Hamid to declare the constitutional reforms in 1908. He, like other writers and poets, took it as fortunate initiative towards the socio-legal reforms demanded by the Arabs. He said

البرق اهدى لنا بشرى بها هدات

اروا حنا بعد طول الخوف والرهب

بشرى كما تبتغي الامال صادقه

اجلها الناس من قاص و مغترب

لقد اقر لعمرى اعينا سخنت

مانا له فئه الاحرار من ارب (37)

(The lightning led to us the tidings, due to which our souls are now pacified after a long period of fear and terror;
The tidings true and pleasing as were hoped and awaited;
every one immigrant and remote respects that.
By God the eyes that were warm before, are not delighted since the group of free men has now achieved its goal! )

Fuād al-Khatib while condemning the Ottomans, titled them 'the children of Chengiz Khan' and equated their atrocities and oppressive actions towards Arabs with those of Mongols who had destroyed the glory of Abbasids in the Islamic history:

يا ال جنكيز ان تثقل مظالمكم

على الشعوب فقد كانت لهم نعما

فالظلم ايقظ منهم كل ذى سنة

ما كان ينهض لولا انه ظلما (38)

(O children of Chengiz! if your atrocities upon the nations are over burdened, those are turned into blessings;
For the atrocity has awakened every one of them.
They might have never got up in case they were not oppressed)

The Arab Christians played crucial role in creating the Arab consciousness devoid of any religious trend. Jurji Zaydan is a clear example in this regard. He glorified the doctrine through his works on Arab history and still more by his series of historical novels, creating a romantic image of Arab past. The Christians, however, felt some doubt about drawing the political conclusion from this, and talking in terms of an Arab nation; for they could not be certain that Arab nationalism would not turn out to be a new form of Islamic self assertion. This doubt they could only vanish in one of two ways. They could identify themselves with majority in a way, which, although equivocal, is not unusual for a minority. Sulaiman al-Bustani arguing for the Ottoman constitution refutes the suggestion that it is a religious innovation by maintaining, exactly as the Muslims have done, that some thing like it had existed, under the first Caliph, or else they could feel the concept of 'Arabism' with the same content as that of 'Lebanon' or 'Syria' and a dream of Arab nation divorced from its religious basis, and incorporating Christians and Muslims exactly in the same way, and under the benevolent protection of liberal Europe. (39)

Such was the line taken by Naqib Azoury, Eilya Abu Mādi, and other Arab Christians. Azoury asserts that there is an Arab nation which includes Christians and Muslims equally; the religious problem of both the communities are really political, and aroused artificially by external forces for their own interests; there should be an Arab Christianity, and Arab Catholic Church, and this Arab nation must be independent of Turks.[40]

following the same views, Eilya Abu Mādi says that both the communities are ascribed to the movement of '*arubah*' that keeps basically no more distinction between the two:

اتباع احمد والسيح هوادة

ما العهد ان يتنكر الاخوان

الله رب الشرعتين وربكم

فالى متى فى الدين تختصمان

مهما يكن من فارق فكلا كما

ينمى الى قحطان اوغسان[41]

(The followers of Ahmad and Christ are moderate and lenient. It is not advisable that the brothers do quarrel in between.
Allah is the Lord of two Divine laws and Lord of yours. To what extent would you dispute in the religion?
Whatever partition is there; both of you ascribed to Qahtān or Ghassān. )

## Against Colonialism

Arab nationalism, not confining to anti-Turks sentiments, covered all the areas of forces of exploitation and corruption and created anger and hatred against all the colonial powers. Umar Abu Risha for instance, becomes too bitter while condemning the colonizers who were the prisoners to Arabs in the Islamic history and were disregarded and misbehaved. Now the time has turned into their favor; they are now imposing war upon the Arabs and are trying to enslave them. He says:

مــــالا بـــنـــــاء السبــــايـــــار كبــوا
لــلا مــــانــى البيض اشهــى مــركــب
ومتــــــى هـــــزوا عــــليــنــــــا راية
مــــا انـطــوت بيــن رخيص السلــب
يــاروابــى القـدس يــامجلــى السنا
يــاروى عيسى عــلى جفن النبى
دون عــليائك فى الرحب المدى
صهــلة الــخيــل ووهــج الــقــضــب
لــمـــت الآمـــال مــنـــا شــمــلــنـــا
ونــمــت مـــابيــنــنـــا مــن نســب (42)

(How much surprising is that the coming generation of the captives, for the sake of shining desires boarded the appetizing ship! When they hoisted against us the flag, it was never folded amidst the chief spoils.
O monticles of Quds, O seeker of Senna!
O visibility of Christ in the form of a Prophet!
In the open space the neighing of horses and the glowing of the camels are below your elevated status.
Our desires are now heightened and our ancestry has grown)

Khalil Mardum, also speaking in the same style, describes the playful tactics of the colonial agencies, their disowning of all the pledges and agreements and their oath-breaking behavior. He says:

اتــى ضـيفــا فــاصبح رب بيت
يـحـكـم بــا لـقطيــن وبــا لعيــال
وســمــى نفســـه قســرا وصـيـا
عــلـى مـفـوضـا فـى كل حال
ومـــنتــد بـــاعــلــى بــرغـم انفــى
ولســـت بـــقــا صــريـوم الــنــزال

(He came as guest and turned into a house lord who initiated deciding about the residents and their families. He forcibly declared himself an executer authorized in all the circumstances; claiming for my mandate despite my unwillingness, but I would not lag behind on the day of confrontation).

He further says:

دعاني للتفاهم بعد أخذ
وردو اختلاف و افتعال
وعاهدني وسماني حليفا
فلم اشفق عليه ولم اغال
لقينا في سبيل العهد مالم
نلاق من انتداب و احتلال
فكم من حاذق فطن تغابي
وداهية تظاهر بالخبال
وكم من ضابط اومستشار
تحذلق بالتحيز والدلال (43)

(He called me for the sake of mutual understanding after a long process of acceptance and rejection, difference and interaction.
He signed a contract with me and called me an ally; I was not afraid of him nor did I bubble up. We, in the process of agreement, travelled amidst deputation and occupation that we had never experienced before.
How many intelligent and skilled people were there who were defaulted and the clevers that appeared to be confused. How many officers and advisers were there who were pedantic of partiality and brokery).

## The Palestine Tragedy

The Palestine tragedy has been a major theme on which Arab writers and poets creating the sense of nationalism in the people, have been emphasizing much more in order to revive the political sovereignty of the country and to regain the full power. The Arab poets are too much enthusiastic in this regard. The poets of Palestine, perhaps first led the movement that was followed consequently by the Jordanians. The movement was fully supported by the poets of *arubah* from Syria, Egypt, Iraq, Morocco, Hijaz and Algiers. To name a few, Ibrahim Tawquān, Haroon Hashim Rasheed, Adil al- Ghazbān, Azizah Hārun are very prominent in this respect. This poetry is known as *sh'ir al-Muqāwamah* (the poetry of resistance). Ibrahim Tawqān while summarizing the whole tragedy, comments upon the defaulters responsible, and is very much vocal to express his anguish and hatred to them:

باعوا البلاد الى اعدائهم طمعا
بالمال لكنما اوطانهم باعوا
قد يعذرون لوان الجوع ارغمهم
والله ما عطشوا يوما ولاجاعوا
وبلغة العار عند الجوع تلفظها
نفس لها عن قبول العار رداع
لكنهم وعذاب الله يمحقهم
للبطن والفرج دون الخير نزاع
تلك البلاد اذا قلت اسمها وطن
لايفهمون ودون الفهم أطماع
يا بائع الأرض لم تحفل بعاقبة
ولاتذكرت ان الخصم خداع
لقد جنيت على الاحفاد والهفى
وهم عبيد وخدام واتباع
وغرك الذهب اللماع تحرزه
ان السراب كما تدريه لماع
فكر بموتك في ارض نشات بها
واترك لقبرك ارضا طولها باع (44)

They sold the country to their enemies for the sake of wealth; instead they have disposed of their homeland.
They excuse, if the hunger seizes them; they would be never in thirst and hunger.
While being in the two options of hunger and shame, a restrained soul will never accept the shame.
But they are-and the divine punishment may destroy them-quarrelling for the stomach and sex, not for the virtue.
The country, when I say, its title is the homeland, they do not understand; and in it lies their greediness.
O seller of the land! You did not mind of any consequence nor did you remember that the opponent is most deceptive.
Alas! You have committed against the generations, who are now the slaves, servants and the subordinates.

The shining gold that you have gained, deceived you; the mirage, as you know very well, is shiny only.
Think over, your last breath be in the land in which you flourished; and leave for your grave.
a piece of land no longer than of two arms).

Ibrahim Tawqān, in another poem, deals in detail with the politics of the "representatives" who lost Palestine. Their representatives used different slogans all misguiding and mischieving. The poet criticized them adversely and disclosed their cheating:

ايها المخلصون للوطنيه
انتم الحاملون عيب القضيه
انتم العاملون من غير قول
بارك الله في الزنود الفتيه
وبيان منكم يعادل جيشا
بمعدات زحفه الحربيه
واجتماع منكم يرد علينا
غابر المجد من فتوح اميه
وخلاص البلاد صار على البا
ب وجاءت اعياده الورديه
ما جحدنا افضالكم غير انا
لم تزل في نفوسنا امنيه
في ايدينا بقية من بلاد
فاستريحوا كيلا تطير البقيه (45)

(O those sincere for patriotism, you yourselves are responsible for the tragedy.
You are the worker without any saying; God may invoke blessings in the young wrists!
A 'statement' of your's is equated with an army along with its full preparations for march;
And a 'get together of yours will certainly revive our lost glory along with the conquest;
And the salvation of the country is on the gate and its rosy celebrations are about to start.
We never denied your credits and merits; we, however, have no desire in our hearts
In our hands is remainder of the country; be satisfied so that the other remainder may not fly from.)

In another poem, Tawqān declares that these so called representatives are the brokers of the country in fact. He says;

اما سماسرة البلاد فعصبة
عار على اهل البلاد بقاوها
ابليس اعلن صاغرا افلاسه
لما تحقق عنده اغراوها
يتنعمون مكرمين كانما
لنعيمهم عم البلاد شقاوها
هم اهل نجدتها وان انكرتم
وهم وانفك صاغر زعماوها
وحماتها وبهم يتم خرابها
وعلى يديهم بيعها وشراوها (46)

(As for the brokers of the country are concerned, their survival is a shame on the frontlet of the people.
The devil declared submissively himself insolvent as his provocating them was completed.
They are enjoying respectfully with the luxuries though the entire country suffers from their mischievousness.
They are upholding the relief of the country though you refuse to acknowledge it; they are leaders of the country in spite of your disliking.
Due to its supporters exclusively, the destruction of the country is completed, and its selling and purchasing is in their hands).

These are few samples of the sentiments from the poetry of resistance regarding the Palestine and other national issues that represent anti colonial and anti imperialist feelings ingrained in the conscience of the Arabs. These poetic creativities enhanced the *arubah* trend and united the Arabic-speaking people gradually.

## Reconciliation with Islam

The Islamic reformists in the 19th and 20th centuries, apart from the nationalists, tried their best to accommodate the national feelings of Arabs with the Islamic ethos of Ummah. Muhammad Rashid Rida is a clear example in this regard. The final object of Rida's political thought was the re-establishment of a truly Islamic State. He disapproved of all attempts to create in the Muslim world state based on a solidarity other than that of religion: among others, national states in which the nation was the final object of loyalty, national sentiment the binding force, and national interest the highest criterion of policy and legislation. This sort of nationalism seemed to Rida, nothing but a new form of the purely natural tribal solidarity which had existed in the days before Islam; its principles were those of the days of religious ignorance-loyalty and honor-not those of the Shariah. The element of Arab national feeling is, however, strong in his writings, and stronger still in those of his friend Shakib Arsalan (1869-1946) [(47)]. When they talk of the problems of Islam they are thinking first of all about Arab Islam, and regard other Muslims, in Arsalan's own phrase, as 'the pupils of the Arabs'. They believed that, because of the special place of the Arabs in the Ummah, Arab nationalism could be reconciled with Islamic unity in a way impossible for any other-even more, that a revival of the Ummah needed a revival of the Arabs. Islamic thought could not flourish unless the Arabic tongue flourished: it was the only language in which Islam could be properly studied and expounded, and therefore it was the duty of any Muslim who could do so to learn Arabic. Moreover, there could be no deep unity in Ummah unless it was a unity of language and in the Muslim Ummah this could be none other than Arabic. The Arabs were the guardians not only of the language of Islam, but also of its holy places. They had done much for Islam, and were capable of doing more, for in the peninsula at least there were still devoted to their religion and untouched by the corruption of the west. [(48)] Rida asserted that the political interests of the Arabs were the same as those of Ummah as a whole, for an independent Arab state would put new life both into the language of Islam and into its law; if the two had not been the same, he would have preferred his religion to his national duties, for they concerned the happiness of the next world as well this. [(49)] To Rida and other Islamists, Islam takes priority over Arabism.

The same line of thought and expression was taken by some of the prominent poets like Ahmad Shawqi[50] , Hafiz Ibrahim[51], Amir Nasiruddin and others. Ahmad Shawqi composed so many long poems in which he glorified beautifully Islam and the Muslim Ummah, and their heroes especially the Prophet of Islam and his pious companions. He admired the Ottoman Caliphs and their victorious Turk army generals. He compared them with those of Islam in the classical period:

ياخالد الترك جُدد خالد العرب[52]

(O Khalid of Turks, revive Khalid of Arabs!)

The constitutional reforms declared by Sultan Abdul Hamid made Shawqi hopeful to further reforms for the revival of Ottoman's lost glory and power. He admiring the Sultan speaks enthusiastically:

بشرى البرية قاصيها ودانيها

حاط الخلافة بالدستور حاميها

اسدى الينا امير المومنين يدا

جلت كما جل فى الاملاك مهديها

وليس مستعظما فعل ولا كرم

من صاحب السكة الكبرى ومنشيها

(Congratulation to all the people whether near or far. The custodian of Caliphate has incorporated the constitution.
The chief of the faithful has conferred upon us a blessing as magnificent as the dignitary confirming himself is magnificent in the dominions.
Any act or benevolence is not so amazing because it is from the man of great power who has commenced with it.)

Hafiz Ibrahim too supports the Ottoman Empire and regards it a shining symbol of Islamic glory and Muslim universal brotherhood, and prefers the religious identity to that of territorialism and nationalism. He clearly demonstrates:

مــالــلـخـلافة الاالتـرك تحـرسـهـا
الله يـحــرسـهـم فـى ال يـاسـين
ولــلاعــاريــب حـق لانـضـيـعـه
وان رمـيـنــا تبـفـريـط وتهـوين
بـنـو ابـيـنـا واخـوان الـزمـان عـلى
مـاكـان مـن شـدة يومـاومـن لين (54)

(What is with the Caliphate? Only the Turks can retain it.
Allah guards them amidst the family of Yāsin.
Arabs certainly have the rights; we cannot forfeit them, though we are accused of humiliating and minimizing them.
They are the sons of our father and are brothers of entire people though there was hardship in one day and softness in the other.)

Admiring the Ottoman Caliph, Hafiz may be seen in another poem:

اثـنـى الحـجـيج عـلـيـك والحـرمـان
واجــل عـيـد جـلـوسـك الـثـقـلان
ارضـيـت ربـك اذ جـعـلـت طـريـقـه
امـنــا وفــزت بـنـعـمـة الـرضـوان
وحـمـيـت بـالـدسـتـور حـولـك امـة
شـتـى الـمـذهـب جـمـة الاضـغـان (55)

(All the pilgrims, and the entire population of Makkah and Madinah praised you, and the people felt reverence to your installation ceremony.
Did you please your Lord as you followed His path as a symbol of peace, and you succeeded to the blessing of Divine pleasure?
You saved through the constitution a nation around you that follows different religions, from a plenty of rancor).

Another poet Ameer Nasir al-Din emphasizes upon the need of strengthening the Islamic unity (*al-rabitah al-Islamiyah* ) in order to support the relevance and meaningfulness of Arab people. He makes the national feelings subordinate to the Islamic one. He says:

نحن الالى بنت العروبة بيننا
ذاك البناء فاظهر الاسلام
نحن الالى بلسانهم قد انزلت
اى الكتاب وذالك الالهام (56)

(We are those, among whom Arabism was founded so strongly, and Islam overcame subsequently.
We are those, in the tongue of whom the verses of the Book were sent down and that was the Revelation!)

## Muslim Nationalists

In the 1920's and 1930's there emerged a new brand of Arab nationalism rather different from the two older forms (the western model of nationalism and the theory of subordinating nationalism to Islam). This new trend emerged due to foundation of the Ahāli group in Iraq in 1931, and the League of National Action in Syria in 1935. The first stood for parliamentary democracy, individual rights and unity of the nation. The second also had a similar programme. These two parties played a certain part in expressing a nationalist doctrine uncompromising and more distorting. The center of gravity was now shifted from Islam as divine law to Islam as a culture; in other words, instead of Arab nationalism being regarded as an indispensable step toward the revival of Islam, Islam was regarded as the creator of Arab nation, the contents of its culture or the objective of its collective pride. For example an Iraqi teacher Abd al-Rahman al-Bazzaz outrightly rejected any contradiction between the nationalism and Islam. The idea of a contradiction, he discussed, emanated from a western conception of Islam and of nationalism, and that so many Arabs had accepted it showed the intellectual domination of west over them. In reality the content of Islam was the same as that of Arab nationalism: and this was true only of the Arabs, not of the other Muslim nations. Muhammad Rashid Rida and other Islamists would have defined Arab culture in terms of Islam: Bazzaz does rather the opposite. Islam is a national religion; the real Islam was the Arab Islam, it was later destroyed by the other nations with their particularism. Islam needed a developed form of what was already present in the nature of the Arabs. Its moral ideas are the same as the natural morality of the Arabs; its political ideal of *shura* is identical with the natural democracy of the beduins. The spread of Islam was the medium through which the Arabs made their great contribution to the history. (57) This brand of nationalism was more alarming and deviated too. The universal character of Islam was now confined to Arabism: the Arabic-speaking nations may appropriate Islamic culture and the Islamic past as their own; other nations are alien to this culture and have been destroying it throughout the Islamic history according to the new perceptions. The scholar who complained of the intellectual domination of the west, himself became a severe victim of westernization and argued in the term that was clearly opposed to the basic tenets of Islam.

*****

## NOTES AND REFERENCES

1. Niharranjan Ray, for example, elaborates that no definition of nationalism seems to meet any given case of a nation. He says, ' Any definition of the term ' nation' is as good or as bad as any other, since no definition would exactly and wholly meet the situation of a given case'. *Nationalism in India*, Aligarh, 1973, p.18.
2. Hertz, Fredrick, *Nationality in History and Politics: Psychology of National Sentiment and Nationalism*, 1944. The scholars have been using this term in different backgrounds. B. G. Ray has discussed this as a factor for confusion. He says: " A good deal of confusion prevails in the intellectual field because thinkers and writers do not care to adopt a universally accepted meaning so far as a particular term is concerned. ......Unfortunately these two terms- humanism and nationalism- have been used in a variety of senses. Ray, B. G. Humanism and Nationalism, in *Nationalism and Humanism*, edited by Mittal, Keval Krishna, Delhi, 1981.p.6.
3. *Encyclopaedia Britannica*, Vol.7, p.195.
4. Tara Chand, *National Integration and Secularism*, Aligarh, 1968, p.3.
5. *International Encyclopaedia of Social Sciences*, Vol.2, p.
6. *The Shorter Oxford English Dictionary*, Vol.2, 1959, p.279.
7. Hertz, Fredrick, *op cit*, p.21.
8. Ray, Punaya, S., in *Nationalism and Humanism,* op cit , p.1.
9. Kohn, Hans, *Nationalism: Its Meaning and History*, Princeton, 1955, p.13.
10. *Nationalism: A report by a study Group of members of the Royal Institute of International Affairs*, London, 1939, p.6.
11. See for detail, Hull, R., *Medieval Theories of Papacy*, London, 1934.
12. Tout, T.F., *The Empire and the Papacy* 918-1213, London, 1924, p.2.
13. See far a detailed study, Mc Ilwain, C.H., *The Growth of Political Thought in the West*, New York, 1932.
14. Bowle, J., *Western Political Thought- From the Origin to Rousseau*, London, 1961, p.242.
15. Bornes, H.L., *An Intellectual and Cultural History of the Western World*, Vol.2, 1965 (New York), p. 548.
16. See far detail, Kausar, Zeenath, *Maulana Azad's Concept of Nationalism*, unpublished dissertation submitted in AMU for the award of M. Phil, pp.59-105.
17. Afghani, Jamal al Din (1838 / 39-1897) writer and pan-Isalimst political activist. Despite his claim to Afghan origin, he was born and raised in Iran of a Shií family (*Oxford Encyclopedia of Modern Islamic World*, Vol.1, p.24). After his education in his home-town of Asadabad in North west Iran, and in Qazwin and Tehran, he went for higher education in the 1850's to the shií shrine cities in Ottoman Iraq. He then seems to have embarked on slow journey that included probably Makkah, and certainly a trip across Iran in to Afghanistan in the early

1860's. In 1869, he went briefly to Cairo and then to the Ottoman capital, Istanbul. He was involved in the council of education and the new university where he gave a series of lectures. From 1871-1879 he lived in Cairo, supported by a grant from the government fund paid by the statesman Riyad Pasha, teaching and re-interpreting Islamic philosophy. He was in Paris from 1881 to 1883 where he along with Abduh, edited *al-Urwah al-Uthqua*. In 1884, Afghani went to Britain, but in the last phase of his life he was again in Istanbul where he died of cancer of the jaw.

18. Abduh, Muhammad (1849-1905) Egyptian scholar and reformer who was regarded as the architect of Islamic modernism. The crucial influence in his development was the impact of Afghani. Abduh was later on made the editor of *al-Urwah al Uthqua*, which was the organ of the pan-Islamism at that time. He was exiled from Egypt between 1882 and 1888 where he made wide contact with kindredmind in Syria and North Africa, with a short sojourn also in France. After his return to Cairo, his thoughts and efforts were drawn increasingly towards education and Islamic reformism. His *Risalah al-Tawhid* is very important in this regard.

19. Rida, Muhammad Rashid (1865-1935) Islamic revivalist and reformer. He was born in a village near Tripoli. After his early education, he attended an Islamic School established by Shaykh Hussain al-Jiśr who believed in the synthesis of religious education and modern sciences. *Al-Urwah al-Uthqua* initiated by Afghani and Abduh, made a deep impact on Rida; it broadened his idea of reform and brought him to a new stage in his intellectual life. In Cairo he published *al-Manár* in 1898, the main objectives of which were to articulate the idea of reform and preserve the unity of Muslim Ummah. Central to his scheme was the concept of the Caliphate and revival of Islamic State. His book *al-Khilafah wa al-Imamah al-Uzma* is very important in this respect.

20-21. Muhammad Ali (1805-1848) and his son Ibrahim are usually depicted as able rulers in Egypt. Arriving with an Ottoman force sent to expel Napoleon Bonaparte's French expedition (1798-1801) Muhammad Ali maneuvered until the Sultan recognized him as the governor of the Egypt. The Ulama of Azhar mosque helped him to power, but he soon curbed their political influence and economic autonomy. He dug irrigational canals, promoted cotton as a cash crop for export, centralized taxes and established monopolies in industry in foreign trade. Western advisers helped him to build a modern army and schools to train officers, administrators and technicians. The historians have endowed him with the title of "Father of Modern Egypt". His son Ibrahim, who ruled only a few months and predeceased his mentally incapacitated father, implemented all the policies of his father.

22. Muhammad bin Abd al-Wahhāb (1703-1791), the ideological founder of the Saudi Kingdom, the most prominent Islamic scholar and activist whose impact upon all parts of the Muslim world is remarkable. He wrote on a variety of Islamic subjects such as theology, exegesis, jurisprudence, and the life of the Prophet Mohammad. A set of issues dominated his teachings, includes *tawhid, tawassul, ziyarah al-Qubur, takfir, bid'ah, ijtihad* and *taqlid.* Shayk al-Islam propagated the Quranic teachings without any compromise with the non-Islamic belief and practices. His book *Kitab al-Tawhid* is on of the source books on the pristine teachings of Quran and Sunnah.
23. *Oxford Encyclopedia of the Modern Islamic World*, edited by John L. Esposito, New York, 1995,Vol.1, p.113.
24. Abu Khaldun Sāti 'al-Husri born in 1880 in San 'a, Yemen, to Syrian Arab parents from Aleppo, moved often as his father filled Ottoman judicial post in Yemen. Anatolia, and Libya. Graduating in 1900 from the Civil Service College in Istanbul, he spent eight years in the Balkan caldron of competing nationalisms, as a school teacher and then as an Ottoman official. With the effective demise of Ottoman Empire in 1918, he switched his allegiance to Arab nationalism and joined Faysal ibn Husayn's regime in Damascus as Director General, then minister of Education. He later on moved to Iraq in 1921 and for 20 years living there in he promoted Arab nationalism at every opportunity. He was exiled in 1941 to Syria where he Arabised the national education system (1944-1946). The following decade he spent in Cairo as Cultural Advisor to the Arab League and first Director of its Institute of Higher Arab Studies. He retired at the age of 77 in 1957 and died in Bagadad in 1968.
25. Gokalp, Mehmet Ziya (1875-1924) Turkish social scientist, writer and nationalist. Born in Diyar Bakr, Ziya attended the Imperial Veterinary School (1896) at Istanbul, where he joined the Revolutionary Committee of Union and Progress. He was dismissed from the School, arrested and jailed when this affiliation was disclosed. After his release from prison he devoted himself to a serious study of Durkheimian sociology. His career as a nationalist thinker started in Thessaloniki in 1911. When the Balkan war (1912-1913) broke out, he established himself in Istanbul and continued to publish in various journals. In 1915, he became a professor of sociology at Istanbul University. He is treated as the father of Turkish nationalism. He has been one of the most influential minds in 20$^{th}$ century political history. He prepared the ground for secularist westernization in the country.
26. *Oxford Encyclopedia of the Modern Islamic World*, Vol.2, p.155.
27. Renan ( Joseph-) Ernest ( b. Feb.28, 1823, Treguier-d. Oct.2, 1892, Paris) French philospher, historian, and scholar of religion a leader of the school of critical philosophy in France. See for detail, *The New Encyclopaedia Britannica*, Vol. 9, pp. 1022-1023.

28. Al-Husri, is instead very much influenced with Ibn Khaldun's theory of the relationship between religion and *asabiyah*: religion can not by itself create a political community, it can only strengthen one already created by natural solidarity derived from a natural relationship. Al-Husri was so much affected with this theory that he named his son Khaldun and thereby added Abu Khaldun to his own name. Ridā, on the contrary, was not in agreement with this theory of *asabiyah*. This theory to Rida was untrue in fact, and the history of Islam showed it; the action of Muhammad (SAW) was not directed by the desire for social prestige, or to increase the authority of his clan, and his success was not due to strength of asabiyah at his disposal. On the contrary, *asabiyah* was subordinated to the imperatives of Islam; and when it revived it destroyed the Islamic state, as Rida maintained. See his book *al-Khilafah wa al-Imamah al-Uzma*.
29. *Oxford Encyclopedia of the Modern Islamic World*, Vol.2, p.156.
30. Hourani, Albert, *Arabic Thought in the Liberal Age 1798-1939*, Oxford University Press, 1970, pp.314, 315.
31. *Ibid*, p.277.
32. Zaghlul, Muhammad, Dr., *al-Qawmiyah al-Arabiyah fi al-Adab al-Hadith*, Egypt, Dār al-Ma 'ārif, 1959,pp.105-106.
33. Al-Kawākibi, Abd al-Rahmān (1854-1902) Islamic reformer and advocate of an Arab Caliphate. He was born in Aleppo, Syria and was educated thoroughly in religion, Ottoman administrative law, Arabic, Turkish and Persian. He began his career in journalism and the law and from 1879 to 1896 held several senior public posts. After suffering from the intrigues of Ottoman officials, in 1898 he fled to Egypt where he remained until his death in 1902. he is best known for his two books *Umm al-Qura* and *Tabāi al-Istibdād*. He published them in Cairo under the pen name of al-Sayyid al-Furati and Traveller K, respectively, to avoid the harassment of the Ottoman authorities.
34. Hourani, Albert, *op.cit.*, pp. 272, 273.
35. Al-Rusafi, Maruf (1877-1945) the national poet of Iraq, one of the members of *al-Majma al-Ilmi al-Arabi*, was born and died in Baghdad. He was elected as a member in the Ottoman parliament and he criticized the Arab reformers severely. He published a daily newspaper *al-Amal* in 1923 that survived only for 3 months. He was elected as a member in the Upper House for five times. He is regarded as a distinguished poet who clearly admired and discredited some time dignitries as well as events of the time.
36. Zaglul, *op. cit.*, p.84.
37. *Ibid*, pp. 85-86.
38. *Ibid*, p.105.
39. Hourani, *op. cit.*, p.277.
40. *Ibid*, p. 278.
41. Zaglul, *op. cit.*, p. 73.
42. *Ibid*, pp. 111-112.

•

43. *Ibid*, pp. 110-111.
44. *Ibid*, pp. 114-115.
45. *Ibid*, p. 117.
46. *Ibid*, pp. 117-118.
47. Arsalan, Shakib, al-Amir ( 1869-1946) the Arab politician and prominent scholar entitled as *Amir al-Bayan* a distinguished personality of Arabic literature, one of the member of *al-Majma al-Ilmi al-Arabi* born in Lebanon learned his education in the Madrasah Dar al-Hikmah, Beirut. Initiating his career as Director of Education in the homeland, he held so many higher posts in his life. He later on migrated to Switzerland where he stayed for 25 years and after coming back he died in Beirut. He dealt with the Islamic politics before the collapse of Ottoman Empire since he was staunch supporter of it. He later on associated himself with the issues of Arab nationalism; and for that he issued French magazine *La Nation Arabe* from Geneva. He frequently visited the European countries and in 1928 America too. Among his contributions *Limāza Taakhkhara al-Muslimun, Hadhir al-Alam al-Islami* (2Volumes), *al-Sayyid Rashid Rida au Ekhāu Arbayina Sinah* are very important.
48. Hourani, Albert *op. cit.*, Pp.299-300.
49. *Ibid*, p.306.
50. Ahmad Shawqui (1868-1932) the most prominent poet in the modern Arab world, entitled as *Amir al-Shu'ra*, was born and died in Cairo. He visited France in 1887 and studied the French literature. After coming back to the country he started his career as the Head of the British Desk in the office of Abbas Hilmi. He represented the country in the conference of Orientalists in Geneva in 1896. He also visited Spain in 1915 and after his return was appointed as a member of *Majlis al-Shuyukh*, and remained in his office till death. He devoted himself for poetry and composed in each and every variety of it. He discussed all the socio-political events of the Egypt and of the Muslim world in his poetry.
51. Hafiz Ibrahim Muhammad (1871-1932) the famous Egyptian poet who recorded the socio-political history of the contemporary country through his firing poetries. He started his career as a lawyer. He later on joined the national movement of Egypt and suffered a lot. After some time he was titled as *Shāir al-Nil*. He associated himself with Mustafa Kamil and became the spokesman of the independence of the country. He was appointed as the Head of the Arabic literary section in Dar al- Kutub al-Misriyyah in 1911 and continued in the same capacity till his death.
52. Zaglul, *op. cit.*, p. 82.
53. *Ibid*, p. 86.
54. *Ibid*, p. 82.
55. *Ibid*, p.87.
56. *Ibid*, p.81.
57. Hourani, Albert, *op. cit.*, pp.308-309.

*****

# 6

# ISLAMIC SHURA AND WESTERN DEMOCRACY

Islamic Shūrā (Consultative System) and the Western democracy have been studied and analysed in modern times from different angles. Most of the Muslim scholars responded to the West with suspicion and resentment at a time when the Muslim states got independence and established their sovereignty against the former colonial powers. The conquest or occupation imported alien concepts and institutions and presented challenges which the Muslim society has been ill-prepared to meet and turn to its own advantage, both spiritually and materially. To these scholars, colonialism and imperialism are deeply embedded in the consciousness as predominantly evil manifestations of the West, which is, moreover, different in religion and morals, in economic aims and practices, in political and social organization. In this background they criticized the Western concepts and terminologies and declared them anti-Islamic. Syed Abul A'la Maududi (1903-1976), Syed Qutb (1906-1966), Mohammad Al-Ghazali (1917-1996), Hamiduddin Farahi (1863-1930) and Said Ramadan[1] are few names in this group.

The other group – West trained and educated intellectuals – advocated a mixture of Islam and the West, liberalism and conservatism, genuine democracy and conviction in faith. They favoured a system built on the full cooperation of thinking citizens and based on majority rule in liberty and freedom, economic equity and social justice all bound together in obedient service to Allah in the personal life. This group while condemns the rejection of everything modern and European but in the field of rational and empirical studies they preached and followed Western political, and social ideas and their adaptation to Islamic social norms. 'Ali Abd al-Raziq (1888-1966), Khalid Muhammad Khalid

Muhammad Khalid (b. 1920), Allal al-Fasi (1906-1973)[2] and others propagated the idea and used the term 'Islamic Democracy' to connote the mixture of Western and Islamic political ideas. The main features of democracy, *i.e.*, government of the people, popular sovereignty, general will, responsibility of the government and the welfare of man as state's goal, were traced into the consultative government led by the Prophet (SAW) and his four caliphs, and the background, world view and socio-political milieu of both were bypassed.

The Western scholars of Islam, the Orientalists, among whom Gibb, Rosenthal, Watt and Piscatori[3] are prominent, view Islam as totalitarian and undemocratic. But there is an important difference between the Islamic World and the Hitler's Germany or Stalin's Russia, they claimed, "Hitler controlled the ideas of National-Socialism and Stalin was the chief official exponent of the ideas of Marx and Lenin. In the Islamic world, on the other hand, the men with actual political power never had control of ideas. The religious institution was part of the establishment but it also maintained a degree of independence. In particular, the theory was everywhere accepted among Sunnites that the most powerful *sultan* is subject to the *Shari'ah* just like the humblest Muslim. If the *sultan* disobeys God's commands, he may escape punishment in the life, but will have to pay in the world to come. Thus, no *sultan* or other ruler of Sunnite Muslims has anything like the power over men's thinking possessed by the occidental totalitarian dictator."[4]

The question arised, in what way then, a ruler in Islam becomes a dictator and the government a totalitarian one? These Western writers, on the other hand, admit that if any country produces a constitution in accordance with the central principles of the *Shari'ah*, and the appropriate laws are accepted and obeyed by both the ruler and the ruled, the state will approximate to a modern European democracy in the concern it shows for the welfare of the ordinary citizen.

Thus, the student of Islamic political system is always surprised to find that most aspects of this subject are shrouded in vagueness, contradiction, and conflicting views. This situation is led by the following factors:

(i) thinking Islam as merely a collection of dogmas and a religion of personal dealings;

(ii) blind imitation of alien concepts and thought and its application in the Muslim world;

(iii) vested interests of the ruling elite and inefficiency of Muslim intellectuals to understand the problems in Islamic perspective;

(iv) studying and applying the Islamic political system apart from its social, economic and moral components.

Among the 'ulamā' and religious scholars the majority – and this formed a fourth group – followed a negative course which is satisfied with expounding rules previously extracted by classical Muslim jurists and which tries to prove the superiority of these jurists over those who subscribe to modern theories. Nevertheless, the followers of this method offer no solution to the difficulties of the problems which face the people nor do they try to distinguish among the pronouncements of the jurists in regard to what they determined as rules which were suitable during their time and that which constituted a statement of rules of Islamic law binding on Muslims throughout the ages. Their works on the political system, still abound in discussion of such old topics as the executive ministry, the ministry of authorizations, the succession to the throne, the oath of allegiance, the qualifications of the people who should decide matters, the condition of the caliph and other topics which, except as historically, are of no value now.[5]

## Islamic Principles of Politics

The Holy Qur'ān has given some basic general principles in the field of politics and constitutional affairs which cannot be omitted from any sound system of government. The Qur'ān does not mention details and particulars. These have been left for the Muslim *ummah* to formulate according to the needs of time and place. These principles are considered to be the "Supreme Values" and have a great affect upon the formulation of the Islamic concept of state, its functions and characteristics of its system of government. To these 'values' both the rulers and ruled appeal when differences arise among them and according to guidelines of these directives all carry out their duties and secure their rights in the Islamic State. These principles are as follows:

1) *Shura* (mutual consultation)

Some details are given in the last part of this chapter.

2) *'Adl* (justice)

The Holy Qur'ān declared:

"Allah commands justice, the doing of good, and liberality to kith and kin, and he forbids all shameful deeds and injustice and rebellion."[6]

"Allah doth command you to render back your Trusts to those to whom they are due; and when ye judge between man and man that ye judge with justice."[7]

"... and let not the hatred of others to you make swerve to wrong and depart from justice. Be just: that is next to Piety: and fear God."[8]

3) *Freedom*

"Seest those not that to God bow down in worship all things that are in the heavens and on earth, - the sun, the moon, the stars; the hills, the trees, the animals; and a great number among mankind? But a great number are (also) such as are fit for punishment."[9]

"But, if as is sure, there comes to you guidance from Me whosoever follows My guidance, will not lose his way, nor fall into misery. But whosoever turns away from My message, verily for him is a life narrowed down."[10]

"Let there be no compulsion in religion: Truth stands out clear from Error."[11]

4) *Equality*

"O mankind: We created you from a single (pair) of a male and a female, and made you into nations and tribes, that ye may know each other. Verily the most honoured of you in the sight of Allah is he who is the most Righteous of you."[12]

The Qur'ān did not tolerate that the society might be divided on the basis of any superiority:

"Truly Pharaoh elated himself in the land and broke up its people into sections."[13]

5) *Permissibility of Calling Ruler to Account*

"Help ye one another in righteousness and piety, but help ye not one another in sin and rancour."[14]

"And follow not the bidding of those who are extravagant, - who make mischief in the land and mend not (their ways)."[15]

"... nor obey any whose heart We have permitted to neglect the remembrance of Us, one who follows his own desires, whose case has gone beyond all bounds."[16]

There is no agreement among contemporary scholars as to the number of these fundamental principles. Some mention only a few of those which have been listed above; others add more such as obedience, assignment of the competent and abiding by the truth. In fact, there is a consensus in the Islamic *Shari'ah* and *fiqh* confirming all these principles. The difference seems to be in determining which is the most important one which each scholar chooses to deal with.[17] Mawlana Maududi has discussed the basic political concepts in detail. He has further declared some selected verses of the Holy Qur'ān as the cogent directives for state policy Allah ordered to the Prophet (SAW):

'Take not with God another object of worship; or 'thou (O man!) wilt sit in disgrace and destitution

1) Thy Lord had decreed that ye worship none but Him,

2) And that ye be kind to parents. Whether one or both of them attain old age in thy life, say not a word of contempt, nor repel them, but address them in terms of honour. And out of kindness lower to them the wing of humility, and say; My Lord! Bestow on them Thy Mercy even as they cherished me in childhood. Your Lord knoweth best what is in your hearts. If ye do deeds of

righteousness. Verily He is Most Forgiving to those who turn to Him again and again (in true penitence).

3) And render to the kindred their due rights, as (also) to those in want, and to the way-farer.

4) But squander not (your wealth) in the manner of a spendthrift. Verily spendthrifts are brothers of the Evil Ones: And the Evil One is to his Lord (Himself) ungrateful.

5) And even if thou hast to turn away from them in pursuit of mercy from thy Lord, which thou dost expect yet speak to them a word of easy kindness.

6) Make not thy hand tied (like a niggards) to thy neck, nor stretch it forth to its utmost reach, so that thou become blameworthy and destitute.

7) Kill not your children for fear of want. We shall provide sustenance for them as well as for you. Verily the killing of them is a great sin.

8) Nor come close to adultery. For it is a shameful (deed) and an evil, opening the road (to other evils).

9) Nor take life – which Allah has made sacred – except for just cause. And if anyone is slain wrongfully, We have given his heir authority (to demand Qisas or to forgive), but let him not exceed bounds in the manner of taking life, for he is helped (by the law).

10) Come not nigh to the orphan's property except to improve it until he attains the age of full strength.

11) And fulfil (every) engagement, for (every) engagement will be enquired into (on the Day of Reckoning).

12) Give full measure when ye measure and weigh with a balance; that is straight: that is the most fitting and the most advantageous in the final determination.

13) And pursue not that of which thou hast no knowledge. For every act of hearing or of seeing or of (feeling in) the heart will be enquired into (on the Day of Reckoning).

14) Nor walk on the earth with insolence for thou canst not rend the earth asunder nor reach the mountains in heights.

15) Of all such things the evil is hatefull in the sight of thy Lord. These are among the (precepts of) which the Lord has revealed to thee (O Muhammad!) (SAW)"[18]

These verses were revealed at a moment of historic significance, *i.e.*, on the eve of the beginning of the Madnī period. The Makkī period was coming to a close and a new chapter was going to be opened in the life of the Islamic movement. On this historic occasion this Islamic manifesto was revealed. It was to act as the source of policy and conduct of the new Islamic state of Madinah. It provided the guiding principles for the all-pervading construction of the new state and society.[19]

Islam was, in fact, the first comprehensive system of life, which pronounced the notion of *Jamā'ah* (group life) and commanded the practice of the ideals of islam for the welfare of man. *Dīn* was regarded as the foundation of the basic law for the guidance of the Islamic government, which stood for the realization of the noble ideal of human welfare both in this world and the next. The early *Khilāfah* based on these principles differed widely from its belated counterpart – the Western democracy.

## Democracy as Defined

Political ideals apart, democracy as a form of government has also varied in the West: there is a constitutional monarchy with a parliamentary sovereignty in England and a presidential type of government in the United State of America. Modern democracy has not, however, lived upto the noble ideals of Islam and consequently a number of evils have crept in the body politic.

Definitions seldom define concepts particularly true with regard to democracy. Being derived from the word *demos* and *kratos*, democracy literally means the power of the people. A survey of the concept of democracy through the ages would reveal that it contains five fold factors:

(i) a government of 'all' or the 'many';

(ii) the body of the people posses sovereign power;

(iii) consent of the majority or the general will of the people is the basis of the state;

(iv) responsibility is laid upon all governmental action, and

(v) the end of state activity is the welfare of man.

Herodotus, in the fifth century B.C., understood democracy to mean 'Mob-rule' or a society in which there is equality of right and the holders of political authority are accountable for what they do. To Aristotle and Plato, democracy meant the "government of the many" and the Greek equivalent of modern democracy was 'polity'. Cicero's thought centred round two doctrines – natural law and the equality of man – now two fundamental principles of democracy. "If a people have a share in the sovereign power", said Jean Bodin, "we call it a popular state". In the words of Hobbes, "an Assembly of all will constitute democracy". Subsequently, Locke emphasized for the first time the principles of consent and majority decision which form the basis of modern democracy. Locke said that "the majority having... upon men's first uniting into society, the whole power of the community naturally in them, may emplcy all that power in making laws for government is a perfect democracy." Montesquieu in his *Spirit of the Laws* (1748) brilliantly remarked that "when in a republic, the body of the people is possessed of the supreme power, it is called a democracy."

The arguments for democracy have been set forth in the three principal theories – the doctrine of natural rights, utilitarianism and political idealism. As a typical theorist of natural rights, Rousseau emphasized that people are both citizens and subjects when they participate in the sovereign authority of the state or when they submit to the law respectively. He proceeds to define democracy in exact words when he says, "the Sovereign may commit the charge of the government to the whole people or to a majority of the people so that more citizens are magistrates than are mere private individuals. This form of government is called democracy."

The theory of utilitarianism as propounded by Bentham, Mill and Spencer, stands for the standard of utility – the "greatest good of the greatest number", and as such makes representative democracy a preferable form of government. The utilitarian argument was that political government has as its end the well-being of the individual. Society should, therefore, be so reconstituted politically that its constitution could secure ample opportunities for happiness of the greatest number of individuals in the community. Democratic government alone satisfies these arguments.

Political idealism regards democracy as the best form of government, which enables the individual to realize fully the most characteristic potentialities of his personality. Accordingly, democracy will largely effect the development of the latent intellectual and spiritual qualities of the individual. Freedom (with which the concept of democracy is vitally concerned) lies, according to Hegel in obedience to the state. With reference to the foundation of government, T.H. Green beautifully summarized that "will, not force, is the basis of the state."

As already observed, democracy found its main support in the writings of the Contractualists, the Utilitarians and the idealists. The doctrine of natural rights was advocated as a defence of democracy in the middle ages. A Leveller's pamphle' during the Puritan Revolution in England asserted that 'we the people", derive from "Adam and right reason" certain "natural rights of liberty, property, freedom of conscience and equality in political privilege." John Locke sought to establish a scientific justification for the Parliamentary Revolution of 1688. Accordingly, Rousseau's *Social Contract,* Paine's *Rights of Man* and the "Declarations" of the French and American Revolutions vindicated the claim that man as man possesses an inherent right to determine the form and personnel of the government. Thus, from the later eighteenth century until recently, the trend towards democracy has been understood as a great process of man's development from the stage of savagery to the height of civilization – from autocracy to democracy. Mac-Iver testifies to this movement by saying that "inspite of reversions, the main trend of the state is toward democracy". Democracy has seen two forms – old and new – direct and indirect. Direct or pure democracy could only become a reality in a small state, where the number of citizens was small enough to form a public assembly the highest and most powerful body of government. Modern states, on the other hand, are nation-states and it is not possible or practicable to call the entire body of citizens at one place. The only other alternative is a recourse to indirect democracy or representative government. In the practical field, the definition of democracy has undergone a great change. Government of all or of the majority was soon found to be an impossibility. The later theorists per force took a more realistic view and sought to define democracy in a more practical manner. Majority rule, popular consent and responsible government were recognized as fundamental principles of modern democratic states.

## Between Democrats and Critics

Modern democracy has both been praised to heavens and ruthlessly criticized. Democracy has, in fact, displayed its own inherent defects in its working, yet the remedy of democracy has been suggested as more and more democracy. Hearnshaw in his famous work *Democracy at the Cross Ways* mentions four postulates of political democracy. He believes in the fundamental honesty of man, his practical common sense; solidarity of the community and the existence of a general will. Dr. Finer observes that under a democratic government, "we have the assurance that the sphere of our private life – our family, our diversions, our worship, our work – will not be invaded except by due process of law in which we have an equal say with any. We rest tranquil that officials and judges will not abuse us and that they themselves will have to answer for discrimination and bias and unauthorized invasions of our private and public life to a public tribunal in which we, as of right, sit as judge and jury."

Democracy has been bitterly criticised as "aimless, inefficient and economically unjust." A government of the people, "millions, mostly fools" – can be knocked to pieces in five minutes. Democracy, it is said, is a government where the people have the 'freedom to starve'; it is the 'paradise of the shrieker'. Popular government has not, it is a legend, existed even in countries, where constitutions have been normally democratic. Consequently, it has never been a valid theory either as a political ideal or as a description of political fact. Some of the recent writers have stressed upon the "false assumptions", the "receding tide', the "impossibility" of democracy and the "historic necessity of oligarchy".

Apart from its varying definitions and conflicting connotations democracy should be studied in the light of its conceptions of life that contains definite values and ideals corresponding to a certain conception of human nature. Western democracy views Greece as the fountain of all democratic norms and thinks Athens as the main centre was ushered by Solon, the Greek father of European democracy, who desired an equitable distribution of wealth and reforms in the society as a whole. Pericles, the leader of the Athenians taught that the highest devotion in a man's life was towards the city-state. In the 5th century B.C. Sophists raised the banner of intellectual revolution and gave the idea that man was the measure of all things, that success in public life was the most important goal in man's social activity and that truth and values were relative. A.H. Amstrong has called this philosophy "humanist agnosticism" and summarized the position of this group into following:

> "A successful civilized human life is the central concern; and there are no absolute standards of unchanging reality, religion or morality with which the individual mind must conform. There was a discussion, already widespread in fifth century Greece before the Sophists appeared, as to whether religion and morality were natural part of the inborn essential order of things or simply an affair of Custom and Tradition. The relativist humanism of the Sophists led them of course to accept the second alternative. Religion and morality were for them a matter of man-made custom."[20]

The attitude of these Sophists can be described, in modern terminology, as relativistic humanism incorporating a secular and utilitarian outlook on democracy, Socrates (470-399 B.C.) on the other hand revolted against this attitude and insisted that knowledge and virtue, which he merged into a single whole, were not the accidental creation of man and circumstances. The truth to him, possessed the quality of permanence and universality.

In their conception of human nature, the Greeks considered themselves as superior to other nations by their very nature. They did not think of humanity as a whole, they thought of it as divided sharply into two sections, Greeks and barbarians, and of the Greek world as a small oasis of intelligence and culture ringed round by a wide and indefinite expanse of barbarism.[21] Aristotle (383-322 B.C.) considered the Asiatics as slaves by nature. They further made classification within their own society. Some people, as Plato (427-347 B.C.) and Aristotle believed, were born to be slaves and some others to rule. The slaves were doomed to a life-long servitude. They were deprived of all the privileges. The position of women in this democracy was not less shocking. The wife was considered to be inferior to the husband due to the order of nature. She had no authority over her children. The state was the highest good to which she had to devote all her thoughts and desires. The belief in the individual was an assumption which played a small part in the ethics of the city-state, where the individual appeared as a citizen and where his significance depended upon his status or his function.

Stoicism founded by Zeno (340-265 B.C.) exerted later a strong influence on European intellectuals. This school of thought was considered to be of oriental origin. The school was characterized by the fact that its members were frequently descended from the Hellenistic mixed races of the orient. This probably explains why Stoicism emphasized the universality of humanity and the equality of all races.[22]

This golden age of Athens is looked back upon with reverence by the Western writers. This is accurately thought of as the beginning of European civilization. Dr. Sabine is surprised to know that modern student sees this age as a very long time ago – so long in fact as to bring into question its relevance for contemporary concerns. To him, “we would be more accurate to call them (Greeks) “moderns” if not quite contemporary.”[23]

The contemporary western democracy has been studied as something more than a form of the state. The concept is broadened to include the form of society. Some political scientists conceived it as a spiritual ideal whose attainment is impossible with the present political organization.[24] The concept of democracy has been continuously changing. Some have changed the view so deftly that Andrew C. MeLaughlin stated: "An embalanced democracy deserves burial."[25]

## Islamic Process of Democratization

In comparison to these in an Islamic democratic system in which Islamic life is to be lived according to Islamic laws and institutions, which, in pursuance of an ethical ideal of Islam – "enjoin what is just and forbid what is wrong,[26] as enunciated in the Qur'ān – gradually unifies individuals and groups into a well-knit people called the *ummah*. "For those who do good is good in this world" and "certainly the Home of the Hereafter is even better."[27] Peace and good relations as the watch words of modern democracy, can exist only when the Islamic conception of the unity of mankind is realized. Love of humanity implies that glory lies not in the mere possession of power, but in the attainment of a noble ideal through the use of legitimate power. Government should not exist for the personal glory of one or many, but for the good of humanity.[28] A rational faith is, therefore, needed in a Divinely ordained organisation, which shall exist for a virtuous life. The spiritual basis of Islamic life is piety or righteousness, which consists in acting according to the law of Islam.

The Islamic state, as mentioned in the Holy Qur'ān, is established for the eradication of evils, promotion of virtues and implementation of social justice.

> "We sent aforetime Our apostles with clear signs and sent down with them the Book and the Balance (of right and wrong) that man may stand forth in justice. And we sent down *Hadid* (iron) in which is (material for) mighty war, as well as many benefits for mankind."[29]

Here the word *hadid* (iron) connotes the political power and function of the prophets is described as to establish justice. In other verses this object has more clearly been defined:

"(They are) those who, if we establish them in the land, will establish regular prayer and give regular charity, enjoin the right and forbid wrong."[30]

"You are the best of peoples, evolved for mankind, enjoining what is right, forbidding what is wrong and believing in Allāh."[31]

The Holy Qur'ān also declared that the obedience to Islamic state and its rulers is only after the obedience to Allāh and His Prophet (SAW) and subservient to both of them:

"O ye who believe! Obey Allāh and obey the Apostle, and those charged with authority among you. If ye differ in anything among yourselves, refer it to Allāh and His Apostle if ye do believe in Allāh and the Last Day."[32]

The Holy Prophet (SAW) has expressed and elucidated this principle in many of his *ahadith*. He said:

"A Muslim must listen to and obey the ruler whether he approves of what is ordered or abhors it, provided he is not ordered to sin. In that case, he should neither listen nor obey."[33]

"There is no obedience in sin. It is only in virtue."[34]

"You will be governed by people some of whose acts and commands would be virtuous and some others sinful. Then whoever expresses his open disapproval over the sinful acts will not be held responsible for them, and whosoever disapproves of them and dislikes them (at heart, although he does not express his disapproval in so many words) will also save his skin; but whosoever approves of them and follows them would be held responsible for them." The *Companions* asked: "When the days of such rulers come, should we not wge war against them?" The Prophet (SAW) said: "No! Not as long they offer *salah* (prayers)."[35]

According to this tradition the symbol of obedience to Allāh and His Prophet (SAW) is performance of prayers. If the rulers discard it also, then they step out of the basic loyalty to Allāh and it becomes permissible to strive to remove them.

The principle of responsible government was for the first time enunciated by Abū Bakr, when he said, "The strongest among you is weak, so long as I exact from him the due; and the weakest among you is strong so long as I do not restore to him his rightful claim. I am only a follower; obey me so long as I follow the truth, but if I go astray, set me aright."[38]

Islam was the first comprehensive code of life, which established a system of responsible government – a government in which both the ruler and the ruled are responsible before the Divine law: none can deviate from the right path. Under the paramountcy of Divine law, there developed a consultative procedure, whereby the ruler is to be aided by the few competent counsellors in determining the policy of government and in the execution of administrative responsibilities. The Caliph or the ruler in Islam is selected as a successor to the Holy Prophet (SAW), or the Caliphate as such means a representative government. Under such a system of government, political authority can only be exercised as a trust: the ruler is the trustee of the subjects and responsible to God for their welfare. Islam is thus, a representative government, a rule of law, a regime of trust and a governance by constitution.

The political ideal of Islam is to enable human beings to act together in the service of God as well as of one another and to build-up institutions by consent and consultation so as to encourage right conduct and justice.

## The Islamic Alternative

The Arabic term used for democracy in the writings of Muslim medieval philosophers are *al-madīnah al-jumā'iyyah* or jima 'iyyāh or still *al-jumma 'iyyah* all derived from the root *JMA*. It has been translated as "corporate association", "conglomerate city", *la cite' luxurious* and, in course, "democracy". It is tempting to try to find some relationship between the term *jumā'iyyah* and the Islamic notions of *Jama'ah* and ijmā'. If there is any relationship it does not go beyond the etymological connotations. As philosophers, the *falāsifah*, could not give any value or weight to the unexamined opinions of the *jamā'ah*. Neither Al-Fārābī nor Ibn Rushd has wavered in his position that the *jumhūr* or *al-'āmmah*, "the people of rhetoric" as Ibn Rushd calls them, are not to be entrusted with decisions regarding important opinions and convictions about ways of life, laws, and moral values, not to say of truth. At one place Al-Fārābī reveals his judgement of the *jamā'ah* "who blindly accept the same opinion and who defer to an *Imām*", and who do not reflect upon the opinions they hold. "To accept something in good faith and likewise to fail to investigate it, may mask (the truth), blind and lead (one) astray".

First impressions show that the *falasifah* were not exactly interested in addressing specifically Islamic political institutions such as *imjā'*, *shūrā*, elections or the like, or to make an independent inquiry into the foundations of the Muslim state, its origin and development. It should be pointed out, however, that Ibn Rushd applied Plato's analysis to the contemporary scene in the West which is entirely absent from al-Farabi's treatises. This may partially be explained by the fact that they were more interested in introducing Plato's political philosophy and in commenting on it than in investigating their own political systems. Another important reason is the tyranny of the rulers who were afraid that any such investigations would be dangerous. Just as theologians attacked philosophical studies that in their judgement tended to undermine the fundamental precepts of the *Shari'ah* so did rulers discourage scientific investigation of the principles of government lest it might undermine the foundations of their authority.

The term *shurā* the Qur'ānic alternative for democracy denotes consultation. The Qur'ān used the word to emphasise on the democratic spirit of Islamic polity which runs through its veins, its organs, institutions and associations. The word signifies that the political body is set up for consultation on any problem. The word *shura* is an act, an idea, a social technique and a political institution.

Prophet Muhammad (SAW) not only duly emphasized the importance and significance of *shurā* in Islamic polity but established the institution for consultation on religious, social, political and administrative problems. In fact, the Prophetic state was based on *shura*.

In Islam, Allāh alone is the *Mālik al-Mulk* (Master and Lord of all), and *Shāri'ah* constitutes the law of the land in an Islamic state. *Majlis al-Shūrā* as compared to parliament is neither sovereign nor omnipotent having a free hand in matters of legislation, taxation and expenditure without any limitations to its powers. It is not a product of various historical developments. It is, rather, the commandment of Allāh, revealed in the Holy Qur'ān to Prophet Muhammad (SAW) some fourteen hundred years ago, that matters of importance not clearly stated in the Holy Qur'ān and *Sunnah* should be decided through mutual consultation. The Holy Qur'ān says:

> Those who hearken to their Lord and establish regular prayer; who (conduct) their affairs by mutual consultation.[37]

*Al-Shūrā* in the above verse is described as the best characteristic of Muslims in collective affairs. It is stated just after the term *al-salāt* (the Muslim form of worship). *Al-salāt* is not only to worship Allāh, but is also practical demonstration of Muslim unity as *ummah wāhidah* (single community). It is to teach Muslims how to organize themselves. No nation or community can achieve its goal of happiness and peace unless it is well organized. It might be for this reason that Allāh made five times' *al-salat* obligatory on all Muslims, male and female. The *masjid* (mosque) is not only the center of worship, but also other community affairs used to be decided there through mutual consultation.

In *al-salāh*, the collective worship (like *salāh al-jamā'ah*) is given preference over individual worship (*salāh al-munfarid*). In fact the collective worship displays the real essence of Islam. It is to tell Muslims how to organize, and how to develop understanding, brotherhood and mutual cooperation. In collective worship, Muslims make straight lines on the basis of 'first come first' without any discrimination between the rich and poor, black and white, Arab and non-Arab. One who is distinguished in *'ilm* (knowledge) and *taqwā* (piety) is to be the *imam* (leader) of the worship. The *imām* is chosen from among those who are present of collective worship. Once he is chosen and leads the worship, the followers are bound to obey him during the worship as long as he follows the rules of *Shari'ah*.

In the above verse Allāh stated al-salāh and al-shūrā together. It seems that He wanted to teach the Muslims to organize themselves and conduct all their mundane affairs through *al-shūrā* as they do the same five times daily in collective worship. It might be for this reason that in the early period of Islam, *al-Shūrā* was conducted in the *masjid*. It is said about 'Umar, the second Khalifah, that whenever he wanted a meeting of the General Assembly (*Shūrā al-Nass*), he used to make an announcement of *salāh al-Jamā'ah* (*i.e.*, to assembly for collective worship). The people of Madinah would get together with this announcement in the al-Masjid al-Nabawī. They would offer two units of voluntary (*nafl*) prayers and then would discuss the problem.

The importance and compulsoriness of *al-Shūrā* is further known from the verse of the Holy Qur'ān where Allāh commanded the Prophet (SAW) to conduct his affairs through consultation. It says:

> And consult them in affairs (of moment) then, when thou hast taken a decision, put thy trust in God.[38]

It is said that this verse was revealed after the battle of Uhud. The Prophet (SAW) before the battle of Uhud, called *al-Shūrā* (the general Assembly) of the Muslims of Madinah as to how to face the enemy, whether to defend the city from inside or fight in the open field. Some prominent *Companions* and 'Abd Allāh b. Ubay, the leader of *Munāfiqūn* (hypocrites) suggested to stay in Madinah and defend the city. The Prophet (SAW) had the same opinion. But a number of the *Sahābah* (Companions) many of whom were young Muslims, favoured fighting in the open field. The Prophet (SAW) accepted the majority opinion and announced the decision of *al-Shūrā* for battling the enemy in the open field. Those Muslims who betrayed them in the battle of Uhud, the Prophet (SAW) stopped inviting them to *al-Shūrā* meetings thereafter. In the above verse, Allāh asked the Prophet (SAW) to invite them also to such meetings for He is one who is the most gentle and kind hearted. The Holy Qur'ān says in the beginning of the same verse.

> It is part of the Mercy of God that thou dost deal gently with them. Wert thou severe or harsh-hearted, they would have broken away from about thee.[30]

In addition to the two verses mentioned above, Shaykh Muhammad 'Abduh is of the opinion that there is an even stronger evidence stressing the mandate of the Shura than the one deducted from those verses. It is, according to him, in the Qur'ānic verse in the Chapter *Āl-i-'Imrān* which states:

> "Let there arise out of you a band of people inviting to all that is said, enjoining what is right, and forbidding what is wrong: They are the ones to attain felicity."[40]

He points out that the verse in the chapter *al-Shūrā* states that consultation as a characteristic is praised by Allāh and that the other verse in *Āl-i-'Imrān* requires the ruler to seek counsel. Continuing his argument he says: "But as there is no guarantee for his compliance with the matter, what would happen if he neglected it? This verse, however, establishes a mandate that there must exist among the people a strong and united group who call for good and for enjoining the right and forbidding wrong, which is a general mandate to be observed by both the rulers and the ruled. Hence, there is no right greater than justice and no wrong worse than tyranny."[41]

Islam, thus, in a period of disorder, persecution and religious intolerance, tyranny and oppression, emerged to better the condition of mankind and to provide a lasting way of life. With much truth Edward Gibbon remarks that the rise of Islam is "one of the most memorable revolutions which have impressed a lasting character on the nations of the globe." This memorable revolution Gibbon aptly describes as follows:

> "The creed of Muhammad (SAW) is free from suspicion or ambiguity; the Qur'ān is a glorious testimony to the unity of God. The Prophet (SAW) of Mecca rejected the worship of idols and men, of stars and planets on the rational principle that whatever raised must set, that whatever is born must die that whatever is corruptible must decay and perish. In the author of the universe his rational enthusiasm confessed and adored an infinite and eternal being, without form or place, without issue or similitude, present to our most secret thoughts, existing by the

> necessity of his own nature, and deriving from himself all moral and spiritual perfection. These sublime truths thus announced in the language of the Prophet (SAW), are firmly held by his disciples, and defined with metaphysical precision by the interpreters of the Qur'ān. A philosophic theist might subscribe (to) the popular creed of the Mohammedans; a creed sublime perhaps for our present faculties."[42]

The European Renaissance became possible due to its contact with Islam in Spain and during Crusades. The conquest of Palestine by the Crusaders brought Europe in contact with Islam. The Islamic Near East was then the centre of culture and civilization. From here, the treasures of Greek thought, which were preserved by Muslims together with other civilizing influences, were transmitted back to Europe via Italy. Referring to this event, Professor Arnold Toynbee writes,

> "Economically and culturally, conquered Islam took her savage conquerors captive and introduced the arts of civilization into the rustic life of Latin Christendom. In certain fields of activity, such as architecture, this Islamic influence pervaded the entire western world in its so-called 'medieval' age; and in the two permanently conquered territories of Sicily and Andalusia the Islamic influence upon the local western 'successor-states' of the Arab empire was naturally still more wide and deep.[43]

In Spain, the Muslims radiated the rays of enlightenment of the whole of Europe for about 780 years (710-1492 A.D.).

> "Muslim Spain", observes Prof. Hitti, "wrote one of the brightest chapters in the intellectual history of medieval Europe. Between the middle of the eighth and the beginning of the thirteenth century, as we have noted before, the Arabic speaking peoples were the main bearers of the torch of culture and civilization throughout the world. Moreover they were the medium through which ancient science and philosophy were recorded, supplemented and transmitted in such a way as to make possible the Renaissance of Western Europe. In all these Arabic Spain had a large share."[44]

This transmitting condition of the Muslim World corresponds to the basic and fundamental principles of Islam, *i.e.*, justice, *shura*, equality, freedom and brotherhood and the concepts of *tawhīd, risalāh* and *Akhirah*. These are quite different from the world view of the Greek and Western democracy. Both can not be identified with each other though there are some apparent similarities between them.[45]

*****

## NOTES AND REFERENCES

1. 'See for the study of these theorists: Maududi, S.A.A., *The Islamic Law and Constitution*, ed. Khurshid Ahmad, Lahore, 1955; Qutb, Syed, *Ma alim fi al-Tariq*, Cairo, - , *Al-'Adalah al-Ijtimāiyah fi al-Islam*, Cairo, n.d., Al-Ghazali, Muhammad, *Min Huna Nalam*, Cairo, -, *Our Beginning in Wisdom,* trans. I.E. al-Farooqui Washington, 1953; Farahi, Hamiduddin, *Fi Malakūt Allāh,* Azamgarh, 1391, A.H.; Ramadan, Said, *Islamic Law, Its Scope, Its Equity,* London, 1961.
2. For western thinking and approach see, Abd al-Raziq, Ali, *Al-Islam wa Usūl al-Hukm,* Cairo, 1924; Khalid Mohammad Khidr; (*Min Huna Nabda*) *From here We Start,* trans. I.R. al-Faruqi, Washington, 1953; al-Fasi, Allah, *Al-Nagd al-'dati*, Cairo, 1952; -, *Usūl al-Hukm fi al-Islam,* in al-Bayyinah, 1.1, Rabat, 1962; -, *Minhāj al-Istiqlāliyah,* Rabat, 1962.
3. For Oritnetalists' thinking see Gibb, H.A.R., *Modern trends in Islam,* Chicago, 1947;-, "The Search for an Islamic democracy", in *The Middle East in Transition,* ed. W.Z. Laqueur, London, 1958; *Studies on Civilization of Islam*, London, 1962; Rosenthal, E.I.J., *Islam in the Modern National State*, Cambridge, 1965; *Political Thought in Medieval Islam,* Cambridge, 1958; Watt, M., *Islamic Political Thought, The Basic Concepts*, Edinburgh, 1968; Piscatori, J.P., *Islam in a World of Nation-States,* Cambridge, 1986.
4. Watt, W.M., *Islamic Political Thought – The Basic Concepts, op.cit.,* pp. 121-122. For a sympathetic view see Mc Elory Paul Simpson, "Democracy in Islam", *The Muslim World,* Vol. 28, pp. 365-371.
5. El-Awa M.S., *On the Political System of the Islamic State*, Indiana, 1980, pp. 117-118. For the application of jurists' classical method on the contemporary political issues see Nadvi, Syed Sulaiman, *Seeratun Nabī*, Vol. VII, Azamgarh, 1987; Khandhlavi, Mohammad Idris, *Nizam Islam wa Dastur Islam*, Lahore 1387 A.H.
6. The Holy *Qur'ān*, XVI:90.
7. *Ibid.*, IV: 58.
8. *Ibid.*, V:9.
9. *Ibid.*, XXII:18.
10. *Ibid.*, XX:123-124
11. *Ibid.*, II:256.
12. *Ibid.*, XLIX:13.
13. *Ibid.*, XXVIII:4.
14. *Ibid.*, V:3.
15. *Ibid.*, XXVI:151-52.
16. *Ibid.*, XVIII:28.
17. See for details, Mutawalli, A. Hameed, *Mabādi Nizām al-Hukm fi al-Islām*, Alexandria, 1964, pp. 239-240; Uthman, A. Karim, *Al-Nizām al-Siyāsī fi al-Islām*, Beirut, 1968, p. 27.
18. *The Holy Qur'ān*, XVII:23-39.

19. Maududi, S.A.A., *The Islamic Law and Constitution*, pp. 189-191.
20. Quoted in Alattas, Hussein, *The Democracy of Islam*, The Hague and Bandung, 1956, p. 12.
21. G.H. Sabine (*A History of Political Theory*, New Delhi, 1973, p. 130) has well analysed this Greek political superiority. He said that the assumed political superiority of the Greeks over barbarians was not viable in the eastern Mediterranean, in view of the economic and cultural relations which had long existed between the Greek cities and the Asiatic hinterland. When Alexander deliberately adopted the policy of merging his Greek and oriental subjects – a policy which must have been flatly contradictory of all that Aristotle had taught him about policies – he was at once accepting a fact whose importance his teacher had missed and also taking a step which made his teacher's political presumptions definitely obsolete.
22. Alattas Hussein, *op.cit.*, p. 19.
23. Sabine, G.H., *op.cit.*, p. 7.
24. Miss Follett, *The New State*, 1918, quoted in Dunning W.R., *A History of Political Theories – Recent Times*, Allahabad, 1969, p. 65.
25. *Ibid.*, p. 79.
26. *The Holy Qur'ān*, XXXI:17.
27. *The Holy Qur'ān*, III:14, XVI: 30.
28. *The Holy Qur'ān*, IV:58; XLIX:13; II:247; XVIII:28.
29. *The Holy Qur'ān*, LVII:25.
30. *The Holy Qur'ān*, XXII:41.
31. *The Holy Qur'ān*, III:110.
32. *The Holy Qur'ān*, IV:59.
33. Bukhārī, *al-Jāmi' al-Sahīh*, Kitāb al-Janā'īz.
34. Muslim, *al-Jāmi' al-Sahīh*, Kitāb al-Imārah.
35. *Ibid.*
36. Safwat, A. Zaki, *Jamharah Khutab al-Arab,* Egypt, 1923, Vol. I, p. 67.
37. *The Holy Qur'ān*, XLII:38.
38. *The Holy Qur'ān*, III:159.
39. *Ibid.*
40. *The Holy Qur'ān*, III:104.
41. *Tafsīr al-Manār*, by Syed Muhammad Rashīd Ridā, al-Manar Edition, 1376, A.H., Vol. IV, p. 45.
42. Gibbon, E., *Decline and Fall of the Roman Empire,* An Abridgement by D.M. Low, London, 1960, p. 665.
43. Toynbee, Arnold, *Civilization on Trail*, Oxford, 1948, p. 185.
44. See for details, Hitti, P.K., *History of Arabs*, London, 1937, pp. 557-590. *The Arabs in Europe: Spain and Sicily.*
45. Dr. Zeenath Kausar (Political Development: Western and Islamic Perspectives", *The Islamic Quarterly*, London, Vol. XXX, No. 2, 1996, pp. 104-117) has advocated this view and the interpretation of the popular vicegerency of *Khilāfah* system in Islam as 'Islamic Democracy" has been criticized by the learned scholar. She has

advised her readers to avoid using this term and has emphasized upon the term '*ikhtiyār*' instead. The term '*ikhtiyār*' however, does not connote the total picture of Islamic system of government. In my opinion the term *shūrā* would be more appropriate to reflect the same.

*****

# 7

# ISLAMIC PLURALISM
## (Some conceptual Dimensions)

### THE *QUR'ĀNIC* GUIDELINES

This chapter aims to analyse the idea prevalent in the West and advocated by some Muslim scholars on Islam in general and on Islamic polity and revivalism in particular, that Islam being the harbinger of universal community which is obligated to order good and forbid wrong and to establish the religion through using all the means, has no room for any pluralistic society in its realm. The chapter further argues with some conceptual dimensions of Islamic pluralism in detail and emphasizes upon the comparison between Islamic *'Ahd* and *Shura* on the one side and western democracy on the other.

The classical and medieval theorists of Islamic polity are of the view that Islam is pre-eminently a religion of initiatives and concentrated upon the creation of a universal community based on the concept of *Ummah* far from all kinds of boundaries and barriers. The holy *Qur'ān* and the Prophetic traditions emphasize upon the need and desirability to fight against all kinds of oppressions, tyrannies, despotic methods and anarchic polytheists, monotheists, and hypocrites who are mischieving, perpetrators of dissension and are creating hindrance in the way of letting the people free to opt any religion or faith.

> "And fight them on until there is no more tumult or oppression and there prevail justice and faith in Allah", (Al-Baqrah 2:193).
> "And Tumult and oppression are worse than slaughter", (Al-Baqarah 2:191).
> "Then fight you all against the one who transgresses until he complies with the command of Allah," (Al-Hujurat 49:9).
> "But if they (hypocrites) turn renegades, seize them and slay them wherever you find them", (Al-Nisa 4:89).

Keeping these above quoted holy verses in view most of the writers on Islam namely orientalists categorize it 'uncompromising' and 'crusading' that is intolerant of the non-Muslims. It was this background in which Bernard Lewis declared that 'Foreign policy is a European concept' and 'is alien and new in the world if Islam'.[1] This is so because Islam emphasizes the division of the world into *dar al-Islam* and *dar al-harb*. The aim of Islamic world is to expand at the expense of the non-Islamic world and Muslims are obligated to resort to holy war to do this, as Lewis has claimed.

Rudolph Peters views that the traditional ideas have such a hold on Muslim intellectuals that any of their 'sweeping assertions about Islam recognizing the equality of all mankind and the reciprocity in inter-state relations amount to no more than gratuitous and non-committal slogans'.[2] James P. Piscatori, after describing all such statements with their arguments has found them very strong but their conclusion wrong and misleading because:

(a) The classical and medieval theory is not as simple and clear-cut as the views summarized above.

(b) The practice of Muslims over time indicates an overwhelming acceptance of the reality of (political) territorial pluralism, and today the consensus of action firmly on this side.[3]

The comments of Piscatori are true but incomplete. Declaring Islam from its teachings of waging war against tyranny or oppression as crusading and uncompromising one is consciously or unconsciously misleading and confusing. IF Islam is very much concerned with establishment of its system in all walks of life and in an ideological sense if the state is universal and all-embracing and 'its sphere of activity is co-extensive with the whole of human life' as Maududi has explained[4], how can it be categorized as intolerant and aggressive towards other cultures and religions? And how these statements are strong and convincing while Piscatori himself knows the complication and gravity of the case under discussion?

Islam is the final revealed religion. It is the divine guidance for mankind till the day of judgement in all circumstances. The holy *Qur'ān* also has the potential for establishing authentic socio-political pluralism. As such it provides for the healthy co-existence of religions, ethnic 2nd linguistic groups, cultures and civilization at national and global levels.

The holy *Qur'ān* vehemently condemns any coercion or compulsion in the matters of religion because it is incompatable with religion. The religion depends upon faith and free will and these would be meaningless if induced by force; and truth and falsehood have been so clearly shown up by the mercy of Allah that there should be no doubts in the minds of any person of good will as to the fundamentals of faith:

> "Let there be no compulsion in religion: Truth stands out clear from Error". (Al-Baqarah 2:256).

> "Say, "The Truth is from your Lord:" Let him who will believe, and let him who will reject it". (Al-Kanf 18:29).

> "Yet no faith will the greater part of mankind have, however ardently you do desire it". (Yusuf 12:103).

This chapter al-Kafirun clearly admits a plural approach to the matters of faith. In matters of faith Muslims must make no compromise, but there is no need to persecute or abuse anyone for his faith or belief. Faith is a matter of personal conviction and does not depend on worldly motives. Worship should depend on pure and sincere faith, but often does not: for motives of worldly gain, ancestral custom, social conventions or indicative instincts, or a lethargic instinct to shrink from enquiring into the real significance of solemn acts and the motives behind them, reduce a great deal of the world's worship to sin, selfishness, or futility. The Prophet (SAW) firmly resisted all appeals to worldly motives.

Islam allows different religions and varying cultures to flourish in the society under its protection:

> "Mankind was but one nation, but different later. Had it not been for a word that went forth before from your Lord, their difference would have been settled between them". (Yunus 10:19)

> "If Allah had so willed, succeeding generations would not have fought among each other, after clear signs had come to them but they chose to wrangle, some believing and others rejecting. If Allah had so willed, they would not have fought each other; but Allah fulfils His Plan". (Al-Baqarah 2:253).

The concept of *Tawhid* and equality requires establishment of the moral obligation of Muslims, individually and collectively, to fulfil their personal, national and international commitments. Numerous *Qur'ānic* verses urging Muslims to fulfil their agreements leave no doubt about the positive moral attitude of Islam in this sphere. It allows no room for double standards. A Muslim can find no refuge in the Islamic frame work of thought or in its principles and values to justify violation of agreements either by intention or by deliberate action.

> "O ye who believe ! Fulfil all obligations"[6]. (Al-Maidah 5:1).

Imam Sarakhsi has opted a unique stand in this regard. To him it is permissible for Muslims to take a truce agreement with a stronger enemy for the sake of gaining time and then break the agreement as soon as they are able to fight successfully against that enemy. This stand is taken on the ground that fighting against non-believers is a duty, and delaying it is similar to giving more time to a borrower to play later.[7] This stand, as Abdul Hamid A. Abu Sulayman examines, is the exception in Muslim jurisprudence, and in his opinion the analogy is a wrong one and the stand is clearly in violation of both the letter and the spirit of all the *Qur'ān ic* verses on the subject. Those same verses do not support static legalistic interpretation relating to the concrete circumstances concerning the Banu Qur'āyzah in conjunction with which *Qur'ān* (8:58) has revealed, as the standard for the interpretation and implementation of the concept of unilaterally withdrawing from or repudiating an agreement.[8]

The western writers like Piscatori and others admit the other view which is 'distinctly at odds with the one which focuses on jihad as an instrument of Islamic militancy and expansionism'. This alternative view, as he has categorized it, is 'of a tolerant non-violent Islam that accommodates itself to the reality of divisions and non-Muslim centres of power'. In this tolerant Islam, as he elaborates, the greater jihad is working for the good and against the evil; rather than relying primarily on the sword, the Muslim is to use his heart, tongue and hands for the good of his own and to build the just society. He is also convinced with the fact that fighting is enjoined in the cause of righteousness, but primarily for self-defense, and in order to protect the non-Muslim subjects, though jihad can take the form of holy war against polytheists, unbelievers, and hypocrites and rebels, and Muslims are required to end the fight if the enemy has the momentary advantage or withdraws from active hostilities. Piscatori agrees with this *Qur'ānic* injunction also that Muslims may conclude a treaty with the enemy; and as the Prophet (SAW) did, they are entitled to receive foreign delegations.[9]

## THE PROPHETIC MODEL

The noble Prophet (SAW) led an exemplary life in his dealing with the non-Muslims. Apart from those pagans and people of the Book, who were fully involved in all kinds of conspiracies against Islam and Muslims, the Prophet (SAW) developed an attitude of all-out war only against the Bedouins and their Qurayshi leadership in their opposition to Islam. This hostile attitude toward the 'savage' Arabs came about because Bedouins were considered to be in a stage of social development not capable of any human responsibility or orderly interaction. The 'savage' pagans, pursuing in many ways a barbaric course of behaviour and life, had to be forced to accept changes that were necessary to put them in the realm of human civilization and orderly social human interaction. A fundamental human change indeed was achieved when Islam introduced basic human rights as Arabia was subdued and started its historic journey of civilization under the banner of Islam.[10]

The Prophet (SAW) of Islam after the migration to Madinah and establishment of Islamic brotherhood therein, implemented the Kitab/Sahifah (constitution) which bound the whole populace, whether Muslim or non-Muslim, into a political and social organization. A careful study of the forty-seven articles of the constitution brings to light the real nature of the prophetic political dealing and his behaviour toward non-Muslim allies. In this constitution Muslim-Ansar and *Muhajirs*-were declared, as is evident from article 1,15 and 25, the only members of *Ummah*, for it was based on the bonds of religion.[11] The Jews of Madinah and their different clans, however, were treated as important allies in all the political and social issues confronting the society. Articles 2 to 11 dealt with blood-wits and ransom-important measures for social security in the tribal structure of the Arab. Each clan of the city was enjoined to pay blood-money as a unit. Articles 12 to 16 guaranteed social security to all the Medinese. All the same, all inhabitants of the city, Muslims, pagans and Jews, were under obligation to abide by the conditions laid down to achieve social security and peace as articles 16,17,21,22,40,41 and 47 unmistakably show. Articles 24 to 35 dealt with different clans of the Jews of Madinah and confirm their social customs and privileges while articles 36,37,38 and 46 dealt with their relationship with the Islamic state and enjoined mutual help and cooperation between them and the Muslims in all matters of common interests or involvement including war. Other articles such as 18,24,38 and 45, specifically mentioned that the Jews and the Muslims would help each other and jointly bear the expenses of war. The obligation to defend the city-state against external foe was squarely laid on all sections of the Madinese population in articles 39 and 44. since the greatest danger in Madinah was from the Quraysh, the people of Madinah were called upon in articles 20 and 43 not to give any help or protection to the Makkans in particular and to other enemies in general.[12]

A study of this constitution shows that the noble Prophet (SAW) duly recognized the Jews of Madinah and concluded with them a treaty including the social and political issues providing full freedom to their religion, customs and traditions as well.

Another revolutionary step in this regard was the treaty of Hudaybiyah conducted by the Prophet (SAW) with the pagans of Makkah in the year 6 A.H. This treaty, was a 'peace offensive' as Imran N. Hosein has rightly called it, that was initiated on the bases of principles to maintain peace and normalcy between the two parties. Article 3 of the treaty established a ten-year truce and article 4 secured self-passage through each other's territories for both the Muslims (for pilgrimage or trade) and the Quraysh for tade. In a choice between peace (even for a limited duration) and the continuation of war, the Prophet (SAW) chose peace. That is the basic and abiding significance of the treaty of Hudaybiah. It is also of immense significance that the Islamic proselytizing activity achieved its greatest successes during the short period of peace which followed the entry-into-force of the treaty. More people embraced Islam during the two years of peace which followed Hudaybiah than had done so during the entire previous period of the mission of the Prophet (SAW). The implication, from the Islamic theoretical standpoint, is clear. Provided that the Islamic state clearly manifests its resolve not to submit to aggression, and not to be intimidated by threats of aggressions, it is peace rather than war which is conducive to Islamic proselytization. This preference for peace also refutes the war held by scholars that jihad must be used as an offensive force for establishing Muslim control over territories occupied by non-Muslims. Muslim control over such a territory, it is felt, is the basic prerequisite for the eventual entry of its non-Muslim residents into Islam.

The duration of ten years for any treaty between Muslim and non-Muslim, has been considered by Majid Khadduri as the maximum period, because the law of Islam and the practice of the Prophet (SAW) allow only brief spans of peace and "in Islamic theory jihad is a permanent obligation upon the believers to be carried out by continuous process of warfare, psychological and political, even if not strictly military."[14]

It appears that Khadduri depended for this point on Imam Shafii's strict position[15] but ignored the equally authoritative opinion of Imam Abu hanifah. Ibn Qudamah quoted Abu Hanifah's argument on this point: "Since a peace treaty is a contract allowed for ten years then it is permissible to extend it in the same way as a contract (which has no such time restriction)... Muslims' interest can be served in peace more than in war.... The time period being specified in ten years means that it also applies to longer periods:.[16] Thus Imam Abu Hanifah's position is that since the treaty is a contract it can be negotiated without time-limits or on the basis of renewable time-periods.

It would very much appear that the essential sunnah in this matter was the 'peace offensive', and the duration of the treaty was a matter regulated by the exigencies of a situation which was subject to change from time to time and from place to place.[17]

The Prophet (SAW) of Islam concluded a treaty after the conquest of Makkah with the Christians of Najran. This treaty gives us an idea of the actual position of the non-Muslims in the Islamic state and it clearly demonstrates the plural nature of the religion of Islam. The document as quoted by the historians reads:

"This is the letter from Muhammad (SAW) the Prophet, the Messenger of God, to the people of Najran. To him belonged the decision upon them in respect of every fruit, yellow, white or black, and every slave, but he was gracious to them and felt (them) all that for the payment of 2000 suits (*hullah*) of clothes, namely, suits of sources (*awaqi*) of which a thousand are to be handed over each (year in ) Rajab (i) and a thousand in Safar (ii) each suit worth one ounce (*uqiyah*). Where these tribute suits exceed or fall short of the ounce, that is taken into account. Najran is to give lodging to my messengers for 20 days or less, but my messengers are not to be kept more than a month. It is obligatory for them to lend 30 coats of mail, 30 horses, and 30 camels if there is war (*kayd*) in the Yemen. Whatever is destroyed of the coats of mail or horses or camels they lend my messengers is guaranteed by my messengers until thy repay it. Najran and their followers have protection (*jiwar*) of God and the *dhimmah* of Muhammad the prophet, the Messenger of God, for themselves, their community, their land and their goods, both those who are absent and those who are present, and for their churches and services (no bishop will be moved from his episcopate, and no monk from his monastic position, and no church-warship) and for all, great or little, that is under their hands. There is no usury, and no blood-revenge from pre-Islamic times. If any of them asks for a right, justice is among them (in their own lands) (to see that they are) not doing wrong and not suffering wrong, it belongs to Najran. If any one takes usury after this, my *dhimmah* is free from (responsibility for) him. No one of them is punished for the wrong-doing of another. On the terms stated in this document (they have) protection (*Jiwar*) of God and *dhimmah* of the prophet for ever, until God comes with His command, if they are loyal and perform their obligation well, not being burdened by wrong..."(18

This document needs no explanation, for it sheds light on the position of Christian non-Muslim in, and their obligations to, the Islamic state very clearly. The Christians of Najran were guaranteed full rights and were exempted from the Islamic obligations.

Piscatori after a lengthy discussion on conceptualizing the territorial and political plurality of Islam has provided numerous examples from the life of the prophet, from Umayyads and Abbasids, from the crusades, Ottoman Persian and other experiences in detail, and has concluded that if they did not exactly concede that the western states were their equals, the Muslim states did regularly enter into territorial and political', with them and concluded peace, even 'peace in perpetuity' with them. The Muslim practice in the history put a full stop to the earlier debate among Muslim jurists as the valid length of a peace treaty between Muslims and non-Muslims".[19]

## The Classical Concept Of '*Ahd* And Modern Democracy

A host of terms in the Arabic language commonly mean agreement or treaty: *ahd* (pledge) *hudnah* or *muwada'ah* (truce),*mu'ahadah* (treaty), *mithaq* (covenant or pact), *sulh* (peach treaty), and *hilf* (alliance) are a few examples.

Legally speaking , '*ahd* indicates consent on lawful matters and the obligation to fulfil the terms of a contract by the respective parties, Jurists advise termination of the '*ahd* either in case of breach of agreement and unilateral renunciation by the other party and / or in case the terms of agreement are known to violate *al-shar*' (lawful standard ). The content of the agreement and the concerned juristical school determine the legality or illegality of the '*ahd* in question. For example, if the political authority concluded a truce for more than ten years, there would be no automatic juristic fiat concerning its legality. While Shafi'i would invalidate it for the extra period beyond ten years, others such as Hanafi jurists, would disagree with this opinion. The act of pronouncing the renunciation of the agreement on the Muslim side is called *nabdh*. Muslim jurists do not agree to any unilateral renunciation of the *'ahd* on the part of the Muslims merely on the basis of suspecting that the other party will breach the *'ahd*. Such an action has to be based on a clear case of breach of agreement. With the exception of the Hanafi school, jurists do not approve of Muslims initiating the breach of any lawful agreement. If the other party did breach the agreement, with or without being aware of its act, the Muslim party has to inform the other party of the termination of the agreement on the part of the Muslims except if the other party attacks the Muslims first.

Because of their attitude toward jihad as a means of spreading Islam, some Hanafis would advise the political authority to renounce a truce unilaterally whenever circumstances change to the Muslims favour. Since they believe that the interest of Islam is best served by undertaking jihad, it behoves the Imam, as circumstances change, to renounce the truce unilaterally. Other jurists, however, do not agree with this interpretation of *nabdh* because it constitutes a breach of an agreement. To them, Muslims interest is a consideration at the time of concluding the agreement but not after that. The *'ahd* was a major diplomatic vehicle in foreign affairs such as peace agreements. Along with *aman* (safe conduct or pledge of security) and *dhimmah*, the *'ahd* was also used to facilitate political, cultural, and social communications as well as regulate trade with non-Muslim peoples and territories.[20]

The classical concept of *'ahd* dealing with the non-Muslims in political, social and commercial affairs may be applied to the modern concept of democracy with certain reservations and essential conditions in terms of the worldview and values. The modern scholars of Islam, Sayyid Abul Ala Maududi, Muhammad Asad, Mazharuddin Siddiqui, Mohd. Salim El-Awa, Dr. Hasan Turabi, Fatima Mernissi, Khurshid Ahmad, Ibrahim

Abu Rabi, John L. Esposito and John O. Voll to name a few, have compared the western democracy with Islamic system of politics. A number of scholars like Tawfiq al-Shawi, Dr. Qahtan Abdur Rahman al-Dawri, Dr. Jamaluddin al-Ramadi, Dr. Yaqub al-Malliji, Dr. Abdul Hamid Mutawalli, Abdur Rahman Abdul Khaliq, Dr. Mahmood al-Babilly, Dr. Uthman Khalil, Maulana Sayyid Jalauddin Umali, Maulana Abdur Rahman Kilani, Maulana Hamid al-Ansari Ghazi and others have viewed Islamic *Shura* as more competent, fruitful and feasible than western democracy and have declared both as the two poles apart.

Islamic state is different from a secular democracy as it is diametrically opposed to the concept of the sovereignty of the people. Allah is the supreme Law-Giver and Shariah is the law of the land. Within the framework of the Shariah new problems are faced and their solution worked out. This represents the cardinal difference between the two. As for as the principles of rule of law, protection of fundamental rights, independence of the judiciary, the right of minorities and choice of policies and rules in accord with the wishes of the people are concerned, Islam ensures them within its own frame work.

The individual is the corner stone of society, which insures his freedom, rule of law and respect for opposition. The people and the press are free to discuss and resolve problems through Shura. The Islamic state and society are concerned with all the physical and worldly problems of justice and social well being. The entire domain of the temporal world is the concern of Islam and the Muslims. Yet the Islamic and secular approaches are fundamentally different. Islam accepts multiplicity of cultures and community lifestyles. Islam is at war with secularism with respect to its claim to solve all human problems without reference to religion, Divine guidance and absolute moral values. On that account Islam and secular democracy represent two worlds apart.[21] Secularization is defined as the deliverance of man "first from religious and then from metaphysical control over his reason and his language"[22]. It is the loosing of the world from religious and quasi-religious understandings of itself, the dispelling of all closed worldviews, the breaking of all supernatural myths and sacred symbol... the defatalization of history, the discovery by man that he has been left with the worlds on his hands, that he can no longer blame fortune or the furies for what he does with it...; (it is) man turning his attention away from worlds beyond and towards this world and this time[23]. Secularization encompasses not only the political and social aspects of life, but also inevitably the cultural, for it denotes "the disappearance of religious determination of the symbol of cultural integration".[24] It implies "a historical process, almost certainly irreversible, in which society and the culture are delivered from tutelage to religious control and closed metaphysical worldviews"[25]. It is a "liberating development" and the end product of secularization is historical relativism.[26] Hence according to them history is a process of secularization.[27] The integral components in the dimensions of secularization are the disenchantment of nature, the desecration of politics and the deconsecration of values.[28]

Sayyid Muhammad Naqib al-Attas while discussing the history of secularism and secularization in detail, has argued that secularization is the result of misapplication of Greek philosophy in western theology and metaphysic, which in the 17th century logically led to the scientific revolution enunciated by Descartes, who opened the doors to doubt and scepticism, and atheism and agnosticism to utilitarianism, dialectical materialism evolutionism and historicism"[29]. To Attas, "Islam totally or secularism, as they do not belong and are alien to it in every respect; and they belong and are natural only to the intellectual history of western Christian religious experience and consciousness. We do not, unlike western Christianity, lean heavily on theological and metaphysical support of the theories of secular philosophers, metaphysicians, linguistics and other scholars, most of whom, if not all, did not even practice the religious life, who knew not nor believed in religion without doubt and vacillation; who were sceptics, agnostics, atheists, and doubters all".[30]

After a careful study of the basic trends in the development of secular democracy and of its political, social and human implications and after a survey of western philosophy and thought, one may conclude that secular western democracy, as

Khurshid Ahmad views, has its own distinct ethos, and its indiscriminate export to other parts of the world can not lead to the establishment of a stable, truly democratic and just political order. The Muslim *Ummah*, therefore, must not follow blindly any of the western models; instead, they should draw upon their own ideological and historical sources and establish institutions that represent their own values and ideals.[31]

Islam-the final revealed religion based on the principles of popular vicegerency (*istikhlaf*), consultation in all walks of life (*Shura*), justice and equity (*adl*), rule of law and equality to all, respect for human rights and contractual obligations, separation of judiciary from executive is a religion very unique. It focuses on humans, their souls and personalities. It concentrates on *Tazkiyah* (purification). The change comes first from within. The society developed by individuals here is ideological, norm-based, permeated with *rabbaniyyah* (Godliness), and *Ihsan* (excellence). Equality, brotherhood, mutual help, social responsibility and justice for all are the salient features of this society. There is no place for any arbitrary power in Islam. Despotic system of governance is not allowed and any totalitarian approach is not approved. The entire corpus of Muslim law in the history has been developed through a rational, democratic and popular process, in which all concerned participate through debate, dialogue and discussion. The entire legal system evolved outside the corridors of political power, and once established, the rulers were as much subject to this law as were common people. This has worked as a great check on arbitrary power and has entrenched the true credentials of participatory democracy in Muslim society.[32] John L. Esposito and John O. Voll accept this unique feature of Islamic history: "In the long-standing concept of oriental despotism, there is no sense of a separation of power or structure limiting the power of ruler. However, such unlimited power was not available to leaders in classical Muslim societies and this situation is visible both in Islamic law of political structures and in actual historical experience... It was the consensus of those scholars and not the commands and rules of the caliphs that provided the basis for formal Islamic law. No ruler was recognized as being above the law and all rulers would be judged by that law".[33]

Against this totalitarian and despotic approach Islam and western democracy are no more incompatible. Islam too advocates people's participation and power-sharing. Here the democratization in the sense of freedom of the people, fundamental rights and mass participation are natural corollaries. Islam, through its system of *shura* desires to maintain the same in the framework of its own values and principles.

## Voices of Democracy, Pluralism and Development

Islamic process of democratization, its basic values for pluralism and development are now advocated by the Muslim intellectuals, activists and the politicians. The Islamists desire to conduct the cultural and civilizational dialogue. They are, however, aware of the shortcomings of western-style development and secular democracy. They advocate the modern trends in Islamic terms and perform *ijtihad* in order to prove the Islamic compatibility with the modern experiences. Active as intellectual and leader of Jamaat-e-Islami Pakistan, Professor Khurshid Ahmad, the Islamic activist Rashid Ghannushi who was sentenced to eleven year's imprisonment in 1981 and was released in 1984 and since 1990s living in Europe as a political exile; and the politician and revivalist Anwar Ibrahim, former deputy prime minister of Malaysia are very important personalities of the Muslim world who are playing crucial role in defining and reformulating the Islamic concept in the contemporary world.

## Rashid al-Ghannushi

The Tunisian Islamic thinker and activist Rashid al-Ghannushi redefines a Muslim plural society in the light of the *Qur'ānic* notions and historical precendents.[34] He shapes the Islamic government as the one in which supreme legislative authority is for the Shariah which transcends all the laws; and in which political power belongs to the *Ummah* which should adopt a form of *shura* which is a system of mandatory consultation It is incumbent upon the community of the faithful to avoid passivism and isolationism. He further argues that every Muslim has a responsibility toward the task of establishing the Islamic government and if it is impossible then Muslims must endeavour to accomplish whatever can be accomplished.

According to Ghannushi, power-sharing in a Muslim or non-Muslim environment becomes a necessity in order to lay the foundations of the social order. "This power-sharing", as he talks in his unique way, may not necessarily be based on Islamic Shariah Law. However, it must be based on an important foundation of *Ummah* (community) so as to prevent the evils of dictatorship, sharing inlay also aim to achieve a national or a humanistic interest such as independence, development, social solidarity, civil liberties, human rights, political pluralism, independence of the judiciary, freedom of the press, or liberty of mosques and Islamic activities,"[35] as he independently of the majority' views, theorizes.

Can any Muslim community afford to hesitate in participating in the establishment of a secular democratic system if it is unable to establish an Islamic democratic one? Ghannushi answers; no'. It is the religious duty of the Muslims, as individuals and as communities, to contribute to the efforts to establish such a system. In this way, he explains, the Muslims would seek the establishment of the government of rationale due to their inability to establish the government of Shariah as Ibn Khaldun puts it.

Ghannushi while theorizing the Muslim participation in a non-Islamic government, has referred several documented cases from the *Qur'ān* and the Islamic history. The *Qur'ān ic* chapter Yusuf provides a detailed account of the Prophet Yousuf who was imprisoned and mistreated, yet he seized the moment when it was right and expressed readiness to take the charge of the most important office in the Pharaoh's government, believing it was his duty to rescue many nations that were threatened by famine and drought. "He did not wait for the Egyptian people to renounce paganism and embrace his Unitarian religion so as to form the foundation of an Islamic government," he elaborates the case in his favour.[36]

The next example is that of the Negus (the Emperor of Ethiopia) who lived during the early years of Islam. The Prophet advised some of his companions who were being severely persecuted to migrate to Abyssinia describing the Negus as "the King in whose country none is wronged." The presence of the small Muslim community in Abyssinia resulted in the Negus embracing Islam, although he did not effect any amendments to his government in the direction of implementing the Shariah, as such an attempt could have threatened his Kingship and endangered the lives of his guests. The Prophet instructed his followers to perform a prayer for the King's soul when the news of his death reached them.[37]

The third example is that of *hilf al-fud ul.* It was an agreement among several pre-Islamic Arab tribes to support the wronged, maintain close relations with relatives and take good care of them. The Prophet did witness the signing of the alliance prior to his prophethood, and said afterwards that if he were to be invited to a similar alliance in Islam he would have accepted without reservation. He further stressed that any good and noble contract made in Jahiliyah is automatically endorsed by Islam. It is thus concluded, Ghannushi says, that the Muslim Community may participate in an alliance aimed at preventing injustice and oppression, at serving the interests of mankind, at protecting human rights, at recognising the authority of the people and at rotating power-holding through a system of elections.

The fourth example that Ghannushi has quoted is that of Omar bin Abul Aziz who is considered as the fifth rightly guided caliph (al-Khalifah al-Rāshid). Although he was a king who inherited kingship, he was unhappy with the monarchy, and in principle did not approve of it. However, he could not alter the system and was unable to restore the right of the *Ummah e.g.* consultative style government due to the accumulation of corruption over the years. Nonetheless, he managed to significantly reform many bad practices and restore justice and fairness through the institution which he himself did not approve of. No one said that he was wrong or misguided in his actions.

Ghannushi discusses in detail the contemporary considerations also and the issues of Muslim minority in a secular state; the conflict between the Islamic movements and the Muslim dictators in power; the possibility of mobilizing the Muslim masses through elections in favour of Islamic changes; and joining a national front against the colonizers were taken into account by him to prove his thesis. It should, however, be emphasized that the problem facing the concept of 'power-sharing' does not lie in the difficulty of convincing the Islamists to accept democracy, pluralism and power-sharing. The problem, he argues, lies in convincing the 'other' that is the ruling regime, of the principle of people's sovereignty and of the right of Islamists – just like other political groups – to form political parties, engage in political activities and compete for power or share in power through democratic means.[38]

## Khurshid Ahmad

Islam's compatibility with modern democratization process is thoroughly examined by Professor Khurshid Ahmad in its proper context. He is fully convinced with the *Shura* system of Islam evolved in Islamic history according to the *Quran*ic perceptions and Prophetic practices especially under the four caliphs. Islam has created a new concept of human vicegerency (*Khilāfah*) based mainly upon the consent of the people. It is not specifically confined to any particular group, clan or clergy. The revealed law provides its jurisdiction and is accommodative and flexible in what is called permissible (*mabāh*). The right to explain and interpret the Book of Alah may be exercised by everyone who has the deep knowledge and ability of understanding and interpreting it. In the jurisdiction of the legal system of Islam the door of *ijtihād* (individual opinion) is always open.

Professor Ahmad is in no mood to sanction the power of authority on the basis of any religious post; all the individuals of a society have the right, rather an obligation to assign the power and rule only to those who receive full support and consent; the political leadership is responsible to God and the people directly. In the political system of Islam the law always prevails in all the circumstances and ensures the fundamental rights to all its citizens including the minorities. In this process the democratic procedure receives the central place. Prof. Ahmad is strongly opposed to see the political objectives and ideals of Islam in the altitude and behaviour of the contemporary Muslim governments though these claim to be 'Islamic'. So many democrats in the modern world are not fulfilling the basic requirements of democracy; this deviation is not to be treated as the failure of democracy itself, he further suggests.[39]

The scholar examines the 'Islamophobia' of the West and assures no danger or threat to the west from the side of the Muslims or the revival of Islam. There is no possibility the Muslims would have violently attacked or posed any threat to the political order of the west. Muslims are trying to settle their internal affairs. They desire only to lead their lives both the individual and collective according to their concepts and values. The revivalist movements in the contemporary world are not allergic to the requirements of science and technology, nor are those opposed to the modernization; these advocate the material progress and modernization but only in the perspective of their culture and values. They explicitly condemn the imposition of the western culture and values openly or secretly upon a nation of a magnificent culture and civilization.[40]

Professor Ahmad is very much vocal in maintaining the Muslim identity at any cost. He advised the Muslims to avoid conflict and to aim mainly the correction at home, the depth in knowledge both the religious and scientific, the unity among the *Ummah*, the improvement of their resources and the furtherance of their power and ability. The Muslims, according to him, neither should live in isolation nor should rely heavily on others. A search in the common points and upon these the maintenance of relations is need of the time. Instead of fighting in the battle fields chosen by others, Muslims must move ahead and create a consensus among the nations on the following five points which may provide a nucleus for the global *dawah* mission of Islam:

i) freedom of all the nations, their sovereignty and security as provided by the U.N. charter. Islam offered the same principle of humanity. It eliminates the roots of colonialism and imperialism;

ii) the pluralism based on the hegemony of a single culture civilization or the country is the greatest danger to the world peace. Everyone must recognize that, each nation has full right to maintain its culture and that the forced or forged uniformity is against the nature and contradictory to the requirements of justice;

iii) all the human affairs must be resolved through dialogue and the use of violence must be subordinated to the law and global justice; against every kind of violence, global mobilization be made and terrorism in all the forms be discouraged;

iv) for the sake of acquiring equity and justice all the peoples and nations must be attached willingly with an international just order. Justice in the only constructive base on which the world peace may be achieved and

v) the respect for the collective self-reliance principle and the regard for a global network under which may come into existence such global institutions that provide to poor the full security from all kinds of exploitations.[41]

The learned scholar suggests honestly the Muslims to keep in mind always their position of the 'the moderate people' created for the implementation of justice, furtherance of good, deliverance from the evil and the testification of the divine message through the deed and behaviour' (The *Qur'ān* 2:143). Has any politics of violence or terrorism entrenched in this *Ummah*, it is surely incompatible with its mission and spirit and appears an ugly spot on its original character. Professor Ahmad explicitly declares that in all the individual and collective spheres Islam condemns the violence, compulsion and terrorism and promotes the love, brotherhood, tolerance, coordination and cooperation wholeheartedly. The objective of jihad, he asserts, is fulfilled through the establishment of justice and the assurance of freedom, dignity, equity and respect to all the people. The jihad in all its forms be it against oneself (*bi al-nafs*) through the tongue and pen, wealth or resource or actual fighting (*qital*) – is bound to its clear moral limitations and objectives; the teaching and propagation of these is incumbent in order to be understood properly and benefited equally by the Muslims and non-Muslims. The true perception of Jihad was to be necessarily understood and taken into full considerations in all the ages and phases of the history. Today in the given situation when the jihad is being defamed and equated with the use of violence and terrorism, the teaching and full consideration of Jihad and its holy requirements and conditions is needed more. Professor Ahmad appreciates the role of the Islamic movements in this field. These movements have revived the concept and spirit of Jihad on the one side, and concentrated on its original character by defining its objectives and mechanism and maintaining its sanctity on the other, as he analysis.[42]

Islam and the Muslim *Ummah* brook no sympathy for arbitrary and authoritarian rule, the scholar explicitly declares. Whatever arbitrary power reigns is a product of colonization and westernization, and not of Muslim ideals, history or contemporary aspirations. They regard the western secular version of democracy as alien to their principles, values and traditions. But they have their own concept and rich tradition of democracy and people's participation that ensures just rule, consultative processes at all levels respect for rights and dissent, the independence of judiciary and politico-cultural pluralism. Professor Ahmad criticizes that whatever despotic or arbitrary rule exists in the Muslim lands is part of an alien and imposed tradition against which the forces of Islamic resurgence are struggling. Islam and true democratization are two sides of the same coin. As such democratic processes and Islam would go hand in hand. The rise and rule of despotisms – civil or military, elected or hereditary – responsible for the negation of democracy and usurpation of fundamental freedom are fruits of westernization and secularization, and not of Islam.. Democratization is bound to be a stepping stone to Islamization. The fulfilment of Islamic aspirations would become possible only through the promotion of democratic process, as he very rationally argues.[43]

## Anwar Ibrahim

He joined the government of Prime Minister Mahathir Muhammad in 1980 and proved himself successful in both worlds, rapidly evolving from a charismatic opposition leader to deputy Prime Minister and Finance Minister. He worked effectively with diverse political forces and navigated Malaysia's complex multi-religious and multiethnic society. He had impressed many at home and abroad with his ability to bridge religions and cultures and to work effectively to achieve common goals. Eighteen years later in 1998 he was tried and convicted on politically inspired charges, an action condemned internationally by many political and religious leaders and human rights organizations. He was released in 2005 on certain political conditions by the Badawi government and now he is engaged in teaching profession in the universities of John Hopkins and Oxford in Great Britain. He is considered a significant voice on issues of socio-political and economic development, advocating pluralism in multi-religious societies and inter-civilizational dialogue as the only alternative to a deadly clash of civilizations.[44]

Anwar Ibrahim believes that both Marxism and the West and their models for secular materialism failed because Marxism "severs man from his moorings in faith... There was no place for ethics, morality or spirituality" and the west also rejects "any reference to moral and ethical considerations, Cultural preservation."[45]

Pluralism and tolerance based upon mutual respect and understanding are corner-stones of Anwar Ibrahim's vision of a civilizational dialogue or *convivencia* that has deep roots in medieval Islamic history.[46] He finds the roots of *convivecia* supported in the *Qur'ān* also as illustrated by verse:

> O mankind! Verily We have created you all from a male and a female, and have made you into nations and tribes that you may come to know one another. (49: 13)

This Islamic form of pluralism is based on the primacy of social and economic justice and equality, recognized as fundamental to all the religions. He says:

> For us the divine imperative as expressed in the *Qur'ān* is unambiguous. Humanity has been created to form tribes, races and nations, whose differences in physical characteristics, Languages and models of thought are but the means for the purpose of lita'arafu – getting to know one another.[47]

It is important to note that while stressing that *convivencia* is a necessity for progress, he firmly argues that it must be an encounter among equals.[48]

In an interview to M. Sajid in New Delhi, Anwar Ibrahim emphasized upon the key role to be played by Indians in the Asian region. He accepted *hindutva* and nationalistic politics of communal Hindus as major obstacles in the way of progress and development. He, however, appreciated the democratic set up of the country. He said that Indian plural – society seems to be based on coordination and mutual cooperation. India through Hindu-Muslim participation in the politics and administration jointly may play a leading role in Asia; for that a strong political will is needed. This pluralism does not mean that individuals would have lost their identity. Giving his own example, Anwar Ibrahim said that he is a practicing Muslim yet he advocates the pluralism. Both the Muslim and non-Muslim populace of Malaysia studies the religious books of one another and has its separate identity also. No politics of any country would be allowed to intensify the gap between the two communities; any violation of human rights is not allowed, he explicitly said. When he was asked whether he had any lenient attitude towards America, Anwar Ibrahim responded in a categorical 'no'. He at the same time argued that apart from America 'others' also are not just. Saddam Husain of Iraq was also anti-America but how did he behave with his people? Several other countries also are severe critique of America but these use all the undemocratic illegal and unconstitutional means to suppress their people and to strengthen their authoritative rule over their citizens; then their criticism against America remains futile and meaningless, Anwar Ibrahim unhesitatingly reacted.[49]

## Conclusion

i) Islamic pluralism as a permanent feature of Islamic political thought has been very clearly designed and articulated in the Islamic texts as well as in the Muslim experiences throughout the history. Religious tolerance, human dignity, equal treatment to all the sections of the society, and respect to the fundamental rights are main features of this phenomenon.

ii) Juristic interpretations of the term *'Ahd* and the connotations of *Shura* in the *Qur'ān* and *Sunnah* may be applied on pluralism in general and democratization in particular within the framework of Islamic *Shari'ah*.

iii) Islamic pluralism should always be ascertained in its paradigm, in its cultural and civilizational perspective and along with the background of its worldview and system of belief and action in total.

*****

# NOTES AND REFERENCES

1. Bernard Lewis, *The Middle East and the West*, Harper Row, New York, 1964. p. 115. Writing in 1932, Robert Montagone similarly concluded that the nation state and plural society are totally alien and a heretical innovation. *Foreign Affairs,* 30, July, 1932, p. 580.
2. Peters, *Islam and Colonialism*: *The Doctrine of Jihad in Modern History*, p. 140. Adda. B. Bozeman (Iran: US Foreign Policy and the Tradition of Persian Statecraft, *Orbis*, 23, Summer 1979 p. 389) too has studied Islam as inimical to the core idea of the state', and has declared it true in the case of Middle East where communities of believers or freely floating sects unconfined by spatial bounds have been the norm.
3. Piscatori, James P., *Islam in a World a Nation-States,* Cambridge, 1986, p. 45.
4. Mawdudi, Abul Ala, *Political Theory of Islam*, ed. By Khurshid Ahmad, Islamic Publications, Lahore, 1960, p. 26.
5. Explaining this holy verse while emphasizing on the conscious and willing submission to Allah, Syed Muhammad Al-Naqib Al-Attas, very nicely argues that in religion there should be no compulsion not only in the sense that, in the act of subjugating to religion and submitting to it, one must not compel others to submit; but in the sense that even with oneself, one must subjugate and submit oneself wholeheartedly and willingly, and love and enjoy the submission. Unwilling submission betrays arrogance, disobedience, and rebellion, and is tantamount to misbelieve, which is one of the forms of unbelief (*Kufr*), it is mistake to think belief in one God alone is sufficient in true religion, and that such belief guarantees security and salvation. Iblis (*satan*), who believes in one true God and knows and acknowledges Him as his Creator, Cherisher, and Sustainer, his rabb, is nevertheless a misbehaviour (*kafir*). Although Iblis submits to God, yet he submits grudgingly and insolently, and his *Kufr* is due to arrogance, disobedience and rebellion. He is the most notorious example of unwilling submission. Unwilling submission, then, is not the mark of true belief, and a *Kafir* might therefore be also one who, though professing belief in one God, does not submit in real submission, but prefers instead to submit in his own obstinate way-a way, or manner, or form neither approved nor revealed and commanded by God. Real submission is that which has been perfected by the holy Prophet (SAW) as the model for mankind, for that is the manner of submission of all the Prophets and Messengers before him, and the form approved, revealed and commanded by God. Thus, the fundamentally, the submission; for the submission confirms and affirms the belief to be true and genuine. *Islam and Secularism*, Kuala Lumpur, 1976, p. 61. Foot note No. 67.

6. To Abdullah Yusuf Ali, the word *'Uqud* implies so many things first, these are the divine obligations that arise from our spiritual nature and our relation to Allah. He created us and implanted in us the faculty of knowledge and foresight; besides the intuition and reason which he gave us, he made nature responsive to our needs, and his signs in nature are so many lessons to us in our own inner life; He further sent Messengers and teachers, for the guidance of our conduct in individual, social and public life. All these gifts create corresponding obligations, which we must fulfil. But in our own human and material we undertake mutual obligations express and implied. We make a promise; we enter into a commercial or social contract; we enter into a contract or marriage: we must faithfully fulfil all obligations in all these relationships. Our group of state enters into a treaty: every individual in that group or state is bound to see that as far as lies in his power, such obligations are faithfully discharged. These are tacit obligations: living in civil society, we must respect its tacit conventions unless they are morally wrong, and in that case we must get out of such society. There are tacit obligations in the character of host and guest, wayfarer of companion, employer or employed etc., etc. which every man of faith must discharge consciously. The man who deserts those who need him and goes to pray in a desert is a coward who disregards his obligations. All these obligations are inter-connected. Truth and fidelity are parts of religion in all relations of life. *The Holy Qur'ān - Text, Translation and Commentary,* Amana Corporation, USA, 1989, p. 243, Note No. 682.
7. Al-Shaybani, Muhammad bin al-Hasan, *Sharh al-Siyar al-Kabir*, dictation of Muhammad Ahmad al-Sarakhsi, ed. Salah al-Munajjid, Cairo, 1958. Vol. 1 pp. 190-191.
8. Abu Sulayman, A. Abdul Hamid, *The Islamic Theory of International Relations: New Directions for Islamic Methodology and Thought*, Herndon, 1987, pp. 1214-125.
9. Piscatori, *op. cit.*, pp. 45-46.
10. Abu Sulayman, A. Abdul Hamid, *op. cit.*, pp. 38-39.
11. Welhausen, on the contrary, perhaps for the first time claimed that non-Muslims, the Jews and the pagans of Madinah were not excluded from the 'Ummah'. The Ummah, as he wrote, embraces a wide area- the whole precincts of Madinah are to be a district of inviolable peace. There are still heathen among the Ansar, and they are not excluded, but expressly included. The Jews are also included, though they have not so close a connection with the Umma as the Muhajira and the Ansar, and have not exactly the same rights and obligations". *The Arab Kingdom and Its Fall*, London, 1973, pp. 11-12. See also Watt, W.M., *Muhammad at Madina*, Oxford, 1956, pp. 225-26 and 241-242. Sayyid Abul Ala Maududi (Islamic Way of Life: Delhi, 1967. p. 17 ff.) and Prof. Muhammad Yasin Mazhar Siddiqui (Organization of Government Under the Prophet, Delhi, 1987, pp. 10-12) have

criticized the statement and proved it as against the words and spirit of the document and as contradictory to the Quranic perception of *Ummah*. See also Akram Diya al Umari, *Madinan Society at the Time of the Prophet*: Its Characteristics and Organization, Vol. I, translated by Huda Khattab, Herndon, 1991, pp. 99-122.

12. Siddiqui, M.Y.M., *Organization of Government under the Prophet*, *op.cit.*, pp. 10-15.
13. Hosein, Imran N., Diplomacy in Islam: Treaties and Agreements – An Analysis of the Treaty of Hudaibiyah, *Muslim Education Quarterly*, Vol. 3, No. 3., 1986. p. 67.
14. Khadduri, Majid, "Introduction" to al-Shaybani, *The Islamic Law of Nations*, Baltimore, 1966, pp. 16-17.
15. Al-Shafii, Abu Abdullah Muhammad bin Idris, *Kitab al-Umm*, Cairo, 1903, Vol. IV, p. 109.
16. Ibn Qudamah, Al-Mughni, Cairo, Vol. IX, p. 286.
17. See for the diplomatic missions in Islam in detail, Afzal Iqbal, *Diplomacy in Islam*, Lahore, 1962; Fahad, Obaidullah, Principles of Diplomacy in Islam, Lahore, 1996; Homoud, Muhammad Ali Nasir, Diplomacy in Islam, Jaipur, 1994, pp. 186-208.
18. Hamidullah, Muhammad, *Majmuah al-Wasaiq al-Siyasiyah li al-Ahd al-Nabawi wa al-Khilafah al-Rashidah,* Cairo, 1941, pp. 81-82.
19. Piscatori, J., *Islam in A World of Nation-States*, p. 62.
20. The whole discussion on *'ahd* is quoted from Abu Sulayman, A. Abul Hamid, *op.cit.*, pp. 20-21.
21. See for detail, Khurshid Ahmad, Islam and Democracy: Some Conceptual and Contemporary Dimensions, in The Muslim World, Vol. 90, Spring 2000, pp. 1-21. It is interesting to note that Piscatori while claims that most Muslims accept democracy as good and believe Islam as intrinsically democratic, he admits the fact also that there are few Muslims who would question that Islam is democratic, for democracy is western concept, displacing rule by Allah with rule by the people, and who would see any argument equating Islam and democracy as an indication of the extent to which Muslims have become westernized (*Islam in A World of Nation-States*, p. 168 foot note No. 7) He, on the other side, claims that some Muslims reject democracy in the particular form of a multi-party parliamentary democracy and propose instead, the tribal custom of *Shura* or consultation as the appropriate democratic form (*Ibid.*, p. 41). The writer overlooked the fact that Islam emphasizes on the spirit and essence not on the form and structure.
22. By the Dutch theologian Cornelis van Perusen, who occupied the chair of philosophy in the University of Leaden. This definition is cited by the Harvard theologian Harvey Cox in his *The Secular City,* New York, 1965, p. 2 and is quoted from a report on a conferences held at the Ecumenical Institute of Bossey, Switzerland, in September 1959.
23. Cox. *Ibid.*, pp. 2 and 17.

24. *Ibid*., p. 20.
25. *op. cit.*
26. *Ibid*., pp. 30-36.
27. *Ibid*., passim, and see p. 109.
28. *Ibid*., pp. 21-23.
29. Al-Attas, *op.cit.*, p. 20.
30. *Ibid*., p. 23.
31. Khurshid Ahmad, *op. cit.*, p. 6.
32. *Ibid*., p. 11.
33. John Esposito and John Voll, *Islam and Democracy*, New York, Oxford University Press, 1996. p. 41.
34. The famous Tunisian Islamic Thinker and activist Rashid Gannushi is very vocal on this point. See his rticle "The Participation of Islamists in a Non-Islamic Government, in *Power-Sharing Islam*, Liberty for Muslim World Publications, London, 1993. pp. 51-63.
35. *Ibid*., p. 56.
36. These two cases are further elaborated in favour of Islamic participation in a non-Islamic government by Maulana Sultan Ahmad Islahi, a researcher of Islamic sociological studies in *Idarah Tasnif wa Tahqiq Islami* Aligarh, also a member of *Majlis Numāindagān, Jamaat e Islami* of India, in his book *Musalmān Aqalliyaton Ka matlubah Kirdar* (Azamgarh 1423 A.H./ 2002 A.D., pp. 103-150). He maintains no scope for any differentiation between the key-posts and ordinary posts to be achieved by the Muslims in such governments (p. 148). He emphasizes upon the active participation in the political/electoral process of a democratic state (p. 150) in order to play a leading role in the construction of legislative assembly and parliament and in the formation of the cabinet of the country. He declares mandatory for the Muslims to qualify the competitive examinations in order to seek appointment in the executive and judiciary (p. 154).

    It is very interesting to note that Maulana Sayyid Abul Ala Maududi had rejected any participation in a government run by the people of infidelity, dominated by non-Islamic elements. In such a non-Islamic government no faithful-individual or group – is allowed to accept any post or employment; that will be treated otherwise, as the service to the system of *Kufr* and infidelity, Maududi concluded (*Tafhim al-Qur'ān*, Delhi, 1970, Vol. 2, pp. 411-412). The same view is taken with the marginal differences by Maulana Amīn Ahsan Islahi (*Tadabbur Qur'ān*, Lahore, 1978, Vol. 3, pp. 483-484) also. Both the scholars have discussed that the Prophet Yousuf was entrusted with the full authority over the country. He was assigned as the sovereign of the state. He did not participate in an un-Islamic government nor took he charge of any finance ministry under the system of *Kufr*.
37. Ghannushi (*Ibid*., p. 58) on this point has quoted *Ibn Taimiyah* who has said: "We know definitely that he (Negus) could not implement the law of the *Qur'ān* in his community because his people would not

have permitted him to do. Despite that, the Negus and all those who are similar to him found their way to the pleasure of Allah in eternity although they could not abide by the laws of Islam and could only rule using that which could be implemented in the given circumstances." *Ibn Taimiyah, Majmū' Fatāwā Shyakh al-Islam*, Vol. 19, pp. 218-219.

38. Ghannushi *Ibid.*, p. 63. He has quoted the Tunisian and Algerian elections in this context, where the victors were punished severely by the dictators in power with the consent of western democracies and support of local theological elites allied with the oppressive regimes in both the countries. These suffice to prove that the root of problem in the Muslim world lies in the hegemony of despotism.
39. Ahmad, Khurshid (Prof.), *Amrīca: Muslim Duniya Ki Be Itmenāni*, Lahore, *Maushurāt*, 2002, pp. 52-53.
40. *Ibid.*, p. 50
41. *Ibid.*, pp. 262-264.
42. *Ibid.*, pp. 266-267.
43. Ahmad Khurshid, Islam and Democracy: Some Conceptual and Contemporary Dimensions; *op. cit.*, p. 19.
44. The portrait of Anwar Ibrahim is taken from Esposito, John L., *Unholy War: Terror in the Name of Islam*, Oxford, 2002, pp. 134-135.
45. Ibrahim, Anwar, "Development, values and Changing Political Ideas", *Sojourn: Social Issues in Southeast Asia* I (February 1986) p. 2.
46. *Convivencia* (Living together) alludes the spirit of Roger II's twelfth-century Sicily and Muslim rule in the Iberian Peninsula in centres like Toledo, Cordova and Granada. In Iberia Christians, Muslims and Jews live together in a context of social intercourse and cultural exchange. It was a time of prosperity and achievements; the arts, literature, poetry, astronomy and medicine flourished. Many Christians became known as Mozarabs because of the extent to which they adopted elements of Arab dress, culture and language, including Arabic names. Some Christian scholars wrote in Arabic instead of Latin. Esposito, *op.cit.*, pp. 135-136.
47. Ibharim, Anwar, "The Need for Civilizational Dialogue", Occasional Papers Series, Centre for Muslim – Christian Understanding, Georgetown University, 1995, p. 5.
48. Ibrahim, Anwar, *The Asian Renaissance*, Singapore, Times Book International, 1996, p. 45.
49. Ibrahim, Anwar, Interview by M. Sajid, *Rafieque e Manzil*, Delhi, Urdu Monthly, Vol. 18 No. 5 (May 2005), p. 18-19.

*****

# BIOGRAPHICAL NOTES

### Abdul Aziz, Shah (1746-1824)

In northern India, he was a prominent ā'lim, a powerful orator, an effective preacher and an expert on Qurān and hadith. He left a deep imprint on Islamic learning through his writings and through his students and followers. At the age of sixteen following the death of his father Shah Waliullah, he assumed the responsibility for administering and teaching at *Madrasah Rahimiyah* founded by his grandfather. Author of twenty two known books, he wrote on topics ranging from Islamic philosophy, Hadith, Tafsir, and the spirit of Sunnis to rhetorics, genealogy, music and Persian literary styles. In the Qurānic studies, his Fath al-Aziz (translation and exegesis of the first two chapters and the last two parts of the Qurān in Persian, in 3 volumes) is a major contribution in its methodological framework and interpretation. His other two important works *Malfūzāt-e-Azizi* and *Fatāwā Azizi* serve as comprehensive sources for religious and social reconstruction against British India. His major preoccupation was to restore the superiority of Sunnism by refuting aspects of Shiism. His most comprehensive work in this regard was *Tuhfah Ithna Ashariyah* completed in 1789-1790. This work not only demonstrates his profound knowledge and understanding of authentic sources of the Shi'i and Sunni Law but also epitomizes the linear development of sectarian polemics written by Sunni Ulama in the seventeenth and eighteenth centuries.

### Abu Sulayman, Abdul Hamid A. (b. 1939)

Born in Makkah, Saudi Arabia and residing mostly in America he obtained his Bachelor's Degree in Commerce from the University of Cairo in 1378 A.H./1959 A.D. and M.A. in Political Science from the same University in 1381 A.H./1963 A.D. He completed his Ph.D. in International Relations from the University of Pennsylvania in 1393 A.H./1973 A.D.

Dr. Abu Sulayman served his home land as the secretary of State Planning Committee in 1383-84 A.H./ 1963-64 A.D. He was appointed as Chairman in the Department of Political Science at King Saud University Riyadh in 1402-04 A.H./1982-84 A.D. He held various positions of repute as founding member of the Association of Muslim Social Scientists (1392 A.H./1972 A.D.), its president (1405-07 A.H./1985-87 A.D.), secretary general of the World Assembly of Muslim Youth (1393-99 A.H./ 1973-79 A.D.), Chairman of the Board, trustee, former president and founding member of International Institute of Islamic Thought, Herndon and Rector of the International Islamic University, Kuala Lumpur, Malaysia (1988-98).

Dr. Abu Sulayman has been instrumental in bringing about many international academic conferences and seminars all over the world on the issues of Islamization of knowledge, social sciences and humanities. He has been travelling around the globe in order to create intellectual awareness in the Muslim Ummah. His books include: *The Islamic Theory of International Relations: New Directions for Islamic Methodology and Thought; Azmat al-Aql al-Muslim, The Islamic Theory of Economics: Philosophy and Contemporary means.*

**Ahmad, Khurshid (Prof.) (b. 1932)**

Obtained the higher degrees in Economics, Islamic Studies and Law from Pakistan his homeland and abroad. As a Professor of Economics he spent most of his life in Karachi University. He is the leader and spokesman of the Islamic Movements around the globe. In the process of a sincere dialogue between Islam and the West he is equally respected in both the communities due to his clear and uncompromising commitment with the Muslim Ummah, but becoming very rational, argumentative and un-provocative. Apart from responding well to the contemporary challenges confronted with the Islamic thought, and creating understanding and coordination between various Islamic Academic Institutions, Professor Ahmad played a key role in the construction and theorization of Islamic Economics in the modern world. He consequently received the Islamic Development Bank's first Award in 1988 and King Faisal Award for the service of Islam in 1990 both treated as very prestigious and respectable in the Muslim world.

He is the Chairman of Institute of Policy Studies Islamabad, Pakistan and the Islamic Foundation in Great Britain. He has successfully worked as Secretary General of Islamic Research Academy, Karachi, member of Senate of Pakistan (1985-1997), Federal Minister for Planning, Development and Statistics in Pakistan National Assembly and Deputy Chairman in the Planning Commission Government of Pakistan (1978-1979). He has been intellectually very active and dynamic as the Chief Editor of Students Voice (1952-55), New Era and Urdu monthly Chiragh Rah (1957-68) and Deputy Editor of Iqbal Review Lahore (1960-64). He is presently the editor of Tarjaman al-Quran, Lahore – the Urdu Journal of global repute founded by Maulana Sayyid Abul Ala Maududi. Prof. Ahmad is writing regularly and extensively in both the Urdu and English languages on all the issues and challenges faced by Islamic movements and the Muslim world today. He is one of the prominent ideologues of Islamic revival in the contemporary world.

### Ahmadullah, Maulvi (1808-1881)

The famous freedom fighter of 1857 independence movement. His original name was Ahmad Bakhsh; the popular name was given by Sayyid Ahmad Shaheed of Mujahidin Movement. Belonging to an educated family of Patna, Bihar, he was socially very influential and occupied official positions in Patna City as Deputy Controller in Income Tax Board Assessors for some time and was the member of Sudder Committee formed under Act XX of 1856 and of the Patna Public Instruction Committee. Deeply influenced by the founder of the Mujahidin Movement, he alongwith the members of his family joined it in 1923 and stayed in Patna to organize the jihad activities. He was treacherously arrested along with Shah Muhammad Husayn (1788-1860) and Waizul Haq on 19th July 1857 by Tylor (1808-1892) – the Chief Commander of Patna, as a precaution in the 1857 movement and was released three months later.

Later he assumed full charge of the Patna Centre and applied himself to re-organise the struggle. The Government kept a close watch on him. His brother Yahya Ali and nephew Abdur Rahim were arrested and tried at Ambala in 1864 for conspiracy to wage war against the Queen. He himself was arrested and tried at Patna in 1864 and was sentenced to death on 27th February 1865, which was later converted by the High Court to transportation for life and forfeiture of all his property He was then transported to Port Blair on 13th April 1865, and his residential house at Sadiqpur was demolished. He died in 1881 during imprisonment and was buried at Bundas Point in the Viper Island. Brother Yahya Ali was similarly deported to the Andamans and he also died there.

### Arnold, Thomas Walker (Sir) (1864-1930)

Born at Devonport on 18th April 1864, Arnold received his early education at the Plymouth High School and the City of London School. In 1883 he moved to Cambridge having won a scholarship at Magdalene College. After completion of his education he joined Mohammadan Anglo Oriental College at Aligarh in 1888. He very soon found a place in the esteem of his Muslim colleagues, Maulana Shibli Nomani, Maulana Abbas Hussain and Maulana Khalil Ahmad. Here he founded a society called Anjuman al-Farz, better known as Duty Society inorder to undertake serious attempts for the betterment of the students. After serving Aligarh for ten years (1888-1898) he joined the Indian Education Service as Professor of Philosophy at the Government College Lahore, where in his familiar circle he came to be known as the 'saint'. Here he shaped the mind of Iqbal, who did his M.A. in Philosophy under his guidance in 1899. He returned to London in 1904 to take charge of his new appointment in the India Office Library; but his love for the teaching profession soon got him the chair of Arabic at the University College London. Later he was selected to be the first Educational Advisor for Indian students at London – the post he continued to hold from 1909 to 1920. Later on he became the Professor of Arabic at the newly-started School of Oriental Studies in the London University. In January 1930 Arnold was invited to deliver a series of lectures at the Cairo University. This visit included a short stay in Cyprus and a still shorter stay in Rhodes and Jerusalem. He died on 9th June 1930 in his homeland.

His main publications include: *The preaching of Islam: A History of the Propagation of the Muslim Faith* (1896), *Ahmad bin Yahya bin al-Murtada al-Mutazilah* (ed.) (1902), *The Caliphate* (1924), *Islamic Faith* (1928), *Painting in Islam: A Study of the Place of Pictorial Art in Muslim Culture* (1928), *The Old and New Testaments in Muslim Religious Art* (1932) etc.

## Ataturk, Mustafa Kamal (1881-1938)

Founding father of the Turkish Republic. Born of modest Turkish parentage in the cosmopolitan Ottoman port of Selanik (now Thessaloniki) into a markedly Muslim environment he opted for a military education, passing out as an infantry staff-captain in 1905. A participant in Young Turk Movement, his early political career ran concurrently with his secret, illegal political activities against Sultan Abdul Hamid II. He was very much active in quelling domestic uprisings in the capital (1909) and Albania (1910) as well as in the defense of Ottoman Libya against Italy (1911-12); but it was the disastrous Balkan War of 1912-13 that really accelerated his conversion to Turkish nationalism. He emerged from World War I a brigadier general, acknowledged as one of the youngest and most outstanding commanders among the combatants and accorded prestige and popularity at home. His supervision and centralization of spontaneous and widespread local resistance, establishing an alternative national assembly to represent the resisting Turkey was founded upon his conviction for fighting with independence.

With the foundation of the Republic of Turkey in 1923, President Ataturk concentrated on the furtherance of his nationalist revolution. Through a series of predominantly political and social reforms, despite internal and international opposition, endeavoured to establish a capitalist nation-state based on popular sovereignty, secular democracy and western model of society. He aimed to secularize the polity and extricate the state from all kinds of relationships of Islamic Shariah.

## Al-Attas, Muhammad Naquib (Syed)

Professor al-Attas has lectured throughout the world and written many books and articles in his academic fields of competence: Islamic philosophy and metaphysics, history, literature, Islamic art and civilization, and education. While his book *Islam Secularism and the Philosophy of the Future* (1985) was in preparation, he was invited to discuss the concept of *din* on the widely-acclaimed BBC Television Series, *Encounters with Islam*.

At the National University of Malaysia he has been Head of the Department of Malay Language and Literature, Dean of the Faculty of Arts, the first holder of the chair of Malay Language, Literature and culture, which he founded in 1973. He has also been Head of the Division of literature in the Department of Malay Studies and Dean of the Faculty of Arts at the University of Malaya; Visiting Scholar and Professor of Islamics at Temple University, Distinguished Professor of Islamic Studies and the first holder of the Tun Abdul Razak Distinguished Chair of Southeast Asian Studies.

In 1975 he was made a Fellow of the Iranian Academy of Philosophy, and in 1979 was awarded the Iqbal Centenary commemorative Medal by the president of Pakistan, Professor Attas is the first scholar in contemporary times to formulate a definitive and comprehensive concept of the Islamic University.

**Esposito, John L.**

He is the university Professor of Religion and International Affairs and Founding Director of the Centre for Muslim-Christian Understanding at the Walsh School of Foreign Service, Georgetown University. A past president of the Middle East Studies Association, he is the author of Unholy *War-Terror in the Name of Islam* (2002), *The Islamic Threat: Myth or Reality, Islam: The Straight Path, Women in Muslim Family Law, Islam and Politics, Makers of Contemporary Islam* (with John O. Voll), *Islam and Democracy* (with John O. Voll), *World Religions Today* (with Darrell J. Fasching and Todd Lewis) and the editor of *The Oxford Encyclopaedia of the Modern Islamic World, The Oxford History of Islam, The Oxford Dictionary of Islam, Voices of Resurgent Islam and others.* He lives in Washington D.C.

**Farahi, Hameeduddin (1863-1930)**

The thinker and interpreter of the Qur'ān mostly known as the scholar who theorized the concept of coherence in the Qu'rān (Nizam al- Qurān). Born in Phariha – a Village in Azamgarh District, he attended the circles of Maulana Faruq Chirayyakoti, Maulana Abdul Hay of Farangi Mahal in Lucknow and Maulana Faizul Hasan Saharanpuri in Lahore for the sake of learning the Islamic subjects. In order to acquire the modern knowledge he was admitted in M.A.O. College, Aligarh in 1891 where he took keen interest in learning the English language and Western philosophy. Here he attended enthusiastically Maulana Shibli Nomani and Prof. T.W. Arnold. He obtained his bachelor's degree in 1895. Starting his professional career as teacher of Arabic language in Madarsatul Islam Karachi in 1897, he occupied high positions in various institutions and universities. He served as Assistant Professor of Arabic in M.A.O. College, Aligarh (1907-1908), Professor of Arabic in Muir College Allahabad (1908-1914), Principal, Darul Uloom, Hyderabad on deputation (1914-1919) and finally as Rector (Nāzim) of Madarsatul Islah, Azamgarh in 1916. His main interest was concentrated upon developing and improving Madrasatul Islah as the highest seat of Islamic Learning where the teaching and reflecting in the holy Qurān would have gained the central position just as the nucleus around which all other sciences and learnings were to revolve. Maulana Farahi with the help of others founded *Dar al-Musannifin* in Azamgarh city in order to conduct researches on Islamic Studies. His academic contributions to Islamic- Qurānic studies are comprehensive covering a variety of subjects as Arabic language and grammar, Tafsir, Hadith, Ilm al-Kalam, comparative religion, Arabic poetry and rhetorics, but the most important field of his interest was the tafsir. He offered a model of his theory of Qurānic coherence in his commentary known as *Tafsir Nizamul Qurān*.

### Faruqi, Ismail Raji Al (1921-1986)

Islamic scholar and activist. Born in Jaffa, Palestine, he received an education that made him trilingual (Arabic, French and English) and provided him with multicultural intellectual sources that informed his life and thought. He studied at the mosque school, attended a French Catholic School, Collegedes Freres in Palestine and earned a bachelor's degree at the American University of Beirut (1941). Having become governor of Galilee in 1945, he was forced to emigrate from Palestine after the creation of the state of Israel in 1948. He then earned masters degrees at Indiana and Harvard Universities and a doctorate in philosophy from Indiana University (1952). He, later on, studied and conducted research at major centres of learning in the Muslim World and the West as visiting Professor of Islamic Studies at the Institute of Islamic Studies and a Fellow at the Faculty of Divinity, McGill University (1959-61), Visiting Professor of History of Religion at the University of Chicago (1963-64), Professor in the Department of Religion at Syracuse University (1964-68), and then Professor of Islamic Studies and of History of Religions at Temple University (1968-86).

During his 30 years professional life, Faruqi wrote, edited or translated 25 books, published more than a hundred articles, was a Visiting Professor at more than 23 universities in Africa, Europe, the Middle East, South and Southeast Asia, served on the editorial boards of seven major journals, founded or patronized over a dozen of the Islamic Institutions, and in 1981 he created the International Institute of Islamic Thought in Virginia. At the heart of his vision, however, was the Islamization of Knowledge. He believed that the cure for Muslim decline was two-fold: the compulsory study of Islamic civilization and the Islamization of modern knowledge. He and his wife Lamya al-Faruqi, also an Islamic scholar, were murdered by an intruder in their home.

### Fasi, Muhammad Allal Al- (1906-1973)

Moroccan intellectual, historian, legal scholar, teacher, poet and political leader, a founder of the Istiqlal Party son of the Mufti of Fez, al-Fasi studied Islamic Law at al-Qarawiyin University. In 1927 he was a founder of the

Moroccan Action Committee, a loose coalition of intellectuals in Fez and Rabat. In 1934 he and his compatriots publicly issued a Moroccan Reform Plan and were arrested. In 1937 his group was banned but it reorganized as the National Reform Party that merged into the Istiqlal Party in 1943. He fled from his homeland in 1947 to Cairo where he remained in exile until Moroccan independence in 1956. From Cairo he travelled and lectured in the Middle East, South Asia, Europe and North America. His most important writings date from this period, including the *Independence Movements in Arab North Africa* (1947), *Self Criticism* (1951), and two collections *From the Occident to the Orient* (1956) and *The Call of Cairo* (1959). He was an Islamic modernist and reformer, advocating Islamic renewal, a return to original sources and avoidance of imitating the West.

**Fazlurrahman (1919-1988)**

Pakistani philosopher, educator and prominent liberal, intellectual of Islam. Born in what is now Pakistan, received his master's degree in Arabic from Punjab University Lahore in 1942 and a doctorate in Islamic philosophy from Oxford University in 1949. He was Lecturer in Persian studies and Islamic philosophy at Durham University from 1950 to 1958, Associate Professor in McGill University's Institute of Islamic Studies from 1958 to 1961, Visiting Professor at Pakistan's Central Institute of Islamic Research (1961-62) and its director from 1962 to 1968. He became controversial figure in the country due to his writings and left Pakistan to join as visiting professor at the University of California, Los Angeles, in 1969. Thereafter he went to the University of Chicago to serve as Professor of Islamic thought. In 1986 he was named Harold H. Swift Distinguished Service Professor at Chicago, a title he held until his death.

Fazlurrahman first achieved international renown with the publication of Avicenna's Psychology (1952).

**Ghazali, Muhammad Al- (1917-1996)**

Egyptian religious scholar and former leading member of *al-Ikhwan al-Muslimun*. Born in Buhayra Province, he graduated from Al-Azhar in 1941 and occupied influential positions in his own country and in other Arab states. In Egypt he was director of the Mosques Department, director general of Islamic *Dawah* and under secretary of the Ministry of Awqāf. He also taught at the Universities of al-Azhar (Egypt), King Abdul Aziz and Umm al-Qura (Saudi Arabia) and was the academic director of Amir Abdul Qadir Islamic University in Algeria.

Al-Ghazali was dismissed from his position in the constituent body of the Ikhwan in December 1953, reportedly after attempting with two other prominent members, to unseat the organization's leader, Hassan al-Hudaybi. He contributed approximately 40 titles including such important works as *Khulq al-Muslim*, *Kaifa Nata'a malu ma'al* Qurān (interview conducted by Omar Ubaid Hasanah), *Kifāh Dīn*, *Min Huna Nálam*,

*Nazarāt fi al-* Qurān, *Fiqh al-Sīrah, al-Islam wa al-Istibdād al-Siyasi, Aqidah al-Muslim* and others. He is treated by the scholars as a reasonable, well-balanced and independent álim. He was strongly supportive of an extensively defined concept of *Shura* and was regarded as somewhat modernist in social and technological matters. He admitted only those Ahadiths as the source in Shariah that have a Qurānic credibility and excluded *akhbār aāhād* if they appeared odd or ill reasoned to him.

**Gibb Hamilton, A.R. (Sir)**

Born in Alexandria Egypt in 1895 and was sent back to his homeland Scotland at the age of five for his formal education. In 1904 he entered the Edinburgh Royal High School and obtained his matriculation in 1912. Here he also received a good education in French, German, and the physical sciences. In 1912 he entered Edinburgh University and joined the Bachelor program in Semitic languages with Hebrew, Arabic and Aramaic. In 1919 he entered the London School of Oriental Studies in the post-graduate program in Arabic and received the degree in 1922. He had already been appointed as lecturer in 1921 and thereafter served as assistant to Professor Sir Thomas Arnold. In 1926-27 he made his first lengthy visit to the Middle East and took the opportunity to begin the study of contemporary Arabic literature. In 1929 he was appointed Reader in Arabic History and literature, and in 1930, on the death of Professor Arnold, he was appointed to the Chair of Arabic. He also replaced Prof. Arnold as English editor of the *Encyclopaedia of Islam* serving as such until 1955 and meanwhile becoming one of the original editors of the completely revised edition.

He was Professor of Arabic at the University of London from 1930 to 1937, and Laudian Professor of Arabic at St. John's College, Oxford University from 1937 to 1955. In 1955 he joined the Harvard faculty as University Professor and James Richard Jennet Professor of Arabic, and two years later assumed the directorship of the Centre for Middle Eastern Studies. In 1964 he retired from the teaching faculty at Harvard as University Professor, Emeritus and James Richard Jewett Professor of Arabic, Emeritus.

His principal publications are as follows: *The Arab Conquests in Central Asia* (London 1923), *Arabic Literature* (London, 1926) *Damascus Chronicles of the Crusades* (London, 1932), *Modern Trends in Islam* (Chicago, 1947), *Mohammedanism* (London, 1949), *Islamic Society and the West* (Part 1, London, 1950; Part 2, London, 1957), *The Travels of Ibn Battuta* (Cambridge, Vol. 1, 1958, Vol. 11, 1961); *Studies on the Civilization of Islam* (Boston, 1962) etc.

**Gibbon, Edward (1737-1794)**

English rationalist historian and scholar best known as the author of "*The History of the Decline and Fall of the Roman Empire*" (1776-88), a continuous narrative from the 2nd century A.D. to the fall of Constantinople in 1453.

This book is comprised of two divisions, equal in bulk and inevitably different in treatment. The first half covers a period of 300 years to the end of the empire in the West, about AD 480. In the second half nearly 1000 years are compressed. Yet the work is coherent whole by virtue of its conception of the Roman Empire as a single entity throughout its long and diversified course. He imposed a further unity on his narrative by viewing it as an undeviating decline from those ideals of political and, even more, intellectual freedom that he had found in classical literature.

*Memoirs of My Life and Writings* is his autobiography dealing in detail with his feelings and behaviours towards others.

### Hamidullah, Muhammad (Dr.) (1908-2002)

Born in Hyderabad obtained his degree of Alimiyah from Madarsah Nizamiyah, Hyderabad in 1924, B.A. from Osmania University and L.L.B. and M.A. from the same. He was awarded D.Phil by the Boun University in 1932 and honorary D. Litt. by the Sorbonne University. In 1938 he returned to Readership in Islamic International law at the Osmania University. Following the collapse of Hyderabad state in 1948 he migrated to Paris. He took up an assignment with Centre Nationale de La Recherche Scientifique in 1954, which ended in 1978. During this period he taught in the several other universities in Turkey and Germany. He wrote extensively across a wide spectrum of Islamic disciplines including the translatin of the Qurān, Hadith, Seerah, Fiqh, Islamic international Law. Islamic history and Arabic epigraphy. He wrote over a hundred books and over 1000 articles in several languages, including French, German, English, Arabic, Turkish, Persian and Urdu. He knew 22 languages including Thai, which he learnt at the age of 84. He is the only scholar in the world to have translated the Qurān in three European Languages: French, English and German. English translation was partly published from South Africa in 1960. The German translation, though complete, remains unpublished.

His most important contribution to Islamic studies is his French translation and commentary of the Holy Qurān published in more than 30 editions and is very popular. His another work '*Introduction to Islam*' is rendered into 22 languages. Some of his English publications include: *The Battlefields of the Prophet Muhammad*, The *First Written Constitution in the World*, *Sahifah Hammam Ibn Munabbih*, *Muhammad Rasulullah*, *The Muslim Conduct of State*, *The 1400th Anniversary of the Completion of Islam*, *Emergence of Islam: Lectures on the Development of Islamic World-view, Intellectual Tradition and Polity*. Some of his Urdu books are: *Rasul Akram Ki Siyasi Zindagi*, *Siyasi Wathiqajāt*, *Seerat Ibn Ishaq*, *Ahd Nabwi Ka Nizam-e-Taleem*,

*Imam Abu Hanifah Ki Tadween Qanun Islami*, *Khutbāt-e-Bahawalpur* etc.

**Hifzurrahman, Muhammad Maulana (1901-1962)**

Born in Seohara, a town in Bijnore District U.P., on 10th January 1901 he completed his education from Darul Uloom Deoband and joined actively Jameat ul Ulama Hind and Indian National Congress. He was also active in the Khilafat Movement in 1919. He was selected as member to the working committee of Jameat in 1932, its General Secretary in 1942, a member of All India Congress Committee in 1936, Vice-President of U.P. Congress Committee from 1946 to 1951, and was imprisoned five times for leading the Congress programmes. He was also a member of Executive Committee Sunni Central Board U.P. and Sunni Majlis Awqāf Delhi (1947), Trustee of Darul Uloom, Deoband, a member of All India Muslim Educational Conference, A.M.U. Court and also of Anjuman Taraqqi Urdu.

He was elected the Congress M.L.A. in 1949 in an uncontested bye-election. He was Congress M.P. from U.P. (1950-52), member of Ist Lok Sabha (1952-57) (Moradabad, U.P.); 2nd Lok Sabha from Amroha in 1957-62 term; 3rd Lok Sabha in 1962 from the same constituency.

His publications include *Islam Ka Iqtisadi Nizam, Qisas al-* Qurān (4 Volms.), *Falsafah-e-Akhlaq, Rasul Karim, Balagh Mubin* etc.

**Hitti, Philip Khuri (1886-1978)**

Professor Hitti was considered a leading authority in the United States on Arabic and Islamic Culture and was one of the first persons in any American University to appreciate and promote the importance of the Arab world in the country.

B.A., Ph.D. American Orientalist Born at Shimian, Lebanon on 24 June 1886, educated at the American University of Beirut and the Columbia University. He served in many capacities as Lecturer in the Oriental Department, Columbia University (1915-1919), Assistant Professor of Semitic Literature, Princeton University (1926-1929), Associate Professor (1929-39), Chairman Department of Oriental Languages (1944), Director Programme in Near Eastern Studies (1947-1954), member, American Oriental Society, American Historical Association etc. He was honoured with Litt.D. by the Princeton University in 1966, L.H.D. by American University of Beirut in 1969.

He was the author of many works on the culture, history, languages and religions of the countries of the Near East. His best known work is *History of the Arabs* which was published in 1937 and is still regarded as a standard work in the field. His other publications include: The Origins of the Islamic State (1916), The Semetic Languages Spoken in Syria and Lebanon (1922), The Syrians in America (1924), Characteristics of Moslem Sects (1924), Syria and the Syrians (1926), Lebanon in History (1957),

Islam and the West (1962), Makers of Arab History (1968), Islam-A Way of Life (1970), Capital Cities of Arab Islam (1973), Usama Ibn Munqidh: A Arab Syrian Gentleman and Warrior in the Period Crusades (1929), The Origins of the Druze People and Religion (1929), Syria – A Short History (1959) etc.

### Ibrahim, Anwar (b. 1947)

Malaysian Muslim activist, thinker and politician. He was born at Cerok Tok Kun, Bukit Mertajam, Penang. His parents were active in the United Malays National Organization (UMNO). He received his education from Malay College in Kuala Kangsar, Perak (1960-1966) and became noted as a debator and a school captain. In the University of Malaya (1967-1970) as a student he presided over the two major organizations (PKPIM), (National Union of Malaysian Students) and PBMUM (Malay Languages Society of the University of Malaya). The establishment of ABIM (Angkatan Belia Islam Malaysia) in 1971 made Anwar the most influential young leader of Malaysia. Through this organization, he had extensive contacts with most Malaysian leaders, Muslim intellectuals and activists at home and abroad. He was arrested for the two years (1974-1976) without trial under the Internal Security Act following the Baling demonstrations. Among his many activities he has served as the leader of Malaysian Youth Council (1972), a member of United Nations Advisory Group on Youth (1973-74), a representative of the World Assembly of Muslim Youth (WAMY) for Southeast Asia (1976-1982), a cofounder of the International Institute of Islamic Thought (IIIT), Washington, D.C., and Chancellor of the International Islamic University at Kuala Lumpur. His 1982 entry into UMNO was a landmark in his political popularity. Within the government, he rose rapidly to positions including deputy minister in the prime minister's department; minister of youth, culture and sports, agriculture minister, and education minister, in 1993 he was minister of finance. In 1993 party elections he won the post of deputy president of UMNO. He then took the charge of Deputy Prime Minister and when most observers considered it likely that he will be the next prime minister, he was tried and imprisoned on politically inspired charges. He was released only in the beginning of 2005.

### Ismail Shaheed, Shah Muhammad (1779-1831)

The prominent reformer and Commander-in-Chief of Mujahidin forces led by Sayyid Ahmad Shaheed. Born on 29th April, 1779 in Phulat District Muzaffar Nagar, U.P., received his early education from his father, Shah Abdul Ghani. After the death of his father he was looked after by his uncle Shah Abdul Qadir. He learnt riding masterly from an expert Rahim Bakhsh and boxing from Mirza Rahmat. He was also a good swimmer. He could stay continuously in the water for three days. He was a good marksman too and could very easily kill even a little bird on a dense tree. At the age of twenty-one he was a complete soldier. He later on moved to Punjab and made a secret tour to the Muslim populace and prepared the maps and sketches of some of the important forts. He joined Sayyid Ahmad Shaheed and travelled to important cities and towns along with Abdul Hai and delivered sermons and lectures in the public, criticizing all the un-Islamic beliefs and practices in his simple style and dignified diction, and mobilizing the people in favour of waging jihād against Ranjit Singh of Punjab. His famous book asserting in Islamic belief and criticizing religious innovations uncompromisingly entitled *Taqwiyatul Imān* is remarkable in the history of Urdu literature. There is a pretty definite collection of his political writings too. These political ideas are scattered in the speeches delivered from time to time and the letters he wrote to rulers and Ulama and in the book *Mansib Imamat.*

At the first battle of Akora (Dec. 1826) Ismail Shaheed directed all the forces and ultimately the battle was won due to his strategic planning. After a long tussle in between the Sikh troops and the Mujahidin both the prominent leaders and majority of their supporters were brutally killed in Balakot in 1831. Those who could escape death went to Sittanah and from there continued to trouble the British for a very long time.

### Kemal, Mehmet Namik (1840-1888)

Ottoman Turkish poet, prose writer and libertarian theoretician. He was born in the small town of Tekirdag. His own career in the Ottoman bureaucracy brought him into contact with the Western culture. The Tanzimat had already inaugurated an era of westernization in the empire. He criticized this trend but his emphasis was on the point that government by an elite was illegitimate according to both Islamic and Western principles. Between 1861 and 1867 he was employed in the Translation Bureau of the Ottoman Porte. He also took over the editing of *Tasvir-i Afkar* newspaper. He left the country for Paris and London with his friend Zia Beg and began the publication of the newspaper *Hurriyet* criticizing the Ottomans for their lack of direction and autocratic policies. He returned to Turkey in 1870 and published his ideas now in *Ibret.* In 1876 once more he was exiled to Cyprus. He returned under amnesty of was, but again exiled to Mytilene. He died in 1888 while serving as an administrator in Mytilene.

It is through his passionate patriotic poetry that Namek Kermal is best remembered by the current generation of Turks. The Turkish Republic made a somewhat biased use of Namek, highlighting those aspects of his thought that focussed on the defense of the fatherland. The Republic completely ignored the idea of Namek that the constitutionalism should be harmonized with Islam.

### Khalid, Muhammad Khalid (b. 1920)

Egyptian writer and essayist. Born in Sharqiyyah Province, he graduated from Al-Azhar in 1947 with an Alimiyah degree from the Facutly of Shariah and then gained a teaching certificate, also from al-Azhar. He worked as an Arabic Language teacher and then in the Cultural Bureau of the Ministry of culture. He later became a supervisor in the Department for the Publication of the Heritage. He has written more than thirty books as well as political and religious articles in newspapers and magazines, such as as-Sharq al-Awsat (London), Al-Muslimun, Al-Musawwar, Al-Ahram and Al-Wafd.

His first book Min Huna Nabda (1950) was confiscated because of objections from al-Azhar and then released by order of the Cairo district court. He expressed his secular views along with the Islamic references in other books also written in the 1950s and early 1960s, such as *Muwatinūn La Ri'āya* (1951), *Ma'an ala al-Tariq – Muhammad wa al-Masih* (1958), *al-Dimiqratiyyah abadan* (1953). In *al-Dawlah fi al-Islam* (1981) he revised to some extent the secularist position of his first book and argued that Islam though does not prescribe the sort of "religious government", it does have a civil as well as a religious mission and does call for the state to apply Islamic principles – liberty, shura and parliamentary democracy. His first work was criticized in Islamic perspective by his contemporary Muhammad al-Ghazali.

**Kandhlavi, Muhammad Idris (Maulana) (d. 1394 AH)**

One of the distinct graduates of Darul Uloom Deoband who learned from the prominent scholars like Syed Muhammad Anwar Shah Kashmiri. He was closely associated to his colleague in the hadith lectures (*dawrah Hadith*), Maulana Qari Muhammad Tayyib Qasimi. He had a unique power of memory and taught the higher classes in the Darul Uloom Deoband. After graduation he started his professional career as teacher in several madrasahs and finally in his mother institution in the position of *Shaykh al-Tafsir* who used to teach the hadith classes also especially that of Sunan Abu Dawud. After partition of the country he preferred the Pakistani nationality and was associated with Jamia Ashrafiyah Lahore as *Shaykh al-Tafsir wa al-Hadith* until his death.

Maulana Kandhlavi was a prominent researcher who used to discuss the issues independently. His most important contribution is the interpretation and edition of *Mishkat al-Masabih* by Wali al-Din Tabrezi into five volumes entitled as *al-T'aliq al-Sahih* published from Beirut. In the field of the biography of the Prophet his voluminous master piece is entitled as *Seerat al-Mustafa* in Urdu. He criticized the liberal scholars of seerah in this volume. He had command over both the Arabic and Persian languages and used to compose poetry spontaneously in both the languages. He had several other academic works his credit.

**Khundmiri, Alam Syed, (1922-83)**

Was an important Marxist intellectual figure of Hyderabad who laid the foundation of Comrades Association in 1939 to propagate the Marxist ideology. He was treated by his circle, a true humanist with rare philosophical insights ranging over a wide field. His three major concerns were Marxism, existentialism and Islam, which he owe together to evolve an organic and dynamic view in his own paradigm. His writings are also suffused with an awareness of history, politics, and economics combined with question of time, self, reason, morality and law.

Alam's other writings include many articles in English and Urdu and the text of a monograph on the renowned painter *Sayeed bin Mohammad* (Hyderabad, 1978). His Ph.D. dissertation entitled *The Concept of Time in Western and Islamic Thought, with Special Reference to Iqbal*, with Annemarie Schimmel's notations, inscribed to Zahiruddin, is with the Iqbal Academy, Hyderabad. His selected essays are edited and published by M.T. Ansari, entitled *Secularism, Islam and Modernity* (New Delhi, Sage Publications, 2001).

### Lewis, Bernard (b. 1916)

Hailed as "the world's foremost Islamic Scholar", as "a towering figure among experts on the culture and religion of the Muslim world", Bernard Lewis in nothing less than a "national treasure, a trusted voice" that politicians, historians and the general public of the west have all turned to for insight in to the Middle East. Over the course of his professional career, he has proven himself as a scholar learned in a number of languages, who has interpreted Islam, the Ottoman Empire and the modern Middle East for the west.

Bernard Lewis started his undergraduate studies in 1933 at the University of London in the subject of history with special reference to the Middle East. A travelling fellowship from the Royal Asiatic Society was given to him and in the academic year 1937-38 he set out his first trip to the Middle East. In 1938 he was appointed as assistant Lecturer in Islamic history in the University of London. A year after he was shifted to intelligence and only on Ist September 1945 he could rejoin the University. In 1949 he was appointed to the new chair in near and Middle Eastern History. He is now Cleveland E. Dodge Professor of Near Eastern Studies. Emeritus, at Princeton University. He is the author of over two dozen books as *The Origins of Ismailism* (1940) *The Arabs in History* and most recently *The Crisis of Islam: Holy War and Unholy Terror*, and *What Went Wrong?* A new collection of his articles published earlier is entitled From *Babel to Dragomans: Interpreting the Middle East* (2004). His books have been translated into more than twenty languages, including Arabic, Turkish, Persian, and Indonesian. He lives in Princeton, New Jersey.

### Mashriqi, Enayatullah Khan (1888-1963)

The famous activist and reformer popularly known as 'Allama Mashriqi'. Belonging to a Pathan family he was born in Ichchrah, Lahore. From his childhood he was brilliant and a record holder. He learnt in the institutions of high repute as Punjab University (M.A. Mathematics) and Cambridge University (Language Tripos, 1911; Machanical Trips, 1912).

He held various academic and administrative positions as the member of International Congress of Orientalists, Vice Principal at Islamia College Peshawar (1913) and Principal (1915) and Assistant Secretary in Department of Education and Lands (1915-1919). He joined Indian Education Service as Principal in Government Training College in North-west Frontier Province, Inspector of Schools and Registrar of Examinations. He resigned from I.E.S. in 1932.

He was an ardent pan-Islamist, unofficially represented India at the Islamic Conference Cairo in 1926, and opposed the proposal to elect the Sultan of Egypt as *Khalifah al-Muslimin* holding that a vassal ruler could not be the spiritual leader of the Islamic world. He founded the Khaksār Movement in 1931, a paramilitary organization with a uniform *Khaki* dress for its followers, a *belcha* (spade) as its symbol, and regular drills and road marches as part of its routine. It's aim was to regenerate society and revive the lost glory of Islam. His book *Tazkirah* provided a naval and controversial interpretation of the Qurān. Mashriqi did not believe in non-violence and urged the Congress and Muslim League to make up their differences and strive for an independent India. In 1948 he announced the disbanding of the organization and to have formed Islamic League in order to transform Pakistan into an ideal Islamic state.

## Nadvi, Muhammad Rais (Maulana) (b. 1937)

Born in Bhatia Marwatia Bazar, a village in Basti District, U.P., Maulana Nadvi earned his early education in Madrasah Badriah Basti and then got admission in Nadvatul Ulama Lucknow in 1957. After obtaining the degree of Alimiyah, he started his teaching profession and served in various classical religious institutions as Jamea Salafiah Sirajul Uloom Jhanda Nagar, Nepal, Madrasah Ahmadiah Salafiah Darbhanga, Bihar and finally the Markazi Darul Uloom Jamia Salafia Varanasi.

Maulana Nadvi emerged as a staunch supporter of Ahl Hadith school and a severe critique of Hanafid and Barelvi schools of thought. He wrote extensively on various controversial issues of juristic nature and advocated a strict adherence to the texts of the Qurān and sunnah directly without any reliance on the juristic interpretations. His publications are popular in especially Ahl Hadith circles. These include: *Tashih al-Aqāid bi Ibtal Shawahid al-Shahid, Al-Lamhāt ila ma fi Anwar al-Bari min al-Zulumaat* (the sixth final volume is in process), *Seerat Imam Ibn Hazm, Seerat Umm al-Muminin Hazrat Khadijah al-Kubra, Islam mein Namaz Jum'ah Ka Hukm, Rakaat Tarawih, Tarikh Ahl Hadith Hind, Zameer Ka Buhran, Deobandi Tahaffuz Sunnat Conference par Salafi Tahqiqi Jayzah, Tanwir al-Aafāq fi Masalah al-Talaq, Rasulullah Ka Sahih Tariqah-e-Namaz*, etc.

## Nadvi, Mukhtar Ahmad (b. 1930)

Former amīr (President), Jameat Ahl Hadith of India, Maulana Mukhtar Ahmad Nadvi S/o Al-Hājj Muhammad Zameer was born in Vishunath Pura, Mau, Uttar Pradesh and earned his education from Jamia Alia Arabia Mau, Madrasah Faiz Aām Mau and Madrasa Dar al-Hadith Rahmaniah Delhi. He obtained the Fadhilah degree from Nadwatul Ulama Lucknow. Among his prominent teachers Maulana Muhammad Ahmad (known as Bade Maulavi Sahab), Maulana Abdullah Shāiq of Mau and Maulana Abdul Qasim Saif of Varanasi are only a few.

He started his career as a preacher and orator in Jame Masjid Ahl Hadith Kolkata, Jame Masjid Ahl Hadith Mominpura and Bengali Masjid Madanpura both at Mumbai. He was associated with the magazine *Ahl Hadith* Delhi as a member of editorial board for ten years. He is the founder and patron of various academic and non-academic institutions as al-Dar al-Salafiah Mumbai, Jamea Muhammadiah Malegaon, Madrasah Aisha Siddiquah Malegaon, Kulliyah Fatimah al-Zahra Mau, Muhammadiah Tibbiya College Malegaon, Aliya General Hospital Mau and Idarah Islah al-Masajid Mumbai.

Maulana Nadvi was elected as vice-amīr from November 1979 to November 1989, acting amīr after the death of Maulana Abdul Waheed Salafi the amīr, in 1989-1990 and amīr from May 1990 to July 1997. After completing his tenure as amīr he is exclusively engaged in writing and guiding the Muslims in various issues. He is editor-in-chief of monthly Saut al-Haqq and al-Balagh. He is presently vice-president of All India Muslim Personal Law Board.

## Nadvi, Sayyid Sulaiman (1884-1953)

The famous Islamic scholar and writer who obtained his Alimiyah degree from Nadwatul Ulama Lucknow where he was a student of Shibli Nomani also. One time he was associated with Sir Syed Ahmad Khan and was deeply influenced by him. He joined hands with Abul Kalam Azad to publish al-Hilal Urdu Journal from Calcutta in 1912. Later on he joined later on Darul Musannifin at Azamgarh and emerged as a distinguished Islamic writer and scholar. He was a pan-Islamist and took active part in all the programmes of the Khilafat Movement. A number of Muslim delegations to Muslim countries were led by him as the Khilafat Delegation to Europe in 1920 and Muslim Deputations (1924 & 1926) to Arab countries to inquire into the Palestinian problem. He presided over the special session of Jameatul Ulama at Moradabad in 1921. He was awarded Honrary LD by Aligarh Muslim University in 1940 and in 1950 he migrated to Pakistan.

Among his publications some are very important like *Hayat Shibli* (1943), *Arab o Hind Ke Tijarti Ta'lluqāt* (1930), *Arbon Ki Jahazrani*. The most important of these is his association with his teacher Shibli Nomani in compiling the *Seeratun Nabi* and completing the remaining volumes after the death of the original writer.

### Ramadān, Saīd (Dr.) (1926-1995)

The ideologue and spokesman of al-Ikhwan al-Muslimun in Egypt who migrated to Europe and played crucial role in the organizational interactions with the West. Born in Tanta, Egypt on 12th April 1926. He was brought up and educated by the leader of Ikhwan and scholar Dr. Al-Bahiy al-Khuli. He graduated in 1946 from the Law College Cairo. He was appointed the editor of *al-Shahāb*, the organ of Ikhwan in 1947-48. In 1951 he published the monthly *al-Muslimun* from Cairo to represent the Ikhwan in the academic and literary circles. The monthly was later on banned by the government due to severe differences with the Revolutionary Council. In 1954 he was detained for some time. He then left the country and travelled to Palestine, Syria, Jordan and Saudi Arabia. In 1953 he was selected as the secretary general of Organization of Islamic Conference. He played a key role in the foundation of *Rabita al-Alam al-Islami* in Saudi Arabia. He permanently settled down in Geneva in 1958 and in order to organize *dawah* activities in Europe he founded the Islamic Centre in 1961.

Dr. Ramadan obtained his Ph.D. degree in Law from the Cologne University Germany. When the Egyptian Government deprived him of its citizenship the governments of Saudi Arabia, Jordan and Pakistan all offered him their visa. He was considered the defender and advocate of Ikhwan in Europe. He married in 1946 with the elder daughter of Hasan al-Banna just after his martyrdom in order to prove his loyalty and affection towards the founder of the Ikhwan. His publications include *Three Major Problems Confronting the World of Islam* and *Islamic Law: Its Scope and Equity*.

### Shahabuddin, Syed (b. 1935)

Prolific writer on Muslim issues in Indian dailies and weeklies. Born in Itki, Ranchi on 4th November and learned from Haridas Seminary Gaya (1946-50), St. Xavier's College Ranchi (1950-52), Science College Patna (1951-55) and (1956-57). He started his career as lecturer in physics, Patna University. He qualified the competitive examination of Indian Foreign Service and worked as Government bureaucrat from 1958 to 1978. In the meantime he was appointed as ambassador to Algeria and then Mauritania in 1973-75, worked as Joint Secretary in the Ministry of External Affairs (1975-78) and sought premature retirement in 1978. He joined Janata Party in November 1978, was appointed as the Convenor of Minority Panel of the Party in October 1979 then General Secretary in May 1980. He was elected to *Rajya Sabha* from Bihar in July 1979. Now he is the president of *All India Muslim Majlis Mushawarat* and is fully involved in defending the Muslim cause in the media and government circles. He has been founding editor of *Muslim India* the unique journal in the field of research and documentation on Muslim issues. Now it is edited and published by Dr. Zafarul Islam Khan.

**Siddiqui, Muhammad Yasin Mazhar (Prof.) (b. 1944)**

A renowned professor in the Department of Islamic Studies, A.M.U., Aligarh, India and an established scholar in Islamic history in general and Ummayad period in particular, was born in a town Gola Gokarannath of Lakhimpur Kheri District U.P. After completing his primary education from the local madrasah Hayatiah Islamiah, he was admitted in Nadwatul Ulama Lucknown in 1953 and from there he obtained the degree of Alim in the first division in 1959 and the degree of Fādil Adab from Lucknow University in 1960. To pursue the modern education he got admission in Jamia Millia Islamia, New Delhi and received higher secondary in 1962, B.A. in 1965 and B.Ed. in 1966. Then he came to Aligarh and mastered in History (1968), completed M.Phil. in 1969 and Ph.D. in 1975.

He was associated as Lecturer with the Department of History for thirteen years (1970-83), then was appointed as Reader in the Department of Islamic Studies, A.M.U., and finally as Professor till the present. He was honoured with the '*Nuqush Award* of Pakistan by the president General Ziaul Haq in 1983 on his remarkable work in Seerah field entitled Organization of Government under the Prophet; and another Nuqush award by the President Muhammad Rafeeq Tārar in 1998 on his contributions in the Qurānic studies. He in addition to his teaching assignment holds the post of Director, Shah Waliullah Dehlavi Research Cell under the Institute of Islamic Studies, A.M.U., Aligarh. His other publications include: *Banu Ummayah Aur Banu Hashim Ke Maasharti Ta'alluqaat* (Aligarh, 2001), *Tarikh Tahzib Islami* Vol. I (1994) Vol. II (1998), *'Ahd Nabawi Ki Ibtidai Muhimmein* (Lahore, 1984), *Ghazawāt Nabawi Ki Iqtisadi Jihaat* (Aligarh, 1999), *Wahi Hadith* (Delhi, 2004) *al-Hajamāt al-Mughrazah ala al-Tarikh al-Islami* (Cairo, 1988), *Makki Uswah Nabawi: Muslim Aqalliyaton Ke Masāil Ka Hall* (New Delhi, 2005), *Shah Waliullah Ki Khidmāt Hadith* (Phulat, 2004), *Abdul Muttalib Hashmi: Rasul Akram Ke Dada* (New Delhi, 2004), *Undlus mein Ulum Qirat Ka Irtiqa* (Aligarh, 1998), *Shah Waliullah ka Falsafah Seerat* (Aligarh, 2000), *Ahd Nabawi Ka Nizam Hukumat* (Aligarh, 1994) and others.

**Toynbee, Arnold (Joseph) (b. April 14, 1889, London – d. October 22, 1975, York, North Yorkshire, England)**

English historian whose 12 – volume *A Study of History* (1934-61) put forward a philosophy of history, based on an analysis of the cyclical development and decline of civilizations, that provoked much discussion.

Toynbee was a nephew of the 19th Century economist Arnold Toynbee. He was educated at Balliol College, Oxford (1911) and studied briefly at the British School at Athens, an experience that influenced the genesis of his philosophy about the decline of civilizations. In 1917, he became *a tutor a fellow* in ancient history at Balliol College and in 1915 he began working for the intelligence department of British Foreign Office. After serving as a delegate to the Paris Peace Conference in 1919 he was appointed Professor for Byzantine and modern Greek Studies at the University of London. From 1921 to 1922 he was the Manchester Guardian correspondent during the Greco-Turkish War, an experience that resulted in the publication of *The Western question in Greece and Turkey* (1922). In 1925 he became research professor of international history at the London School of Economics and director of studies at the Royal Institute of International Affairs in London.

While the writing of the *Study of History* was under way. Toynbee produced numerous smaller works and served as director of Foreign Research of the Royal Institute of International Affairs (1939-1943) and director of the Research Department of the Foreign Office (1943-1946); he also retained his position at the London School of Economics until his retirement in 1956. A prolific writer, he continued to produce volumes on world religions, western civilization, classical history, and world travel throughout the 1950s and 1960s. After World War II, he shifted his emphasis from civilization to the primacy of higher religions as historical protagonists. His other works include *Civilization on Trial* (1948), *East to West: A Journey Round the World* (1958), and *Hellenism: The History of a Civilization* (1959).

### Al-Umari, Akram Dia al-Din (Dr.) (b. 1942)

Born in 1361AH/1942 AD at Mosul in northern Iraq, Dr. Umari obtained his degrees of B.A. and M.A. from Baghdad University in Islamic history in 1382 AH/1962 and 1386AH/1966 respectively. He completed his Ph.D. from 'Ayn Shams University Cairo in 1394AH/1974 AD. He taught at Baghdad University from 1386 to 1396AH/1966 to 1976 AD. He was the Chairman of the Department of Graduate Studies at the Islamic University of Madinah and Chairman of the Academic Council from 1397 to 1402 AH/1977 to 1982AD. He is presently Professor of History of the Sunnah at the Graduate Department of the Islamic University of Madinah.

Dr. al-Umari has authored and edited nearly twenty works on Islamic history and in particular, on the subject of the Prophet's sirah. Among the most important of those works are the following: *Buhuth fi al-Sunnah al-Mushriqah, Al-Mujtama al-Madani fi Ahd al-Nubuwah* (2 volumes), *Al-Risalah wa al-Rasul, Al-Sirah al-Nabawiyah al-Sahihah, Qiyam al-Mujtama al-Islami min Manzur Hadāri* and *Al-Turāth wa al-Mu'āsarah*. Among the edited works are the following: *Al-M'arifah wa al-Tarikh* by Yaqub bin Sufyan al-Fasawi, *Azwāj al-Nabiy* by Muhammad bin Zubālah, *Tariqat al-Nabiy* by Hammad ibn Ismail al-Ansari and *Musnad Khalifah Ibn Khayyat* by Ibn Khayyat al-Usfuri al-Basari.

**Watt, Montogomery, W.**

The British orientalist who has been involved in the study of Islam and in contact with Muslims since 1938. From 1947 to 1979 he was Head of the Department of Arabic and Islamic Studies at the University of Edinburgh, and then Professor Emeritus.

His Ph.D. thesis on *Free Will and Predestination in Early Islam* presented to the University of Edinburgh in 1944 and published later in 1948, demonstrated an unusual gift for textual interpretation, combined with a certain lucidity of arrangement which made the argumentation immediately clear to the reader. His two books on the life and epoch of the Prophet *Muhammad at Mecca* (1953) and *Muhammad at Medina* (1956), later on summarized in one single volume (*Muhammad: Prophet and Statesman*, 1961) and translated, in one or the other version into several languages, combined both qualities the ability to read a text as what it is, and the abstraction necessary for defining the cipher of a movement or period – in the most fruitful way. Another work *Islam and the Integration of Society* (1961) is basically an explanation of how Islam succeeded in incorporating the divergent elements which shaped its civilization and how its initial pluralism developed into the uniform and almost monolithic world view which characterized it until the intervention of modern European ideas.

Watt maintained the importance of the intellectual as an 'ideational' factor in history. He discussed the problem in a paradigmatic way in his profound study on al-Ghazali (*Muslim Intellectual*, 1963). This aspect may be seen in his other surveys and introductions as *Islamic Philosophy and Theology* (1962), *A History of Islamic Spain* (1965), *A Companion to the* Qurān (1967), *Islamic Political Thought: The Basic Concepts* (1968), *The Influence of Islam on Medieval Europe* (1972) and *The Majesty that was Islam* (1974). Some other works include, *Formative Period of Islamic Thought* (1973), *Islamic Revelation in the Modern World* (1970), *The Reality of God* (1957), *The Cure for Human Troubles* (1959), *Truth in the Religions* (1963) and *Islam and the Christianity Today* (1983).

**Wellhausen, Julius (b. May 17, 1844, Hameln, Hanover, Germany – d. January 7, 1918 Gottingen, Germany)**

German biblical scholar best known for his analysis of the structure and dating of the Pentateuch. He studied at the University of Gottingen and taught there briefly before becoming professor of the Old Testament at Greifswald in 1872, a position he resigned 10 years later because of conflicts with his academic supervisors. After teaching at other German Universities, he returned to Gottingen in 1892, remaining there until his death.

His major writings put forth the view that the books of the Pentateuch were not written by Moses but were the result of oral traditions that evolved over time from a nomadic religion through the prophets, as it is presented in the Old Testament. He dissected two distinct narrative structures from genesis, determining that these narratives were the oldest portion of the Pentateuch, while the laws and rituals were the latest elements. His New Testament studies, particularly his assertion of the priority of the Gospel according to Mark over the hypothetical "Q" document believed to be the basis for the gospels of both Mathew and Luke, were not as well accepted as his Old Testament work. His another work *The Arab Kingdom and its Fall* has mainly by discussed and analysed the events leading to the fall of Arabs in the middle of the $8^{th}$ century and represents a comprehensive account of the whole period.

**Yahya Ali, Maulvi (1828-1868)**

Son of Elahi Bakhsh and brother of Maulvi Ahmadullah of Patna was a Leader of the Mujahidin movement of Sayyid Ahmad Shaheed. He in the repressive campaign against the Wahhabis in 1864 was arrested and sent to Ambala for trial alongwith Maulavi Muhammad Jafar and Muhammad Shafi and was sentenced to death for abetment of war against the Queen. The sentence was later commuted to transportation for life. He was deported to Andaman's where he died.

*****

# CREDITS

### 1. Classical Political Thought

This paper with the older title "A Critical Study of Classical Political Thought in Islam" first appeared in the quarterly journal *Islam and the Modern Age*, New Delhi, Vol. XXII, No. 2, May 1992, pp. 115-136. It was further developed and presented in the 'Workshop on Legacy in Islam, organized by Institute of Objective Studies, Aligarh Chapter on January 30, 1995 in the Faculty of Arts, A.M.U., Aligarh.

### 2. Some Misperceptions about Islamic Political Theory

This article was first published with the title "Some Reflections on Islamic Political Theory" in Hamdard Islamicus, Karachi, Vol. XXII, No. 2, April-June 1999, pp. 7-12, a quarterly journal of Studies and research in Islam published by Bait al-Hikmah at Madinah al-Hikmah. The editor added a note on the article that it is a critique of our classical and medieval political thinkers and scholars who appear to have tried to relate interpretation of political theories and concepts to their own contemporary conditions. It means that modern Muslim thinkers, following their example, can adopt a similar approach and practice *ijtihād*.

### 3. Islamization of Political Science

This was presented in the seminar on "Research Methodology in Islamic Perspective" organized by the Department of Philosophy, A.M.U., Aligarh and Institute of Objective Studies, New Delhi in February 1999, and was published in the *Journal of Objective Studies*, New Delhi, Vol. 3, No. 1, 1991, pp. 107-123.

### 4. Liberation Struggle or Islam: Reflections on the Mujahidin Movement of India

Originally presented as a paper to the National Seminar on 'The Role of Muslims in the Freedom Movement of India' organized by the Department of Islamic Studies, A.M.U., Aligarh on 18-19 March 2005, and is still unpublished.

### 5. Arab Nationalism

This paper was presented to the National Seminar on 'Trends in the Modern Arabic Poetry, organized by the Department of Arabic, A.M.U., Aligarh on 11-12 March 2004, and was published later on in the proceeding of the seminar entitled "al-*Naza'āt al-Jadeedah fi al-Sh'ir al-Arabi al-Hadith*, Department of Arabic, A.M.U., Aligarh, 2005, pp. 68-92. The seminar aimed to highlight the new trends, concepts and tendencies – both literal and intellectual – incorporated in the modern Arabic poetry. It was earnestly felt in the seminar that the modern Arabic literature whole heartedly accepted all the new trends in its paradigm and specific cultural milieu without compromising its values, characteristics and components.

## 6. Islamic *Shura* and Western Democracy

Under the title 'Islamic *Shura* and Western Democracy: Introductory Outlines' It was published in *Hamdard Islamicus, Karachi*, Vol. XXVI, No. 4, October-December, 2003. pp. 59-69. The learned editor of the Journal added three footnotes to enrich the discussion: i) upon the prophetic tradition quoted in the article qualifying the permissibility of rebellion against those rulers who discard the performance of prayers, the editor comments on it saying that it may be noted that when the first caliph sent forces to quell the rebellion by dissenters, non-payers of *Zakah* or recanters he also prescribed joining in the prayers with the army of Islam as a test for assessing their loyalty and status of the rebels; ii) on the role of Masjid in Islamic society as referred in the article, the editorial note reads that during the period of the holy Prophet and his pious Caliphs the affairs of state were also dealt as there was no *dar al-amārah*; and iii) on the point raised in the discussion about the revelation of the Qurānic chapter III verse, No. 159 after the battle of *Uhud*, the editorial note goes on adding that whenever the Prophet was compelled to take any important decision on his own or in consultation with his companions, verses of the Qurān in support or warning came *e.g.* the case of treatment of the pagan prisoners after the battle of *Badr*.

## 7. Islamic Pluralism

An earlier version of this paper was presented to the National Seminar on '*Muslims in Pluralistic Society: Prospects and Challenges*' organized by the Department of Islamic Studies, A.M.U., Aligarh on 14-15 February 2002, and is still unpublished. The paper has been largely revised and some new fruitful discussions have been added. In the said seminar 37 research papers in Urdu, Arabic and English languages were presented by the scholars of various disciplines in order to chalkout a plan of action for future challenges. The issues discussed in detail revolved around minority-based Muslim Ummah. An urgent need to demonstrate tolerance even in intolerable situations, dignity and farsightedness and to maintain faithly approach and Godly method while facing the complicated problems of plural society, and in order to realize all these noble ideals, building up a new fiqh – may be titled *fiqh al-Aqalliyāt* was finally concluded.

*****

# GLOSSARY

| | |
|---|---|
| *aāl e imran* | Children of Imran, One of the Chapters of the Qur'an. |
| *Abbasids* | Islamic empire lasted from 750 to 1258 A.D. ruled by 37 caliphs, ascribed to Abbas bin Abd al-Muttalib (d. 32/653). The revolution brought in to being under Abu Muslim Khurasani after overthrowing the Umayyads. |
| *absolutism* | The principle that those in government should have unlimited power. |
| *adab al-katib* | The literature on secretarial works and their technicalities |
| *adalat/adalah* | Social justice |
| *ādil* | Just |
| *adl* | Justice |
| *agnosticism* | The theory that one can not know whether or not God exists. |
| *ahādith* | Sg. Hadith. |
| *ahl – bid'ah* | The people who created or practiced naval things contrary to the Islamic texts. |
| *ahl al-hall wa al-aqd* | People of loosening and binding, a title given to the religious scholars, political leaders and intellectuals who have the authority and influence in the society and the government. |
| *ahl al-sunnah* | The people who follow the traditions of the Prophet (SAW), constituting the majority who are usually referred to as Sunnis. |
| *Ahmadiyah* | A sect founded by Mirza Ghulam Ahmad (1839-1908) better known a Qadiyaniyat being ascribed to Qadian, a town in Punjab. |

| | |
|---|---|
| *akhbār ā hād* | Pl. of *Khabr wāhed*. Those traditions narrated through a single channel. |
| *ākhirah* | The next world, the world, the world of resurrection and eschatological realities. |
| *al-'aammah* | The masses. |
| *al-ahkam al-sultaniyah* | The ordinances of government |
| *al-Azhar* | A mosque in Cairo founded by Jawhar al-Siqilli by the order of the Fatimid Caliph al-Muizz li Din Allah in 972 A.H., called with the name of Fatimah Zahra the daughter of Prophet (SAW). The mosque turned into an University in 1936 and the faculties of Shariah and Arabic Literature were established. After 1961 all the departments of languages and humanities were added to convert it into a fully fledged university. |
| *al-Baqarah* | Cow, one of the chapters of the Qur'an. |
| *al-basar* | The act or potential of seeing. |
| *al-din* | The religion of Islam |
| *al-fuād* | The act or potential of feeling in the heart. |
| *al-Hudaybiyah* | A valley near Makkah, became popular due to the treaty signed therein between the Prophet (SAW) and the Makkan pagans emphasizing on no war to be initiated from any side for ten years. |
| *alim* | Religious Scholar |
| *alimiyah* | A degree in Madrasah system equivalent to +2 system of modern education. |
| *al-khulafa al-rashidūn* | The rightly-guided caliphs, applied to first four caliphs of Islam. |
| *allāma* | The most authentic and the greatest scholar |
| *al-madinah al-jamā'iyah/al-jimā'iyah/al-jummā'iyah* | The democratic state. |

| | |
|---|---|
| *al-masjid al-harām* | The sacred mosque at Makkah |
| *al-Qāidah* | A global organisation of militancy and terrorism founded by Bin Laden for the cause of Islam. |
| *al-rabitah al-Islamiyah* | The Islamic league. |
| *al-risālah* | The message of Islam as propagated by the Prophet (SAW). |
| *al-sam'* | The act or potential of hearing |
| *al-tajamm'u al-haraki* | Dynamic concrescence |
| *al-takāful al-ijtimāi* | Mutual social responsibility. |
| *andalusia* | Applied to peninsula of Iberie by the Arabs when they captured it. It became independent of Abbasids and turned into Umavid Kingdom during the period of Abdur Rahman I in 752 A.D. The Kingdom was later on pieced into various petty states in 1031 and, then confined into Granada Emirate (1236-1492) and the term also was applied in that in limited sense. Today it is the name of southernmost region of Spain and Seville is its capital. |
| *ansār* | Helpers, those in Madinah who helped the Prophet in establishing the first Islamic Community after his migration from Makkah to that city. |
| *apostates* | Those who abandon their religious faith |
| *aristotelian (ideas)* | Of or pertaining to the Greek Philosopher Aristotle (d. 322 B.C.) or his philosophical system. |
| *asabiyah* | Derived from the root 'asab (to bind) and asābah (union), it refers to a socio-cultural bond that can be used to measure the strength of social groupings. It was a familiar term in the pre-Islamic era and became a popular concept when Ibn Khaldun (1332-1406) used it in his |

| | |
|---|---|
| | work *Muqaddimah*. *Asabiyah*, then, can be understood as social solidarity, with emphasis on group consciousness, cohesiveness and unity. |
| *asālah* | Innovative application of original Islamic principles to changing situation not compromising with the Islamic basics. |
| *asharism/asharite* | The doctrine founded by Abu al-Hasan Ashari (874-936 A.D.) |
| *asrār e shariah* | Secrets of Shariah, an Islamic discipline developed by the Muslim scholars in order to discuss the logic and reasoning of Islam. |
| *athār* | *(sg. athar)* Sayings of the ancestors |
| *autocracy* | A system of government in which one person has total power. |
| *axiom* | A statement regarded as obviously true. |
| *āyah* | *(Pl. Āyāt)* Sign, symbol, or portent. The phenomena of the created order both macrocosmic and microcosmic are identified as 'signs of God'. |
| *Ayah al-Kursi* | 'Verse of the Throne', verse No. 255 of the IInd Quranic Chapter. |
| *ayn al-yaqeen* | Empiricism or knowledge based upon observation and experiment. |
| *azm* | Determination. |
| *banilisrael* | The children of Israel |
| *barelvi school* | A sect departed from the hanafids founded by Maulana Ahmad Raza Khan better know in his circle as 'Fadhil Barelvi' who tried his best to 'preserve Islam not as represented in the basic texts, but as perceived and practiced in the society'. |
| *Bathism* | The ideology and approach of the Arab Socialist B'ath Party (*Hizb al-Ba'th al-Arabi al-Ishtiraki*) founded in Syria in the early 1940s by |

| | |
|---|---|
| | militants of the Arab Revival Movement, which was led by the two Damascene teachers Michel 'Aflaq and Salahuddin al-Baytar, in conjunction with followers of the philosopher Zaki al-Arsuzi of Antioch. In reaction to Ottoman domination and European colonization, the Party took as its slogan the revitalization, reunification and liberation of "one Arab nation with an eternal mission", and advocated a revolutionary process of reversing (*inquilāb*) the course of history. At its first congress in Damascus in April 1947, the Ba'th promulgated a constitution as its fundamental text. |
| *bātiniyah* | The esoterics, who adhere to the esoteric meanings and commentaries of the Qur'an in its symbolical perspective. The Sunnis applied the term for various deviant sects mostly political, the most important was that of Karmatians. |
| *begāngān baeedul watan* | Origin Persian, strangers of the remote homes. |
| *behaviouralism* | The doctrine that objective investigation of stimuli and responses is the only valid psychological method. |
| *belcha* | Spade |
| *bolshevism* | Origin Russian bol'she' 'greater'. Being a member of the majority group within the Russian Social Democratic Party, which seized power in the Revolution of 1917. |
| *Brahmo Samaj* | The Hindu quasi-Protestant Reform Movement 'Society of Worshippers of Brahma, founded in Calcutta by Ram Mohan Roy in 1828. It discards Hindu rituals and adopts some Christian practices in its worship. Influenced by Islam and Christianity it denounces polytheism and idol worship and Caste system. |
| *buhrān* | Crisis |
| *bureaucracy* | A system of government in which most |

| | |
|---|---|
| | decisions are taken by the state officials rather than by elected representatives. |
| *buwayhids* | A Persian dynasty ruled form 932A.D. to 1055 A.D. founded by Abu Shuja‘ Buwayh whose sons Ali Imad al-Dawlah, Ahmad Muizz al-Dawlah and Hassan Rukn al-Dawlah reigned in the cities of Isfahān, Shiraz, Kirman and Baghdād (945 A.D.) and the Caliph became a puppet ruler in their hands. |
| *caliphate* | The highest institution of politics in Islam. |
| *Chishtiyah* | A prominent Sufi order that derives it name from Chisht, a village near Herat where the founder of the order, Khawajah Abu Is'hāq resided for sometime in the twelfth century. In India it was introduced by Muinuddin Sijzi (d. 1236) who chose Ajmer in Rajputana state as the location for his hospice. The main doctrine was that of wahdatul Wujud, and practices included, *dhikr*, *muraqabah*, secluded worship for forty days (*chillah*) and *majlis samā'* (assembly devoted to spiritual music). |
| *constitutionalism* | The theory to run the government according to the constitution. |
| *cosmopolitan* | Origin from Greek *Kosmos* 'word' + politises 'citizen', consisting of people from many different countries. |
| *crusade* | Any of a series of medieval military expeditious made between the Christians of Europe and the Muslims for the sake of the Holy Land of Palestine. |
| *crusader (modern)* | The western man with the zeal of crusade against Islam. |
| *daf'e madharrat* | Advoidance of harm in general. |
| *dar al-islam* | The land or abode of Islam. |
| *dawah* | Invitation to accept the religion of Islam. |
| *dawrah hadith* | A full fledged course of learning the selected |

| | |
|---|---|
| | sources of *hadith* in Islamic seminaries in *Nizami* curricula. |
| *dhikr* | Remembering God with the specific words in mysticism having two kinds: *Khafi* (remembering secretly) and *jali* (doing loudly in public or congregation. |
| *dhiya* | Waste |
| *dictatorship* | Government by a ruler with total power over a country. |
| *din* | Religion |
| *din al-fitrah* | The primordial religion which man carries at the depth of his nature and with which Islam identifies itself. |
| *disequilibrium* | (pl. disequilibria) Lack or loss of equilibrium, instability, an imbalance. |
| *diwān* | Office |
| *emeritus* | Origin Latin, honourably discharged from service; (of a former office holder, esp. a professor) retired but allowed to retain his title as an honour. |
| *empricism* | The theory that all knowledge is derived from experience and observation. |
| *epistemology* | The branch of philosophy that deals with knowledge. |
| *exactitude* | The quality of being exact. |
| *Fadhilah* | A degree in Madrasah system equivalent to B.A. in most of the seminaries.. |
| *Falahi* | A graduate of Islamic seminary Jamiatul Falah, Bilariaganj, District Azamgarh, U.P. |
| *fanatic* | Origin Latin *fanaticus* 'of a temple'. A person filled with excessive enthusiasm for an extreme political or religious cause. The British historians called the Muslim freedom fighters of 1857 as 'fanatics'. |

| | |
|---|---|
| *fard 'ayn* | Individual religious obligation in Islam. |
| *fard kifayah* | A collective religious duty in Islam that may be performed by an individual or a group of individuals representing the whole population of a town. |
| *fascism* | A right-wing system of government characterized by extreme nationalistic beliefs and strict obedience to a leader or the state. |
| *Fatimids* | The dynasty ruled from 909 A.D. to 1171 A.D. ascribed to Fatimah the wife of Ali and founded by Ubaidullah al-Mahdi. It was first established in Tunisia. The whole of North Africa then was captured and even Egypt was conquered by the powerful ruler Muizz Li Din Allah through his general Jawhar who founded Cairo City. |
| *fatwa* | The authoritative opinion of a high cleric in matters affecting the community of Islam. |
| *fay* | Technically a property abandoned by the enemy or taken from him without a formal war, distinguished from the spoils or booties. |
| *fiqh* | Islamic jurisprudence |
| *fitnah* | Anarchy, disorder, persecution. The Holy Qur'an has used it sometimes for an aggressive paganism (2: 193). |
| *fuqaha* | *(sg. Faqih)* Experts of Islamic Law, jurists. |
| *furū'* | (sg. Far') branches |
| *ghassān* | An ancient Arab dynasty of Yemenid origin, migrated on the eve of the explosion of Ma'arib dame and settled down in the areas of Hurān, eastern Jordan, Lebanon Phyniqiah and Palestine and embraced Christianity in the last decade of the third century. Their prominent kings are al-Harith bin Jabalah (529-569), al-Mundir bin al-Harith (569-581) and al-Numan bin al-Mundir (d. 595 approximately). |

| | |
|---|---|
| *gheelah* | Intercourse with wife during the period when child depends upon his mother's milk. |
| *habeas corpus* | Origin Latin. You shall have the body (in court) a written order that an arrested person be brought before a judge or into court, to decide whether his detention is lawful. |
| *Hadid* | Iron, one of the Quranic chapters. |
| *hadith* | Saying or practice of the Prophet (SAW). |
| *hafiz* | One who memorizes the Holy Qur'an by his heart. |
| *hakimiyah* | Sovereignty |
| *halal* | Permissible in Islamic Law. |
| *hanafid* | A follower of Imam Abu Hanifa. |
| *hanbali* | A follower of Imam Ahmad bin Hanbal. |
| *hanzal* | An Arab plant like bitter cucumber. |
| *haqq al-yaqeen* | The absolute knowledge. |
| *harām* | Prohibited in Islamic Law. |
| *haramayn sharifayn* | The two sacred mosques at Makkah and Madinah |
| *hellenistic* | Having to do with Greek culture from 323 B.C. to 31 B.C. Origin named after *Hellen*, the mythical ancestor of all the Greeks. |
| *hijra* | Migration for the cause of Islam. |
| *hinterland* | Origin German, the remote areas of a country, away from the coast and major rivers. |
| *hudūd* | (sg. Hadd) Islamic punishments clearly defined in the Islamic texts. |
| *humanism* | A system of thought that regards humans as capable of using their intelligence to live their lives, rather than relying on religious belief. |
| *ibādah* | Worship |

| | |
|---|---|
| *idealism* | The belief that ideals can be achieved, even when this is unrealistic. |
| *ijma* | Consensus of opinion among the Muslim scholars of a period. Imam Shafi'i has sanctioned another kind also that is *ijma sukuti*: a consensus not verbally declared, but practiced and executed and is not openly opposed. |
| *ijtihād* | Use of human reason in the elaboration and interpretation of the Shariah, original juristic opinion. |
| *ikhtiyār* | Having option. |
| *Iikhwan/al-Ikhwan al-Muslimun* | The Muslim Brotherhood |
| *ilm* | Knowledge |
| *ilm al-umran* | Sociology that was founded by Ibn Khaldun and developed in the modern period by Ali Shariati of Iran and Malek Bennabi of Algeria. |
| *ilm al-yaqeen* | Rationalism or inference based upon the judgement. |
| *imam* | He who stands before, leader of prayer, authority in religious sciences, caliph. In Shi'ism the term is used in a special sense and refers to those descendants of the Prophet (SAW) who bear within themselves the 'Prophetic Light'. |
| *imam al-haramayn* | Leader of prayers in the Two Holy sacred Mosques |
| *imamah* | The virtue and function of an Imam. |
| *iman* | Faith |
| *imārah* | The virtue or function of an amir. |
| *Indian Wahabis* | Indian Muslims who follow the teachings of Muhammad bin Abdul *Wahhab* (1703-92). The British called every Muslim who rebelled against them as *Wahabi*. In fact this term was |

| | |
|---|---|
| | coined by the British to defame the freedom fighters. |
| *insān kāmil* | The universal or perfect man, used in both the mysticism and Muslim philosophy. The human being who has attained the fullness of the human state and has become the perfect mirror, in which are reflected God's Names and Qualities. |
| *intizār* | Anticipation of the return of the Hidden Imam as believed by Shia community. |
| *irtifāqāt* | Pl. of *irtifāq*, to be gentle, soft, gracious, courteous or civil. The term was coined by Shah Wali Allah of Delhi (1703-1762) to represent the development of human societies through four *irtifaqāt* or stages of increasingly refined order and elaboration of arts of civilized life. These four stages are roughly equivalent to: following natural or instinctive laws, integrating family life and social transactions, developing a local political order, and finally the extension of this to the international level , which Wali Allah identifies with the Islamic Caliphate. |
| *ishrak fi al-adāt* | Association with God in performing various rituals and celebrations. |
| *ishrāk fi al-ibadāt* | Association with God in the worships and religious obligations. |
| *ishrāk fi al-ilm* | Association with God in the field of knowledge. |
| *ishrāk fi al-tasarruf* | Association with God in His doings and disposals. |
| *ishtirakiyah al-Islam* | The socialism of Islam. |
| *Islamic modernism* | The trend of modernization and westernization in Muslim society. |
| *Islamization (-of knowledge)* | Reconstruction of modern thought especially of social sciences in Islamic perspective. The movement launched in modern times by Ismail |

| | |
|---|---|
| | Raji al-Faruqi Shaheed (1921-1986) in Virginia. |
| *Ismā'ilies* | The Shia sect that believes in the leadership of Ismail bin Jafar al-Sādiq after the death of his father. Today the title is applied to the followers of Agha Khan. |
| *istihsān* | Juristic preference |
| *istislah* | Seeking public interests while legislation is going on. |
| *istislāh* | An important method of Islamic jurisprudence that signifies the public interest in the process of legislation. |
| *jabre e tarikh* | Historical determinism |
| *jalaliyah* | A Sufi order also known as Maulawiyah founded by Jalaluddin Rumi (604-672/1207-1273) the great Persian poet and practicing Sufi who was entitled as Jalbi Afandi. Born in Balkh (Iran), Learnt from his father Bahauddin. He travelled Baghdad, Makkah and Syria, and settled down Later on in Quniah where breathed his last. His *mathnawi* as of global repute. |
| *jalb manfa'at* | The achievement of general welfare of mankind |
| *jamā'ah* | Group, association. |
| *jamaat Islami* | Islamic organization founded by Maududi in India in 1941. |
| *jihād* | Striving utmost for the noble cause. |
| *jihād iitiraz* | To launch protest against a tyrant which is termed as *amr bi al-Maroof* in Prophetic traditions. |
| *jumhūr* | The common people. |
| *kalam* | Literally 'word'. One of the names of the Qur'an as well as one of the attributes of God. Later it became the title for theology or that discipline which sought to defend the tenets of the faith through the use of rational arguments. |

| | |
|---|---|
| *khaki* | Mean, humble, made of soil. |
| *khawārij* | One of the oldest Muslim sects rebelled first against Ali who had accepted the principle of arbitration after the battle of Siffīn (37-657) and then fought against Muawiyah. They later on organized themselves into a militant socio-religious organization and were always busy in conspiracies and rebellions against the remaining groups. They were further divided into various minor groups as Azāriqah, Ibādhiyah, Sifriyah and so on. Among its dignitaries are Tirmāh bin Hakim, Dhahhāk bin Qays Shaybani, Qatari bi al-Faja'h etc. |
| *Kaybar* | Oasis in al-Hijaz (presently Saudi Arabia) that was captured by the Prophet in 628 from the Jews. |
| *khilafah ala minhāj al-nubuwah* | Caliphate on the pattern of the prophethood. |
| *khilāfah nubuwah* | Caliphate representing the Prophethood |
| *khilāfah rahmah* | Caliphate of benevolence. |
| *khilāfah rāshidah* | The rightly-guided caliphate. |
| *khilafat* | See caliphate |
| *kuffār farang* | Origin Persian. The British infidels. |
| *kufr* | Paganism |
| *la zarar wala zirar* | Do not harm anyone nor tolerate. |
| *liberal Islam* | The term is coined by the West to differentiate between those who strictly follow the religion and those who are not so committed with it. |
| *lutf* | Kindness, benevolence |
| *m'utazilah/mùtuzili/mutaz ilite* | A Muslim sect in early history of Islam founded by Wāsil bi al-Ata who departed from the circle of al-Hassan al-Basari (d. 110/728) on the issue of the position of a Muslim committing a severe crime, whether he remains a Muslim or turns |

| | |
|---|---|
| | into a Kafir. The sect propagated the five fundamentals of its own definition contrary to Sunnis, i) tawhid, ii) Adl, iii) al-manzilah bayn al-Manzilatayn, iv) amr bi al-Maroof wa nahy' 'an al-Munkar and (v) W'ad wa way'id |
| *Machiavellianism* | The theory in politics propounded first by Machiavelli (1469-1527) the Italian statesman and philosopher, who wrote "*The Prince*", which advised rulers that to gain and retain power they might have to use deception, cruelty, and other unethical methods. |
| *madariyah* | A distinctive regional Sufi order founded in India, with a narrow outreach by Badiuddin Shah Madari, an immigrant (Syrian ?) who settled in Jaunpur where he died *circa* 1440, his tomb at Makanpur (near Jaunpur) becoming the focus of a remarkable festival (*'urs*) and fair. This occasion also acquired notoriety through the rite of fire-walking performed by the Madari *faqirs*. This group is regarded as a bi-shar' (anti-Islamic Law) order, but it is more of syncretistic sect than an order. |
| *Madinah (-Munawwarah/al-Nabi)* | The second sacred place of the Islamic world called as Yathrib before the migration of the Prophet to that city. |
| *madinah al-fādilah* | 'the virtuous city' reminds one first, and most properly, of the famous book written by al-Farabi 257-339/870-950) designated as the 'second teacher' in the history. He has been called the founder of Islamic Political Philosophy. |
| *Madni* | Relating to Madinah; a Quranic Surah revealed therein. |
| *madrasah* | An Islamic seminary |
| *majlis al-shura* | The consultative assembly. |
| *Makki* | Relating to Makkah; a Quranic Surah revealed therein. |

| | |
|---|---|
| *mālik al-mulk* | The Owner of Power/domain. |
| *Mamluks* | The Turk and Mongol slaves who initially assisted Ayyubids through military power and consequently captured the power and established in Egypt two powerful dynasties: i) Bahris (1253-1382) the famous rulers of this dynasty are Baybers, Qalawūn and Khalil Ashraf, and ii) Burjis (1382-1517). First ruler of this dynasty was Burqus and Tumān was the last. |
| *maqāsid* | Pl. of maqsad, objectives. |
| *marjá taqlid* | Source of imitation. |
| *mas'uliyat* | Responsibility |
| *masālih mursalah* | The wider interest of the community being taken into account while the legislation is processed, as a principle of Islamic jurisprudence. |
| *masjid* | Mosque |
| *Masjid al-Nabi/al-Masjid al-Nabawi* | The Prophetic mosque. |
| *maslahah* | Public interest is regarded in Shariah as a basis of Law. According to necessity and particular circumstances, it consists of prohibiting or permitting a thing on the basis of whether or not it serves a "useful perpose" or *maslahah*. It can be defined as the establishment of legal principles recommended by reason of being advantageous. |
| *Mediterranean* | Of, or pertaining to, or characteristic of countries bordering the Mediteranian sea. |
| *minhāj al-karamah* | The method of respect and dignity. |
| *minhāj al-sunnah* | The method of the Prophet (SAW). |
| *modernization* | Adaptation of the modern ideas. |
| *Mohammadans* | Muslims, following Muhammad as their |

| | |
|---|---|
| | Prophet. The term was wrongly coined by the West. |
| *monarchy* | Government by a monarch/king or queen. |
| *monotheism* | The doctrine or belief that there is only one God. |
| *muaiyyidāt* | Sanctions |
| *mubāya'ah* | The mutual pact between the head of the Islamic community and leader or people of Islamic community as well as the initiatic pact made between the spiritual guide and the disciple. |
| *mudhakkirah* | Memoir |
| *mufassirin (sg. mufassir)* | Commentators of the Qur'an. |
| *mufti* | Islamic scholar capable of issuing legal verdict according to Shariah. |
| *mujaddid* | *(Pl. Mujaddidin)* Renovator |
| *mujahidin* | *(sg. Mujahid)* Fighters in the way of Islam. |
| *mulk* | The royal authority, the power, the state. The term in its political meaning as an institution was used under the Umayyads (661-750) who were critized for betraying an ideal. The Qur'an cites the Hebrew prophet Tālūt emphasizing that God alone made and unmade (326) whom He endowed with knowledge and power, not wealth. Their signs were the Ark, a *sakinah*, and Moses' and Aaron's relics. |
| *mulukiyah* | Monarchy |
| *mumin/ pl.: muminin* | Faithful |
| *munāfiqun* | (sg. Munāfiq) hypocrites, one of the chapters of the Qur'an. |
| *muraqabah* | Vigilance upon the spiritual path; meditation and self-reflection. |
| *murshid* | The guide in mysticism. |

*mustabidd* — Authoritarian, dictator

*mutal'ah* — Study

*muttahidah qaumiyat* — United Nationalism

*muttaqi* — God-fearing Muslim

*Muwahhidūn* — The Islamic dynasty in al-Maghreb founded by al-Mahdi Ibn Tumart in 1146 after capturing Morocco the Capital of al-Murabids. Among its prominent rulers are Abdul Mumin bin Ali. Yousuf bin Abdul Mumin, and Yaqub al-Mansur, after whose demise the decline started. Consequently the Hafsids established independly their own in Tunisia in 1228 and Banu Abdul Wad also did in Tilmissan in 1235.

*mysticism* — A systematic teaching about the Divine Reality and a method of realization that permits the seeker to reach it in one way or the other. Some scholars use this term as an equivalent to Islamic *tasawwuf*.

*Nadvi* — A graduate of Darul Uloom Nadwatul Ulama Lucknow.

*nafl/nāfilah* — *(Pl. Nawāfil)* Supererogatory rites and performances.

*Naqshbandiyah* — A Sufi order which is attributed to Ahmad Ata Yaswi (d. 1116). In India it was established by Muhammad Bāqi Billah (1563-1603) and was fully developed by Shaykh Ahmad Sirhindi in the seventeenth century. The main doctrine is *Wahadat al-Shuhūd*, which has been defined as belief in 'God witnessing to Himself in the heart of His votary (*'ābid*). This union with God (Jam') leads to a unification (*ittihād*) which is not a unification of substance, but operates through the act of faith and of Love. Sirhindi's severe attack on Ibn Arabi's Wahdat ul Wujud changed the mystical moorings in India.

*Nasāra nikohidah khisāl* — Origin Persian, Christians of tyrannizing habits.

| | |
|---|---|
| *nationalism* | Devotion and complete surrender to one's nation. |
| *nationalist Islam* | Islam as understood and advocated by the nationalists. |
| *nāzim* | Rector, manager |
| *nazism* | Origin German, from the pronounciation of *Nati-* in *National socialist*: the approach and behaviour of the far-right National Socialist German Workers' Party. |
| *niyābah* | Deputation |
| *nizam/nazm* | Coherence |
| *occidental* | Relating to the countries of the West. |
| *oligarchy* | Origin from Greek *oligoi* 'few'+*arkhein* 'to rule' means a small group of people having control of a state. |
| *orientalists* | European non-Muslim experts of Islam. |
| *orthodox* | In line with traditional or generally accepted beliefs. |
| *Pahlavi dynasty* | An strong dynasty (1343-1399/1925-1979) in Iran founded by Reza Shah Pahlavi (1878-1944) who despite socioeconomic reforms developed no institutions to depersonalize the state. He sought to modernize Iran and took a hostile stand towards the people and the religious scholars. |
| *pan-Islamism* | The unity among the Muslim world advocated by Jamaluddin Afghani. |
| *Patna propaganda* | The remnant from the Balākot battle field of British India continued hostility against the British through their permanent centre in Patna supervised by the Ulama of Sadiq Pur. This centre is described in British history as the 'Patna Propaganda'. |
| *Pentateuch* | Origin Greek. The first five books of the *Old* |

| | |
|---|---|
| | *Testament* and Hebrew scriptures. |
| *phenomenon* | A fact or event that appears or is perceived by one of the senses or by the mind. |
| *Platonic (ideas)* | Of, pertaining to, or associated with the Greek Philosopher Plato (429-347 B.C.). |
| *pluralism* | The existence or toleration in society of a number of groups that belong to different races or have different political or religious beliefs. |
| *polygraph* | A person who imitates or copies another |
| *prophecy* | Prophethood, the power and functions by virtue of whose possession a person becomes a Prophet (SAW). It is God – gifted not to be attained by human beings themselves. |
| *protagonist* | A person who actively supports a cause or idea. |
| *protestant* | A member of follower of any of the Western Christian Churches that are separate from the Roman Catholic Church. |
| *puritan* | A member of a group of English Protestants in the 16th and 17th centuries who sought to simplify forms of worship. |
| *Qadiriyah* | A Sufi order founded in Iraq by Hanbalite scholar and Sufi Abdul Qadir al-Jilani (1077-1166), established in India, under the Mughals, by Shah Nimatullah and Makhdum Muhammad Jilani, and was fully propagated under Muhammad Mir (1550-1635), popularly known as Miān Mir, the preceptor of Shah Jahan's son, Dara Shukoh, and daughter Jahan Ara. The Qadiris were generally tolerant of the non-Muslims and this attitude must have been one of the formative influences on the syncretistic thinking of Dara Shukoh. |
| *Qahtān* | Father of the Arab tribes in Yemen, according to Arab narrations, was divided later on into two branches: i) Himyar most of them being urbans ii) Kahlan most of whom were Bedouin. |

| | |
|---|---|
| *Qasimi* | A graduate of Darul Uloom Deoband. |
| *qasr* | Palace |
| *qawmiyah arabiyah* | Arab nationalism. |
| *qawwāli* | A group song genre of Indian Light Classical music which presents mystical poetry in Persian, Urdu and sometimes in Hindi, to be performed in Sufi assemblies in order to produce religious emotion. It symbolizes now the secular character and composite culture especially in South-east Asia. |
| *qisās* | The principle, introduced by the Qur'an, of retaliation for harm inflicted. Where a life is lost and the victim and perpetrator are of equal status, the death of the perpetrator is an expiation for the death of the victim. In harm short of the taking of life, a similar harm to the perpetrator is an expiation. Along with the establishment of these principles, Islam explicitly recommends the substitution of compensation on another plane, *i.e.* pardon for the guilty person, or material compensation for the harm suffered. (5:45) |
| *qiyās* | Analogical reasoning used in certain schools of Islamic Law. In logic and philosophy, it means syllogism. |
| Quds | Sanctuary, Jerusalem. |
| *Quraysh* | The ancient Arab tribe seized power in Makkah both in the religious and temporal spheres before the advent of Islam. Its prominent branches are Umayyah, Naūfal, Zuhrah, Makhzum, Jumah, Sahm, Hashim etc. |
| *rā'ina* | Literally means "Please look at us, attend to us". Verse No. 104 in the second chapter of the Qur'an. This word was disapproved by God because it was ridiculed by enemies by a little twist to suggest some insulting meaning. So an unambiguous word "Unzurna" with the |

| | |
|---|---|
| | same meaning was suggested. The general lesson is that we must guard ourselves against the cynical trick of using words which sound complimentary to the ear but have a hidden barb in them. |
| *rasul* | Messenger, he who has been chosen by God to bring His message to mankind. |
| *rawāfid* | (sg. *rafidi*) renefades, apostates, a term coined by Sunnis to apply on Shia community that denounces the first three caliphs of Islam. |
| *rawshanfikrān* | Enlightened thinkers |
| *renaissance* | The revival of art and literature under the influence of classical styles in the 14th – 16th centuries. |
| *republic* | A state in which power is held by the people and their elected representatives, and which has an elected head rather than a monarch. |
| *retrogressive* | Returning to an earlier and worse state. |
| *Rifayiah* | A sufi order founded by Abul Abbas Ahmad al-Husayni al-Rifāī (d. 578/1182) who was a follower of Shafiī school, born in a village 'Hasan' of Iraq and died in Umm Obaid a town in between Wāsit and Basarah. Among his academic works are: *Tafsir Surah al-Qadr, al-Tariq ila Allah, Sharh al-Tanbih fi al-Fiqh*, His utterances are compiled in a treatise called *Raheeq al-Kauthar*. |
| *riyasah aammah* | Leadership combining both the religious and temporal. |
| *sadd al-dhari'ah* | The obstruction of ostensibly legitimate means to illegitimate ends as a principle of Islamic Legislation. |
| *sahābah (sg. sahābi)* | Companions of the Prophet. |
| *salafi* | A follower of *salaf* (predecessors); Ahl al-Hadith. |

| | |
|---|---|
| *salāh* | The canonical daily prayers which are obligatory for all Muslims to perform five times a day. |
| *salah al-munfarid* | The individual prayer. |
| *simā'* | Ecstatic listening to music and religious poetry known as *qawwāli*, a feature of Chishtiyah order of tasawwuf. |
| *Sawād* | Name of the cultivated lands in Iraq. Historically it was applied to the area between Dajlah and Furat rivers, sometimes used as synonym to Iraq. |
| *scripturalist* | One who follows scriptures strictly. |
| *sh'ir al-muqāwamah* | The poetry of resistance. |
| *shahādah* | Martyrdom for the cause of Islam and the Muslims ranked highest in the degrees of spirituality by the Prophet (SAW) of Islam. |
| *shariah/shar'* | Islamic Law rooted in the Qur'an, *Hadith*, *Qiyas* and *Ijma*. |
| *shawkah* | Power, authority. |
| *shaykh (tasawwuf)* | A teacher, a revered person, more especifically a spiritual master. |
| *shaykh al-Islam* | The highest religious post under Ottomans. |
| *shirk* | To associate others with Allah in His Attributes. Names or Powers, believing that there are realities independent of Allah. |
| *shura* | Consultation, the democratic politics of Islam based upon *Khilafah* and people's consent. |
| *shura al-nās* | Lower chamber of consultation. |
| *Siffin* | A place on the Syrian frontiers on the river of Furat. On this spot Ali and Muawiyah had fought in the early history of Islam in 37 A.H./657 A.D. and after an agreement between the two it was stopped. |

*sine qua non* — Origin Latin: a thing that is absolutely necessary.

*sirāt mustaqim* — The straight path, which defines the life of Islam in general and the spiritual life in particular. The famous book of Sayyid Ahmad Shaheed.

*siyasah aqliyah* — The rational politics

*siyasah diniyah* — The religious politics

*siyasah madaniyah* — The civic politics

*social contract* — An unspoken agreement among the members of a society to cooperate for the benefit of all, for example by giving up some individual freedom in return for protection from the state.

*socialism* — A political and economic theory which holds that a country's land, transport, natural resources and chief industries should be owned or controlled by the community as a whole.

*socialist Islam* — Socialist brand of Islam portrayed by the communists.

*sophist* — In ancient Greek, a scholar, a teacher especially a paid teacher of philosophy and rhetoric, one associated with specious reasoning and moral scepticism.

*stoicism* — The thought and approach of the ancient Greek school of philosophy founded by Zeno (C 300 B.C.) and characterized by its austere ethical doctrines.

*Suhrawardiyah* — A Sufi order founded by Shaykh Najibuddin Abdul Qāhir Suhrawardi (d. 1169) and developed by his nephew Shihabuddin Suhrawardi (d. 1234) in Iraq. The Indian preachers of the order remained on cordial terms with the rulers; they were hanafids and stressed the importance of ritual prayers. Shaykh Bahauddin Zakariya established the order in Multan in the thirteenth century and

| | |
|---|---|
| | Jalaluddin Tabrezi in Bengal. |
| *sultan* | The ruler, the emperor, the power, the domain |
| *sunnah* | The tradition of the Prophet embracing his manner and ways of doing and acting in different circumstances in life. The term is sometimes applied to that of the holy Caliphs and companions. |
| *tabāi al-istibdād* | The nature and attributes of the tyranny. One of the titles of Kawākibi (1849-1902) of Ottoman Syria. |
| *tafsir* | Commentary of the Qur'an |
| *tafwīd* | Delegation |
| *tahdith* | Modernization |
| *tājirān mata'i farosh* | Origin Persian, merchants selling the commodities. |
| *tamim* | Generalization, nationalization of economic resources. |
| *tanzimāt* | The movement of modernization of military and society under Ottomans. |
| *taqiyah* | Dissimulation, hiding of one's religious beliefs in the face of danger, one of the doctrines of Shia sect. |
| *taqwā* | The term essentially signifies "God-consciousness" and "God-fearing" and, by extension, "piety". *Taqwa* and its derivatives occur more than 250 times in the Qur'an, it has been rendered variously as: fear, God-fearing, Godliness, piety, right conduct, righteousness, virtue, warding-off-evil, wariness. A survey of its usage in the Qur'an indicates that *taqwa* is often paired with faith, goodness, justice fairness, equity, guidance, truthfulness, perseverance fulfilment of promises, generosity. It is contrasted with *fujur* (perversity), *fisq* (deviation) and *zulm* (oppression). Some modern scholars like Abul Ala Maududi (d. |

| | |
|---|---|
| | 1979) Sayyid Qutb (d. 1966) and Fazlur Rahman (d. 1988) have paid particular attention to *taqwa* within the context of the need to regenerate Islam in the modern world. |
| *Taqwiyah al-Imān* | Strengthening the faith, the book composed by Shah Ismail Shaheed (1779-1831). |
| *tarikh* | History |
| *tasawwuf* | Esoterism in Islam as opposed to exoterism. |
| *tasawwur* | Concept |
| *tawakkul* | Trust and reliance on God |
| *tawil* | Inner, esoteric commentary or hermeneutics of the Sacred Text. The esoteric commentaries may also be called symbolic ones. Tawil applies to all kinds of symbols, whether in nature, in the world of man, or in the text of the revelation. |
| *tazkirah* | Reminder |
| *textualism* | Strict adherence to a text, especially that of scriptures. |
| *The enlightenment* | A European intellectual movement of the late 17th and 18th centuries emphasizing reason and individualism. |
| *the mutineers* | Indians who rebelled against the British in 1857. The British records declared them as rebels while the Indians pay their tributes to them as being the first freedom fighters of the country. A mutiny is an open rebellion against authority, especially by soldiers or sailors against their officers. |
| *theo-democracy* | The term used by Maududi (1902-1979) to connote the spirit of Islamic State based upon the concept of sovereignty of God and the people's consent in the issues not discussed in the Islamic texts. |
| *two-nation theory* | Theory that holds the Hindu and Muslim two |

| | |
|---|---|
| | different nations in the subcontinent and consequently advocates the separate states for each. |
| *ulama (sg. 'ālim)* | Class of learned men in Islamic society usually but not completely identified with those learned in the Islamic law. |
| *umm al-qura* | Mother of the towns, applies to Makkah. One the titles of Kawakibi. |
| *ummah* | The Islamic community. |
| *ummah wāhidah* | The one unified people of global character distinct from other ntions and peoples. |
| *urf* | Custom and Legal usage to be considered as important in the process of Islamic Legislation. |
| *urubah* | Arabism, Arab nationalism. |
| *usul al-fiqh* | Jurisprudential source methodology. |
| *utilitarianism* | The belief that the greatest happiness of the greatest number should be the guiding principle of right behaviour. |
| *Wahabi* | Literally a follower of Muhammad bin Abdul Wahhab. It is applied to Ahl Hadith (who follows the traditions of the Prophet and not any juristic school). |
| *Wahabi treatises* | The treatises compiled by *Ahl Hadith* scholars in British India to promote hatred and hostility against the government and to propagate the religious duty of waging jihad incumbent upon the Muslims. |
| *Wahadat al-Wujud* | 'the transcendent unit of bing', the doctrine held by many Sufis according to which only God possesses Being, all that exists deriving its existence from the One Being Who alone is. It was first theorized by Muhiuddin Ibn al-Arabi (d. 638/1240 A.D.) |
| *wahy* | Revelation of God |
| *wathiqah* | Legal document |

| | |
|---|---|
| *Western Islam* | Islam as conceived in Western perspective |
| *wilāyat* | Domination, rule, also the inner and esoteric function of the Prophet (SAW) which, according to *Shi'ism*, was transmitted to the Imams. In Sufism it is associated with esotericism as such. |
| *wilāyat e faqīh* | Domination of the jurists. The theory was developed by Khumayni (1902-1989) of Iran as the mandate of the jurist to rule, both in a series of lectures in Persian, which were published in Beirut in 1970 under the title of *Wilayat e faqih*, and in a work of jurisprudence on transactions, published in the second volume of *Kitab al-Rāy* in 1971. He argued that the right to rule devolves from the Imams to the mujtahids during the Occultation of the Twelfth Imam, and further, that if one of them were able to exercise that right by establishing a government, it would be incumbent upon other mujtahids to obey him. |
| *zakah* | Religious tax which is obligatory on every Muslim who qualifies it, and which constitutes one of the pillars of Islam. |
| *ziaamah āmmah* | The general leadership. |
| *zionism* | A movement for (originally) the re-establishment of a Jewish nation in Palestine and (since 1948) the development of the State of Israel. |
| *zulm* | Oppression, tyranny |
| *zulm (shia)* | Oppression of the Imam's justice as theorized by Shia community. |

*****

# BIBLIOGRAPHY

Abd al-Raziq, Ali, *Al-Islam wa Usūl al-Hukm*, Cairo, 1925

Abu Daud, *Sunan*, ed. Izzat Ubaid, Hims, 1969

Abu Sulayman A. Abdul Hamid, *The Islamic Theory of International Relations: New Directions for Islamic Methodology and Thought*, Herndon, 1987.

——————, *Islamization of Knowledge: General Principles and Work Plan*, International Institute of Islamic Thought, U. S. A., 1989.

——————, *Crisis in the Muslim Mind*, eng. Tr. Yusuf Talal Delorenzo, Herndon, IInd edition. 1994; Urdu tr. Dr. Obaidullah Fahad, *Fikr Islami Ka Buhrān*, Lahore, 2001.

Abu Ubaid al-Qasim b. Salam, *Kitab Al-Amwal*, Vol. 1, Cairo.

Ahmad b. Hanbal, *Musnad*, Vol. III.

Ahmad, Aziz, *Islamic Modernism in India and Pakistan*, London, 1967.

Ahmad, Irfan, The Islamic Method, *Islamic Thought*, Aligarh, Vol. VIII, No. 2, 1961.

Ahmad, Khurshid Dr. *Socialism or Islam*, English tr. Sharif Ahmad Khan, Hindustan Publications, Delhi

——————, Amricā: Muslim Duniya ki Be-itmenāni, Lahore, *Mausharat*, 2002

Ahmad, Moinuddin, *Sayyid Ahmad Shahid: His Life and Mission*, Lucknow, 1975

Al- Attas, Syed Muhammad Al- Naqib, Islam and Secularism, Kuala-Lampur, 1976.

Allal al-Fasi, *Maqasid al-Shariyah al-Islamiyah wa Makarimuha*, Morocco, 1963.

——————, *Al-Naqd al-`dati*, Cairo, 1952

——————, *Minhāj al-Istiqlāliyah*, Rabat, 1962

——————, Usūl al-Hukm fi al-Islam, in *al-Bayyinah*, I. I. Rabat, 1962

Arnold, S. T. W., *The Caliphate*, London, 1965

Asma Rashid & Malek Bennabi, *International Seminar on Malek Bennabi* (Programme Leaflet), University of Malaya, Kuala-Lumpur, 1991

Al-Baghdadi, Abdul Qadir, *Usool al-Din*, Istanbul, 1928

Babely, M., *al-Shura Fi al-Islam*, Beirut, 1968.

Berkes Niyazi, *Development of Secularism in Turkey*, McGill, 1964

Bhutti, Muhammad Ishaq, *Yādgār Majallah Ahl e Hadith, A Historical Document on the Academic, Dawah, Organizational, Missionary and*

*Welfare Contributions*, (Urdu)ed. Asghar Ali Imam Mahdi Salafi and Khalid Hanif Siddiqui Falahi (co-editor), Delhi, 2004

Bornes, H.L., *An Intellectual and Cultural History of the Western World*, Vol.2, 1965 New York

Bowle, J., *Western Political Thought- From the Origin to Rousseau*, London, 1961

Bukhari, *Sahih*, Cairo Vol. I Part 11.

Bukhsh, S. Khuda, "Ibn Khaldun and His History of Islamic Civilization", *Islamic Culture*, Hyderabad, 1927

Cassirer, Ernst, *The Myth of the State*, New Haven and London, Reprint 1986.

Clinard, Marshall. B., The Sociologist's Quest for Respectability, *The Sociological Quarterly* 7, 1966.

Cox, Harvey, *The Secular City*, New York, 1965.

Dahl, R. A., The Behavioural Approach in Political Science, Epitaph for a Monument to a Successful Protest, *The American Political Science Review*, Vol. 55, Dec. 1961.

Dar, Basheer Ahmad, *Religious Thought of Sayyid Ahmad Khan*, Lahore, 1957.

Dehlavi, Mirza Hairat, *Hayat Tayyibah*, Lahore, 1958.

Deutscher, Irwin, "Words and Deeds: Social Science and Social Policy", *Social Problems*, 13, 1966.

Dunning, W. R., *A History of Political Theories – Recent Times*, Allahabad, 1969

Easton, David, The Current Meaning of Behaviouralism, in Charlesworth, J. C. *Contemporary Political Analysis*, New York 1967.

El-Awa, MS., *On the Political System of the Islamic State*, Indiana, 1980.

Eldersveld, S. I., Research in Political Behaviour, in *Introductory Reading to Political Behaviour*, Chicago, 1961.

Enan, M. A., *Ibn Khaldun: His Life and Works*, Lahore, 1946.

———————, *Ibn Khaldun: His Life and Works*, Lahore, 1941

Esposito, John L., & Voll, John O, (editors) *Islam and Democracy*, New York, Oxford, 1996

———————, *Makers of Contemporary Islam*, Oxford University Press, 2001

Esposito, *Unholy War: Terror in the name of Islam*, Oxford, 2002

Al-Faruqi, Ismail Raji, "Towards a New Methodology for Quranic Exegesis", *Islamic Studies*, March, 1962.

*Al-Furqan Monthly*, Lucknow, July 1993

Fahad, Obaidullah, Dr., Tahrik Shahidayn Ka Tasawwur Islam, *Majallah Al-Furqān*, Sidhdharth Nagar, Vol. 11, No. 4, July-August 1998.

———————, *Principles of Diplomacy in Islam*, Lahore, 1996.

Farahi, Hamiduddin, *Fi Malukūt Allāh*, Azamgarh, 1391 AH.

Faruqi, M. Y., Early *fuqaha* on the Significance and Role of the *Khilafah*, *Hamdard Islamicus*, Karachi, Vol. XIV, NO. I.

Fawzia Bariun, "Malek Bennabi and the Intellectual problems of the Muslim Ummah", *American Journal of Islamic Social Sciences*, Herndon, Vol. 9 No. 3, 1992

Fazlur Rahman, *Islamic Methodology in History*, Islamabad, 1984.

*Foreign Affair*, 30, July, 1932

Al-Ghazali, *Fadaih al-Batiniyah*, Leiden, 1956.

—————, *Kitab al-Iqtisad fi al-Itiqad,* al-Mahmudiyah, Egypt

Al-Ghazali, Muhammad, *Min Huna Nalam*, Cairo

—————, *Our Beginning in Wisdom*, trans, I. E. Al-Farooqui, Washington, 1953

Ghannushi, Rashid, "The participation of Islamists in a Non – Islamic Government", in *Power – Sharing Islam*, London, 1993.

Gibb, H. A. R., "The Search for an Islamic Democracy, being Social Reform: Factor X", in the *Middle East in Transition*, ed. W. Z. Laqueur, London, 1958.

—————, *Modern Trends in Islam*, Chicago, 1947.

—————, *Studies on the Civilization of Islam*, London, 1962.

Gibb, HAR., and Eowen, Harold, *Islamic Society and the West*, Vol. 1, Part II, Oxford, 1957

Gibbon, E., *Decline and Fall of the Roman Empire*, An Abridgement by D. M. Low, London, 1960

Hamidullah, Muhammad, *Majmuah al- Wasaiq al- Siyasiyah li al- Ahd al- Nabawi wa al- Khilafah al- Rashidah*, Cairo, 1941.

Haq, Ahsanul, *Reinterpreting Islam in Iran: Life and Thoughts Of Ali Shariati*, Aligarh, 1995.

Hardy P. Dr., *The Muslims of British India*, Cambridge, 1972

Hass, Michael ad Maried, Henry, S. *Approaches to Political Science*, California, 1970.

Hertz, Fredrick, *Nationality in History and Politics: Psychology of National Sentiment and Nationalism,* 1944.

Hitti, P. K., *History of Arabs*, London, 1937

—————, *The Arab in Europe: Spain and Sicily*, London

Homoud, Muhammad Ali Nasir, Diplomacy in Islam, Jaipur, 1994.

Hosein, Imran N., Diplomacy in Islam: Treaties and Agreements – An Analysis of the Treaty of Hudaibiyah, *Muslim Education Quarterly*, Vol. 3, No. 3, 1986.

Hourani, Albert, *Arabic Thought in the Liberal Age 1798-1939*, Oxford University Press, 1970

Hull, R., *Medieval Theories of Papacy*, London, 1934.

Hussein, Alattas, *The Democracy of Islam*, The Hague and Bandung, 1956.

Al-Iji, *al-Mawaqif*, Vol. VIII

Ibn Abdul Barr, *Jame Bayan al Ilm Wa Fadhlih*, Al-Maktaba al Ilmiyah, Madinah

Ibn Abi Shaibah, *Kitab al-Musannaf*, Vol. 2
Ibn al-Farra, *al-Ahkam al-Sultaniyah*, ed. Mohd. Hamid al-Fiqi, Cairo, 1966
Ibn Khaladun, *Kitab al-Ibar*, Dar al- Kitab al- Labnani, Beirut, 1956.
——————, *Al-Muqaddimah* Maktabah Tijariah Kubra, Egypt.
Ibn Qudamah, Al- Mughni, Cairo, Vol. IX
Ibn Taimiyah, *Al-Siyasah al Shariyiah*, Kuwait, 1986.
——————, *Majmū' Fatāwā Shaykh al- Islam*, Vol. 9.
——————, *Minhaj al-Sunnah*, Vol. I, IV
Ibrahim, Anwar, "Development, Values and Changing Political Ideals", *Sojourn: Social Issue in South East Asia I* (February) 1986.
——————, "The Ned for Civilizational Dialogue", *Occasion Paper Series, Centre for Muslim – Christian Understanding,* Georgetown University, 1995.
——————, Interview by M. Sajid, *Rafique e Manzil*, Urdu Monthly Vol. 18, No. 5, May 2005
——————, *The Asian Renaissance*, Singapore, Times Book International, 1996.
*International Encyclopaedia of Social Sciences*, Vol.2
Iqbal, Afzal, *Diplomacy in Islam*, Lahore, 1962.
Iqbal, M., *The Reconstruction of Religious Thoughts in Islam* Ashraf Publications, Lahore, 1954.
Islahi, Maulana Amin Ahsan, *Tadabbur Qur'ān*, Lahore, Vol. 3, 1978.
Islahi, Maulana Sultan Ahmad, *Muslamān Aqalliyaton ke matlubah Kirdar*, Azamgarh, 2002.
Al-Juwaini, *al-Irshad*, Egypt 1950
Al-Juwayni, Imam al-Haramayn, *Giyath al-Umam*, Mustafa Hilmi, Alexandria, 1979
Jafer Thanesari, Muhammad, *Tawārikh Ajib or Kala Pani*, Ambala, 1302 A.H.
Jami`i, Shabbir Ahmad, Ijtimai Ijtihad Ke Asaalib, in *Maqaalaat Seminar Bar Ijitmai Ijtihad*
Al-Kholi al-Bahi, "On Property and Ownership Between God and Man", in *Minbar al-Islam* eng. Tr. Cairo, January, 1962
Kalid Mohammad Khalid, (*Min Huna Nabda*), *From here we Start*, trans. I. R. al-Faruqi, Washington, 1953
Kausar, Zeenath, Dr., "Political Development: Western and Islamic Perspective", *The Islamic Quarterly*, Vol. XXX, No. 2, London, 1996
——————, *Maulana Azad's Concept of Nationalism*, unpublished dissertation submitted in AMU for the award of M. Phil
Khadduri, Abdul Majid, "Introduction" to al- Shaybani, *The Islamic Law of Nations*, Baltimore, 1966.
Khan, Qamaruddin, *The Political Thought of Ibn Taimiyah*, Adam Publishers & Distributors, Delhi, 1988.

Khandhlavi, Mohammad Idris, *Nizam Islam wa Dastur Islam*, Lahore, 1387 A. H.

Kohn, Hans, *Nationalism: Its Meaning and History*, Princeton, 1955

Lambton, K. A. S., Khilafah in Political Theory, in *Encyclopaedia of Islam*.

Laoust, Henry, *Nazriyyat Ibn Taimiyah fi al-Siyasah*, Arabic Tr. by M. Abdul Azim Ali, Cairo, 1979.

Lewis, Bernard, *The Middle East and The West*, Harper Row, New York, 1964.

Al-Mawardi, Abul Hasan Ali, *Al-Ahkam al-Sultaniyah*, Cairo, 1966

Mahmud Husain, The Successor of Sayyid Ahmad Shahid: Jihad on the North-Western Frontier in *A History of the Freedom Movement*, Pakistan Historical Society, Karachi, Vol. 11, 1960

Mahr, Chudhary Ghulam Rasul, *Sarguzashat Mujahidin*, Lahore 1956

*Makātib Sayyid Ahmad Shaheed*, Lahore, 1395 A. H. /1975 A. D.

Manzoor. S. Pervez, Islamic State Between the Mystique of Khilafah and the Logic of Mulk, *Muslim World Book Review*, Vol. 9, No. 1, London, 1988

Mashriqi, Inayatullah Khan, *Molawi Ka Ghalat Mazhab*, No. 4

————————, *Tazkirah*, Lahore, 1980

Maududi, Sayyid Abul Ala, *Tarikh Azādi Hind Aur Musalmān*, Vol. 1, Lahore, 1987

————————, *The Holy Quran: Translation and Brief Notes With Text, Trans.* Muhammad Akbar Muradpuri and Abdul Aziz Kamal, Lahore, 1987

————————, *The Islamic Law and Constitution*, tr. Khurshid Ahmad, Lahore, 1967.

————————, *Political Theory of Islam*, ed. By, Khurshid Ahmad, Islamic Publications, Lahore, 1960.

————————, Islamic Way of Life, Delhi, 1967.

————————, *Tafhim al- Qur'ān*, Delhi, 1970.

Mc Ilwain, C.H., *The Growth of Political Thought in the West*, New York, 1932.

Metcalf, Barbara D., Barelwi, Sayyid Ahmad, in *The Oxford Encyclopaedia of the Modern Islamic World*, ed. John L. Espisito, Oxford, Vol. 1, 1995

Mian, Muhammad, Maulana Saiyid, *Ulama e Hind Ka Shandar Mazi*, Vol. 11, Delhi, 1957

Miss Follett, *The New State*, 1918

Moten, Rashid, Islamization of Knowledge, *The American Journal of Islamic Social Sciences*, Vol. 7, No. 2, 1990.

Muhammad, Shan, *Syed Ahmad Khan: A Political Review*, Meerut, 1969.

Mujeeb, Muhammad, *The Indian Muslims*, London, 1967

Mutawalli, Abdul Hamid, Prof, *Mabadi Nizam al-Hukm fi al-Islam*, Alexandria, 1964.

Nadvi, Mukhtar Ahmad, *Kiya Musalman Khawatin Ka Masjid Mein Aaana Fitnah Hai?*, Mumbai

——————, *Majallah Al-Balagh*, Mumbai, Vol. 15 No. 9, 2005

Nadvi, Rais Muhammad, *Rasul Akram Ka Sahih Tariqah Namaz*, Varanasi, 1996

Nadvi, Syed Sulaiman, *Seeratun Nabi*, Vol. VII, Azamgarh, 1987

Nadwi, S. Abul Hasan Ali, *Religion and Civilization*, Academy of Islamic Research, Lucknow, 1970.

——————, *Sirat Sayyid Ahmad Shahid*, Vol. 6, Lahore, 1958

Nasr, Sayyed Hussain, *Islam and the Plight of Modern Man*, London, 1975.

Nasr, Sayyed Vali Reza, Islam and the Social Sciences, *Hamdard Islamicus*, Karachi, Vol. XIII, No. 2, 1990

*Nationalism: A report by a study Group of members of the Royal Institute of International Affairs*, London, 1939

Nawawi, Abu Zakariya, *Riyadh us-Salaheen*, Vol. 1, Damascus, Dar al- Mamun, 1976

Naziri, Mufti Jamil Ahmad, *Rasul Akram ka Tariqah Namaz*, Jamiah Arabiyah, Mubarakpur, Azamgarh, 1987

Niharranjan Ray, *Nationalism in India*, Aligarh, 1973

Peters, Islam and Colonialism: *The Doctrine of Jihad in Modern History*.

Piscatori, James P., *Islam in a World a Nation-State*, Cambridge, 1986.

Quraishi, Ishtiaq Husain, *The Muslim Community .in Indo-Pak Subcontinent*, Hague, 1962

Qutb, Syed, *Al-'Adalah al-Ijtimā`iyah fi al-Islam*, Cairo. n. d.

——————, *Ma'alim fi al-Tariq*, Cairo

Al-Rayyis, Ziauddin, *Al-Nazriat al-Siyasiyah al- Islamiyah*, Cairo, 1990.

Rahmani, Nazir Ahmad, *Ahl Hadith Aur Siyāsat*, Jamia Salafiah, Varanasi.

Ramadan, Said, *Islamic law, its Scope, Its Equity*, London, 1961.

Ray, B. G. Humanism and Nationalism, in *Nationalism and Humanism*, edited by Mittal, Keval Krishna, Delhi, 1981

Rosenthal, E. I. J., "Ibn Khaldun: A North African Muslim Thinker of the Fourteenth Century", John Rylands Library, *Manchester Bulletin*, Vol. 24, 1940

——————, *Islam in the Modern National State*, Cambridge, 1965.

——————, *Political Thought in Medieval Islam An Introductory Outline*, Cambridge, 1962.

Al- Shafii, Abu Abdullah Muhammad bin Idris, *Kitab al- Umm*, Cairo, 1903, Vol. IV.

Al- Shaybani, Muhammad bin al- Hasan, *Sharh al- Siyar al- Kabir*, dictation of Ahmad al- Sarkhshi ed. Salah al- Munajjid, Cairo, 1958

Al-Shahrastani, *al-Milal wa' al-Nihal*, Vol. I, Cairo, 1910
Al-Sibai, *Ishtirākiyah al-Islam*, Damascus, 1960.
Sabine G. H., *A History of Political Theory*, New Delhi, 1973.
Safwat, A. Zaki, *Jamharah Khutab Al-Arab*, Vol. 1, Egypt, 1923
Sardar, Ziauddin, *The Touch of Midas*, Manchester, 1984.
Sattar, E. M., *Ibn Khaldun: The Author of the Muqaddimah*, Dacca, 1980.
Seoharvi, Hifzur Rahman, *Islām kā Iqtisādi Nizām*, Delhi, 1951.
Shah Waliullah, *Izalah al-Khifa*, Urdu Tr. Abd Al-Shakur, Vol. I, Karachi.
Shahabuddin, Sayyid, Muslim Muasharah Huquq Niswan Ki Maghribi Tahrik Ki Zad Per, *Roznamah Rashtriya Sahara*.
Sherwani, H. K., *Studies in Muslim Political Thought and Administration*, Lahore, 1942.
Siddiqui, Bakhtiyar Hasan, T. W. Arnold: Life and Works, *Iqbal*, Lahore, Vol. XVI, January, 1968
Siddiqui, Muhammad Yasin Mazhar, Prof., *Organization of Government Under the Prophet*, Delhi, 1987
——————, *Tārikh-o-Tahzeeb Islāmi*, Vol. II, Qazi Publishers, New Delhi, 1998.
Siddiqui, Nijatullah Dr. Maqasid Shariat: Yek Asri Mutalah, *Tarjuman Darul Uloom*, New Delhi, Vol. No. 4, December, 2004
Simpson, Mc Elory Paul, "Democracy in Islam", *The Muslim World*, Vol. 28, The Hastford Seminar Foundation, New York, 1938
Sindhi, Ubaidullah, Maulana, *Shah Waliullah Awr Unki Siyasi Tahrik*, n. d.
*Sirat Ibn Hisham*, Vol. 2
Al-Taftazani, *Sharh al-Maqasid*, Vol. 2, Lahore, 1981
Al-Tusi, Nizam al-Mulk, *Risalah Imamah*, Tehran, 1335 A. H.
*Tafsir al-Qurtubi*, Vol. 4
*Tafsir al-Tabari*, Vol. 7
Tara Chand, *National Integration and Secularism*, Aligarh, 1968,
*The Holy Quran*, Eng. Tr. Yusuf Ali, Qatar, ed., II
*The New Encyclopaedia Britannica*, Vol.7, 1994
*The Oxford Encyclopaedia of the Modern Islamic World*, see article by R. Hrair Dekmejian, Vol. IV, 1995
*The Shorter Oxford English Dictionary*, Vol.2, 1959
Tout, T.F., *The Empire and the Papacy* 918-1213, London, 1924
Toyenbee, Arnold, *Civilization on Trail*, Oxford, 1948
Al Umari, Ahsan Diya, *Madinan Society of the time of the Prophet: Its Characteristics and Organization*, Vol. I, tr. By Huda Khattab, Herndon, 1991
Uthman, A. Karim, *Al-Nizām al-Siyāsi fi al-Islām*, Beirut, 1968
Vincent, Andrew, *Theories of the State*, Oxford, 1987.
Watt, W. M., *Islamic Political Thought ... The Basic Concepts*, Edinburgh, 1968.

———————, *Muhammad at Madina*, Oxford, 1956
Welhausen, *The Arab Kingdom and its fall*, London, 1973.
Zaghlul, Muhammad, Dr., *al-Qawmiyah al-Arabiyah fi al-Adab al-Hadith*, Egypt, Dār al-Ma'ārif, 1959.

*****

# INDEX

## A

## B

## C

## D



## E

## G



## H

# I

## L

## M

## N

## O

## P

## Q



## R

## S

## U

*****